A Culinary Journey

ALSO BY NANCY KEENEY FORSTER

Encounters: A Lifetime Spent Crossing Cultural Frontiers

*Journeys in Learning Across Frontiers: Stories,
Strategies and Inspiration from the IB Community*

(co-edited with Sue Bastian, Anne-Marie Evans,
and Lisa Nicholson)

A Culinary Journey

Recipes and Reminiscences of
an American Diplomat's Wife

NANCY KEENEY FORSTER

Nancy Keeney Forster

Illustrations by
Cindy Salans Rosenheim

Wind Shadow Press
Tiburon, California

Wind Shadow Press
Tiburon, California
www.windshadowpress.com

ISBN 978-0-615-73907-6
Library of Congress Control Number: 2013930277

Forster, Nancy Keeney

A Culinary Journey: recipes and reminiscences
of an American diplomat's wife / Nancy Keeney Forster

Typesetting by Jill Ronsley, suneditwrite.com

This book is dedicated
to those who joined our Culinary Journey—
family, friends and visitors at our table—
and to the many friends
who graciously shared their recipes.

Contents

Introduction

IN SEPTEMBER OF 1949, less than two months after our wedding, my husband Cliff and I arrived as newlyweds in Manila. Serving as a diplomatic hostess in far-flung places had not been factored into my education or my own life goals. I didn't even know how to cook.

Our first overseas post was in Davao City, on the southern Philippine island of Mindanao. We lived in the simplest of homes. The first few weeks, simply putting our own meals on the table was an adventure and a challenge, and entertaining was beyond me. But I had married a Foreign Service officer, and home hospitality for local citizens and out-of-town visitors was in my job description. My learning curve was swift.

Our final overseas post, in 1983, was in Tokyo, where I entertained formally and cooked for friends and family in a spacious American Embassy home staffed by a resident cook and maid. In the intervening decades, the recipes I collected and the menus I developed became my travel guide for a wonderful journey across borders and cultures. They helped me grow from a fearful novice to a confident hostess who managed sit-down dinners for thirty-six (including the parents of the future Empress of Japan and the President of Israel), receptions for two hundred (including Bozo the Clown and the Los Angeles Philharmonic Orchestra), celebrations of holidays and rites of passage. Sometimes several events occurred in one week, often without help in the kitchen (relying on the efficiency and good will of my three children), largely in foreign climes and cultures, coping with temperamental utilities and a long supply line to familiar groceries. I wouldn't have missed a day of it.

I continued to enjoy entertaining after my official role as diplomatic hostess had ended, collecting recipes from new homes in Hawaii and California and when traveling abroad. This later journey, in part, has been through changing food styles. In the early years, we weren't counting calories or cholesterol or sodium content—the richer the dish, the better. In recent years, thickening waistlines and rising blood pressure have forced a new learning process. I have learned to keep it lean but make it tasty, too.

The recipes in these pages were gathered from colleagues in the Foreign Service; Japanese, Burmese, Israeli, and Filipino friends; articles in local newspapers; gleanings from magazines; and a full shelf of cookbooks. Many of the dishes have evolved over time to become very much my own.

As a senior citizen with husband retired from the diplomatic circuit, my audience diminished considerably, but the recipes remained treasured, as did the pleasure of trying some of them on more intimate gatherings of family and friends. Culling some of my favorites and weaving them in with reminiscences of where and how they were used, I have compiled my own culinary tour guide.

Please, come journey with me from that frontier town in the southern Philippines right after World War II; through tours in Japan, Burma, Israel, and Washington D.C.; and finally to retirement and new civilian careers in Hawaii and California.

Welcome to our table, whether you have come for lunch or dinner, for tea or cocktails, or to spend a leisurely weekend as our houseguest. *Bon Appétit!*

1

Hash Again?

"NANCY, I REALLY ENJOYED this meal, but do you think we could have something besides canned corned-beef hash and spinach tomorrow?"

I burst into tears. I was as sick of this dinner as Cliff was, but I didn't know what else to prepare.

Our home in Davao was a newly built house surrounded on three sides by a water-buffalo market. Our living room furniture was locally harvested and crafted rattan, cushions stuffed with ka-pok that we picked off trees on a nearby farm and finished with slipcovers that I made on my portable sewing machine. Our kitchen had minimal equipment (anything electric being subject to the whims of frequent power outages) and shopping for food was dauntingly different from the grocery stores back home.

The year was 1949, and Cliff was launching his U.S. Foreign Service career in this Filipino frontier town situated four degrees north of the equator. I was launching a career of my own, that of diplomatic wife and hostess. A twenty-year-old bride fresh out of college, I'd had little experience in the kitchen and none in open-air food markets that sold chickens alive and where the fresh vegetables were potentially full of dangerous intestinal parasites. At this time and in this place, the only "safe" dinner I knew how to prepare was out of the cans we had brought along as part of our household shipment.

When Cliff asked the question about the hash, it was the fourteenth night we'd had this particular menu. There were only twenty-four cans in each case, and we faced a cooking and eating crisis.

More than sixty years later, I can look back with fondness on the first menu of my diplomatic career.

CANNED DINNER À LA AMERICAN BRIDE IN DAVAO

Canned corn beef hash (sautéed, garnished with ketchup)
Canned spinach (warmed in saucepan, garnished with vinegar)
Canned peaches

I WON'T PROVIDE RECIPES for these dishes. The instructions for each would be the same: "Open can with can opener, do minimal preparation, and serve."

2

Dan to the Rescue

DAN WAS THE ANSWER to our prayers. An ex-Philippine Scout, he had cooked his way across the Pacific on a freighter and for some years he slung hash (pardon the term) for cowboys in New Mexico and Arizona. He fortuitously appeared at Cliff's office in the Davao U.S. Information Service (USIS) library the day after the "hash again?" incident. He was looking for a job. Charmed by his tales of adventure, by the eagles tattooed on his biceps, and by his promise to serenade us with his guitar when dinner was done, Cliff brought him home.

During the days before Dan came to us, I had been putting myself through a crash course on cooking techniques and recipes, courtesy of the women's and household magazines that came to our library to showcase American culture. I was building up a world-class collection of chicken recipes, looking forward to a day when someone else would do my market shopping, bring home the chicken, and kill it for me. One article I read included a helpful hint for tenderizing home-killed chicken: feed the bird a jigger of whiskey just before the slaughter and the bird will relax, thereby dying with tender muscles. Dan liked this idea, and frequently suggested chicken for our menus. You can guess who enjoyed the relaxing jigger of whiskey!

With Dan in the kitchen and going to market, a storeroom full of canned foods other than hash and spinach, and my library research providing recipes for him, we were ready to launch our diplomatic entertaining.

THE FIRST DINNER PARTIES

(using mostly canned or packaged foods)
Turkey or chicken tetrazzini
(*or* Ham with dark cherry sauce)
Curried carrot and beet salad
(*or* Three bean salad)
Grapefruit upside down cake
(*or* Chocolate mousse)

TURKEY OR CHICKEN TETRAZZINI

2 to 3 cups cooked turkey or chicken
½ pound macaroni or spaghetti, cooked and drained
1½ to 1¾ pounds sautéed mushrooms (canned may be substituted)

½ cup blanched slivered almonds
3 tablespoons melted butter
2 tablespoons flour
2 cups turkey or chicken broth
Salt and pepper to taste
1 cup heated whipping cream
Parmesan cheese

Combine first four ingredients. Make sauce of butter, flour, and broth, seasoning to taste. Add cream. Add sauce to turkey mixture and place in greased casserole. Sprinkle grated Parmesan cheese over top. Bake in 375 degree oven until lightly browned and heated through, about 30 minutes. (This dish remained a favorite for family and buffet dinners long after we left Davao.)
Serves 8 to 10.

HAM WITH DARK CHERRY SAUCE

1 (5-pound) canned ham
1 (1-pound) can pitted sweet
   cherries
1 tablespoon cornstarch

¼ teaspoon ground cloves
⅛ teaspoon ground pepper
¼ cup toasted, slivered almonds

Heat ham according to directions on can. Empty cherries and their juice into saucepan. Blend in cornstarch and spices. Heat, stirring constantly, until thickened. Stir in toasted almonds. To serve, slice ham and spoon sauce over top.

   Serves 10.

CURRIED CARROT AND BEET SALAD

1 (1-pound) can julienned
   carrots
1 (1-pound) can julienned beets
¼ to ½ teaspoon curry powder

2 tablespoons vinegar
4 tablespoons oil
Salt and pepper

Combine vegetables, then combine remaining ingredients as a dressing and pour over vegetables. Chill thoroughly.

   Serves 10.

THREE BEAN SALAD

1 (1-pound) can cut green beans	1 teaspoon salt
1 (1-pound) can cut wax beans	½ teaspoon freshly ground pepper
1 (1-pound) can red kidney beans	1 cup granulated or brown sugar
1 small onion, sliced, separated into rings	½ cup red wine vinegar
	½ cup olive oil

Drain green and wax beans well. Rinse and drain kidney beans. Combine beans, onion, salt, pepper, and sugar in deep bowl. Warm vinegar but do not boil. Stir in oil and pour over beans. Toss lightly, cover, and refrigerate overnight. Drain before serving.

Serves 10.

GRAPEFRUIT UPSIDE DOWN CAKE

½ cup brown sugar, packed	1 egg
1 can grapefruit sections	1½ cups cake flour
⅓ cup butter or margarine	1¾ teaspoons baking powder
¼ teaspoon salt	¼ cup grapefruit juice from can
½ cup sugar	

Cover bottom of well-greased 8x8x2-inch pan with brown sugar. Drain grapefruit sections, reserving juice. Arrange fruit on top of brown sugar. In a mixing bowl, cream shortening, salt, and sugar until fluffy. Beat in egg. Sift flour, measure, and sift again with baking powder. Add dry ingredients alternately with grapefruit juice to creamed mixture. Pour batter over fruit and brown sugar. Bake in moderate oven (350°) for 45 minutes or until done. Top each serving with whipped cream, if desired.

Serves 6 to 8.

CHOCOLATE MOUSSE

1 (8-ounce) package chocolate   2 tablespoons fruit brandy
   bits   4 egg whites
⅓ cup hot coffee   3 tablespoons sugar
4 egg yolks

Combine chocolate bits and hot coffee in blender container. Whirl at high speed until smooth. Add egg yolks and brandy. Whirl 30 seconds. Beat egg whites in medium size bowl until foamy and double in volume; gradually beat in sugar. Fold in chocolate mixture until no streaks of white remain. Spoon into 8 parfait glasses or a serving bowl. Chill at least 1 hour. Garnish with whipped cream.

    Serves 8.

I DECIDED TO PLANT a vegetable garden to supplement the cans, starting out with seeds for carrots, beets, and lettuce sent from New York by my mother. (Oh, how we hungered for fresh lettuce! Even a few of the wilted outside leaves on an iceberg head—which, in our American supermarket culture, I had thrown into the garbage —would be gourmet fare now!) We had moved, and now lived on the second floor of a two-family house, on a lot that flooded regularly after the daily tropical rains. This meant that my "garden" would have to be in the concrete planting boxes that surrounded our patio on top of the carport.

    My crop was a dismal failure. The lettuce in the intense heat shot straight up in a direct line from seed to stalk, with only a few puny leaflets, and back to seed. The carrots and beets, I should have realized, were root vegetables, and with only a couple of inches of soil their growth was cruelly stunted. So our fate was more canned or well-cooked vegetables and fruits (unless the fresh ones could be peeled).

We were provided with a freezer shipped from Manila by the embassy. When friends or colleagues from Manila came to visit, we used them as couriers—to bring in steak, lamb chops, cheese, celery, and proper lettuce. When the first beefsteak came into our kitchen, Dan gave it his very best efforts. He cooked it, and cooked it, and cooked it some more to make sure it was well prepared. "Medium rare" had not been part of his cooking vocabulary. We ended up cutting it into chunks and using it in my mother's favorite stew recipe.

Kate Blanke's Favorite Beef Stew

¼ pound bacon
2 pounds stewing beef
Seasoned flour (2 tablespoons
  flour, 1 teaspoon salt, ¼
  teaspoon pepper, ½ teaspoon
  dried herbs)
2 chopped cloves garlic
1 cup bouillon

1 cup canned tomato sauce
12 peppercorns
1 bay leaf
½ cup sherry or dry white wine
6 medium potatoes, peeled and
  quartered
6 pared quartered carrots
1 to 2 stalks sliced celery

Cut bacon into ½-inch pieces, sauté in large skillet, and pour out all but about 2 tablespoons of fat. Brown beef in drippings with bacon, sprinkle meat with seasoned flour. Combine garlic, bouillon, tomato sauce, peppercorns, and bay leaf in a separate pan and heat until boiling. Place meat in a heavy saucepan and pour sauce over it. Simmer, closely covered, about 2 to 3 hours, or until meat can be easily pierced with a fork. During the last hour of cooking, add the sherry. Cook celery, potatoes, and carrots separately until nearly tender and add these vegetables during the last 15 minutes of cooking. This one-dish meal may be made a day ahead. Accompanied by French bread, it makes a one-dish meal.
  Serves 6 to 8.

THE USIS LIBRARY IN Davao was located in a building with a colorful history. During World War II, the Japanese government's press service had used it as their southern headquarters. Postwar it had been turned into a hotel, one that according to local lore was a high-class brothel. By the time we arrived, half of the upstairs, including the former lobby and two office rooms, had been rented by the U.S. government. The Filipino library staff worked out of the offices, and the hotel lobby had been turned into a library with shelves for the books, racks for the magazines, a few library tables, and rattan chairs for the patrons. To create an office space for Cliff, a desk and a few chairs were arranged by the staff on an open-air porch above the main entrance. His porch/office had a good view of the rest of the building, which was still a hotel, and still of questionable repute. On a lazy tropical afternoon, beautiful ladies would lean out the bedroom windows, smile, and wave at Cliff.

When Cliff's boss came on an inspection trip from Manila, he decided this was not quite the proper setting for a U.S. cultural showcase and the American Foreign Service Officer who had been assigned to show the flag and win friends. The hotel's lease was bought out and the entire building was transformed to conform more to official taste. Additional furniture was ordered from Manila, partitions were removed between bedrooms, and walls were repainted.

Renovation completed, it was time to celebrate the enlarged facilities with a formal "opening" presided over by dignitaries from the capitol. The American ambassador came in an embassy plane, bringing along the vice president of the Philippines and an entourage of reporters and other VIPs. My job was to provide a buffet luncheon for twenty-four in our very modest second-floor home at the end of an unpaved street.

LUNCHEON FOR VIPs FROM MANILA

Dry martinis, straight up, and soft drinks
Chicken curry, with condiments
Hot cooked rice
Tomato aspic salad, with Rose Keeney's cooked salad dressing
Rum lime sherbet
Pineapple bars

CHICKEN CURRY

2 tablespoons bacon fat or
  salad oil
2 large onions, chopped
2 tablespoons flour
½ teaspoon sugar
½ teaspoon salt
1 tablespoon curry powder
  (or more, to taste)
2 cups chicken broth
Salt and pepper

3 to 4 cups cooked chicken
Hot cooked rice
Condiments: crisp crumbled
  bacon, mango chutney, sliced
  bananas, toasted shredded
  coconut, chopped salted
  peanuts, chopped hard-boiled
  eggs, canned French-fried
  onions

Brown chopped onions in oil. Stir in dry ingredients. Add broth slowly, stirring smooth after each addition. Taste and if needed add salt and pepper and more curry powder. Add cooked chicken. Serve with rice and condiments.

Serves 8.

TOMATO ASPIC SALAD

3½ cups tomatoes (fresh or
  canned)
1 teaspoon salt
½ teaspoon paprika
1½ teaspoons sugar
2 tablespoons lemon juice
3 tablespoons chopped onion
1 bay leaf

4 ribs celery, with leaves
1 teaspoon dried basil or tarragon
2 tablespoons gelatin
½ cup cold water
Optional: sliced olives, chopped
  celery, chopped green peppers,
  grated or chopped carrots, sliced
  avocados

Simmer together first 9 ingredients for 30 minutes, then strain. Soak gelatin in cold water, then dissolved in strained hot juice. Add water to make 4 cups of liquid. Chill the aspic. When it is about to set, add 1 or 2 cups, if desired, of the optional ingredients. Chill until firm. Remove from mold and serve with mayonnaise or cooked dressing.

Serves to 8 to 10.

ROSE KEENEY'S COOKED SALAD DRESSING

6 tablespoons sugar
2 teaspoons salt
3 heaping teaspoons prepared
  mustard
3 tablespoons flour

2 eggs
1½ cups milk
8 tablespoons vinegar
2 tablespoons butter

In the top of a double boiler, add the first 7 ingredients in order named, blending thoroughly after each addition. Cook over hot water, stirring constantly. When thickened, add butter (optional) and blend again. Cool.

Makes 3 cups.

Rum Lime Sherbet

⅔ cup sugar
1½ cups water
¼ cup rum
1¼ teaspoons gelatin dissolved
   in ¼ cup cold water

½ cup lime juice
2 drops green food coloring
2 egg whites

Boil sugar and water, stir in rum and dissolved gelatin. Cool slightly and add lime juice and coloring. Beat egg whites until stiff but not dry, and add to lime mixture. Place in ice tray and cover with wax paper. Freeze in ice tray until partially frozen. Remove and place in chilled bowl. Beat until evenly blended. Spoon back into tray and freeze until firm.

   Serves 6.

Pineapple Bars

1 cup flour
1 teaspoon baking powder
½ cup butter or margarine
1 egg white
1 tablespoon milk
1 (20-ounce) can crushed
   pineapple

1 egg
¼ cup melted butter
1 cup sugar
1 cup flaked coconut
1 teaspoon vanilla

Sift flour, measure 1 cup, and sift together with baking powder. With knives or pastry blender cut in butter until mixture is crumbly. Beat egg and milk together; stir into flour mixture. Spread over bottom of 8-inch square baking pan. Thoroughly drain pineapple and spread over top. Combine egg, remaining butter, sugar, coconut, and vanilla and spread this topping over pineapple layer. Bake 35 to 40 minutes at 350°. Cool and cut.

   Makes 16 squares or 32 bars.

THAT DAY WAS TO become a test of my crisis-management skills. It rained so hard the night before that our yard was more flooded than usual and we had to build a temporary bridge across large puddles with planks of wood. The electricity was off all morning, which meant the aspic and sherbet remained liquid. Tillman Durdin of *The New York Times* sequestered himself in our bedroom to type out his story on my Underwood in time to dispatch it on the one afternoon plane leaving Davao for Manila. He stuck his head out the door at regular intervals asking for a refill in his martini glass. But we made it through the meal with all guests fed and apparently happy. (They drank their salad and dessert.) No one fell off the planks as they wove back across the makeshift bridge to their waiting cars. I breathed a sigh of relief, went into the kitchen to congratulate Elise (the maid) and Dan for a job well done. But the excitement wasn't yet over: I found Dan chasing Elise around the kitchen table with a carving knife, demanding "just one little kiss." He had obviously been imbibing the sherbet rum and/or chicken whiskey to bolster his confidence for the big day.

"I looked out from the kitchen," he told me later with a great big smile, "and the ambassador was taking a second helping."

This was the pinnacle of Dan's diplomatic cooking career. He disappeared shortly thereafter, presumably to take to sea again and to rejoin a more macho society. And, once again, I was the chief chef.

The first cake I baked was soggy in the middle and leaden on the edges, but nevertheless Cliff and I each ate a piece before we set out on a day trip in the "mobile unit" to show movies to Bogobo tribal members on the lower slopes of Mount Apo. This self-contained four-wheel-drive vehicle had its own generator and was used to bring movies to settlements that had no electricity. In those days the USIS theatrical fare was purely educational: how to control pests that were attacking local agriculture, scenic views of U.S. national parks, a cartoon showing why one should wear shoes to avoid getting hookworm. After a showing of the hookworm film in a town

at the very end of the road going northwest, the local shoemaker took an arduous bus ride into Davao to thank Cliff in person. His business had picked up exponentially after the USIS visit.

When we returned home that night of my first cake, I had a stomach ache that intensified as the night wore on. In the wee hours, Cliff walked up the street to neighbors who had a telephone (which we did not) so he could call a doctor. When Dr. Durban informed me that my stomach ache was acute appendicitis and that he was taking me to the hospital immediately for surgery, I was relieved. At least my cooking wasn't so dreadful that it had created the intense pain I was suffering!

In the months to come, I learned to bake a cake that never failed—and is even good for one's health.

BLENDER CARROT PECAN CAKE

1 cup pecans	1 teaspoon salt
1¼ cups vegetable oil	3 cups sliced carrots
4 eggs	2 cups sifted flour
2 cups sugar	1 teaspoon baking soda
2 teaspoons cinnamon	2 teaspoons baking powder

Chop pecans in blender and set aside. Place oil, eggs, sugar, cinnamon, and salt in blender container. Blend 5 seconds, then gradually add carrots. Blend until just grated. In large mixing bowl, sift together dry ingredients. Add the contents of the blender. Mix well. Stir in chopped pecans. Pour into greased tube pan and bake about 1 hour 10 minutes at 325°. Allow to cool slightly, then frost with cream cheese icing.

Serves 8.

CREAM CHEESE ICING

4 tablespoons butter

1 (8-ounce) package cream
  cheese

2 cups sifted powdered sugar

1 teaspoon vanilla

1 cup grated coconut

½ cup chopped pecans

Blend together butter and cheese while they are at room temperature. Slowly add powdered sugar. Add vanilla, coconut, and pecans, mixing well.

THE FILIPINOS LOVED TO entertain. A favorite event was a "merienda," a large gathering of family and friends, sustained by a lavish table of food, enlivened by music and dancing, and lasting for many hours. Cliff and I often enjoyed the creative nature of Filipino hospitality. At a luncheon in our honor on a small island to the north of Mindanao, our hosts at a small elementary school spelled out the name "Forster" in sliced beets on top of the potato salad. On another excursion, to a remote Bogobo village, we climbed narrow paths behind two men carrying a pig lashed to a pole across their shoulders—following our dinner up the mountain.

EATING FILIPINO STYLE

Chicken adobo

Sour beef stew

Lumpia (Filipino spring rolls) with sweet and sour dipping sauce

Baked bananas with coconut

(*or* Baked bananas in rum)

CHICKEN ADOBO

4 pounds chicken pieces
1½ cups distilled white vinegar
2 garlic cloves, crushed
2 bay leaves
1 teaspoon cracked black pepper

1 cup water
¼ cup soy sauce
3 tablespoons vegetable oil
Hot cooked rice

In large kettle, combine chicken, vinegar, garlic, bay leaves, pepper, and water; bring mixture to a boil and simmer it, covered, for 20 minutes. Add soy sauce and simmer, covered, 20 minutes more. Transfer chicken to a plate and boil liquid for 10 minutes, or until it is reduced to about 1 cup. Let sauce cool, remove bay leaves, and skim fat from surface. In large skillet heat oil over high heat till hot but not smoking and sauté chicken, patted dry, in batches, turning it, for 5 minutes or until browned. Transfer chicken to rimmed platter, pour heated sauce over it and serve with rice. (Optional garnish: tomato wedges and cubes of fresh pineapple.)

Serves 6 to 8.

SOUR BEEF STEW

1 pound beef
½ pound pork (or additional
    beef)
2 lemon grass stalks or 1
    tablespoon fresh ginger
1 lime or lemon
2 medium unripe tomatoes

6½ cups water
2 cups shredded cabbage
2 tablespoons fish sauce or light
    soy sauce
Cracked black pepper

Cut beef and pork into bite-size cubes. Place lime cut into large quarters in large saucepan; add quartered tomatoes and water and bring to boil. Simmer 10 minutes. Strain out lime seeds. Add meat and lemon grass or ginger; cover and simmer about 1¼ hours until tender. Add cabbage, fish or soy sauce, and pepper and simmer again briefly. Remove lemon grass and lime pieces.

Serves 8.

LUMPIA

½ pound ground pork
½ pound ground beef
½ cup chopped onion
½ pound raw shrimp, chopped
(optional)
2 eggs, beaten
½ cup chopped mushrooms
½ cup grated carrot
¼ cup chopped green onions

2 cups shredded Chinese cabbage
3 cloves garlic, minced
2 tablespoons soy sauce
Salt and pepper to taste
50 lumpia (or spring roll)
wrappers
Milk for sealing wrappers
Vegetable oil

In large skillet, sauté pork, beef, and onion; drain excess fat. Add shrimp and cook 1 minute. Remove from heat and add eggs, vegetables, and seasonings. Set aside to cool. Put heaping tablespoon of mixture on each lumpia wrapper. Roll up, forming a small cylinder. Tuck ends into roll and seal wrapper with milk. Deep fry in oil until brown. Serve with Sweet and Sour Dipping Sauce.

Serves 25.

SWEET AND SOUR DIPPING SAUCE

1 cup water
½ cup sugar
¼ cup vinegar
½ cup ketchup
2 tablespoons soy sauce

Dash Tabasco
Salt and pepper to taste
2 tablespoons cornstarch
¼ cup water

In a saucepan, bring water, sugar, and vinegar to a boil. Add ketchup, soy sauce, Tabasco, salt and pepper. Dissolve cornstarch in water and add to sauce. Cook until thickened. Serve with lumpia.

Makes about 2 cups.

BAKED BANANAS WITH COCONUT

¼ cup melted butter
6 firm bananas
2 tablespoons orange juice
¼ cup brown sugar

¼ teaspoon ground cinnamon
⅛ teaspoon ground nutmeg
½ cup shredded coconut

Preheat oven to 350°. Roll peeled bananas in butter, coating entire surface. Place in shallow baking dish and sprinkle evenly with orange juice, brown sugar, and spices. Bake 10 minutes. Sprinkle with coconut and bake 15 minutes more. Watch that coconut does not burn.

Serves 6.

BAKED BANANAS IN RUM

1 cup sugar
½ cup lemon juice
1 tablespoon butter

2 tablespoons white rum
6 firm bananas
Ice cream or whipped cream
(optional)

Simmer sugar, lemon juice, and butter 10 minutes, then add rum. Placed peeled bananas, halved lengthwise, in buttered baking dish. Pour syrup over them. Bake 30 minutes at 400° and turn once after 15 minutes. Serve topped with ice cream or whipped cream, if desired.

Serves 6.

As our first Christmas approached, the Filipino staff at the Cultural Center worried that we would be homesick and felt it was important that we have a holiday tree. The tropical pine trees that grow in the mountain highlands of the island have long droopy needles on branches more reminiscent of willows than of northern fir or spruce. Nevertheless, our friends brought us a jeepload of cut casuarina branches, which they tied together to simulate the shape of a Christmas tree, and we managed to find some dusty tinsel and a string of lights in one of the Chinese-owned shops on Davao's main street. (Actually, we preferred the Filipino Christmas decorations—delicate paper lanterns in the shape of a star, which they hung, lighted, in their windows.) We celebrated by inviting all our staff and their children for a party at our house, with presents for the children under the casuarina Christmas tree.

Christmas Party for USIS Staff and Their Families

Eggnog
Hot tea punch
Chicken almond puffs
Garlic cheese roll and crackers
Tuna pate and crackers
Sliced canned ham and dinner rolls with butter, mustard, and/or mayonnaise
Coconut meringue cookies
Ginger snaps

EGGNOG

12 eggs
1 pound powdered sugar
½ teaspoon salt
¼ cup vanilla
8 cups canned evaporated milk

3 cups water
4 cups dark rum, brandy,
    bourbon, or rye
Grated nutmeg (freshly grated is
    best)

Beat eggs until light in color. Gradually beat in sugar, salt, vanilla. Stir in milk diluted with water. Add liquor. Cover tightly and permit eggnog to ripen in refrigerator for 24 hours. Stir and top each serving with nutmeg.

Serves 40.

Note: To serve 6, I use 3 eggs, ¼ pound powdered sugar, 1 tablespoon vanilla, ⅛ teaspoon salt, 2 cups canned milk, ¾ cup water, and 1 cup liquor.

HOT TEA PUNCH

6 cups boiling water
3 tea bags
½ cup sugar

Grated nutmeg (freshly grated is
    best)
¼ cup lemon juice
1 teaspoon grated lemon rind

Pour boiling water over tea bags. Let steep 5 minutes; remove bags. Add other ingredients and warm over low heat. Serve hot, or make ahead and serve cold.

Serves 8.

CHICKEN ALMOND PUFFS

1 cup flour	½ cup finely diced cooked chicken
¼ teaspoon salt	2 tablespoons chopped roasted
½ cup butter or margarine	almonds
1 cup chicken broth	1 pinch paprika
4 eggs	1 teaspoon curry powder

Sift flour, measure, and sift again with salt. Combine butter and broth in large saucepan; keep over low heat until butter is melted. Add flour all at once and stir vigorously over low heat until mixture forms a ball and leaves sides of pan. Remove from heat. Add eggs, one at a time, beating thoroughly after each addition. Continue beating until a thick dough is formed. Stir in chicken, almonds, paprika, and curry. Drop by small spoonfuls onto greased baking sheet. Bake at 450° for 10 minutes; reduce heat to 350° and bake 5 to 10 minutes longer, until brown. May be made ahead and stored for several days in a container with a tight fitting lid.

Makes 4 to 5 dozen.

GARLIC CHEESE ROLL

2 pounds Velveeta cheese (at	2 cloves garlic, minced
room temperature)	2 cups pecans or walnuts
8 ounces cream cheese	Paprika and cayenne pepper

Mix the first four ingredients thoroughly in a food processor. Form into 2 to 3 rolls, 1½ to 2 inches in diameter. Sprinkle a layer of paprika mixed with a dash of cayenne on wax paper and roll the cheese in the spices until it is well coated. Refrigerate 24 hours. Slice and serve on round crackers, such as Ritz.

Makes 2½ pounds.

TUNA PATE

8 ounces cream cheese, softened
2 tablespoons chili sauce
2 tablespoons snipped parsley

2 tablespoons finely minced onion
½ teaspoon Tabasco
2 (7-ounce) cans tuna, drained

Blend cream cheese, chili sauce, parsley, onion, Tabasco. Gradually stir in flaked tuna. Beat until mixture is thoroughly blended. Pack into 4-cup mold or small bowl. Chill at least 3 hours. At serving time unmold and serve with small crackers.

Makes 3 cups.

COCONUT MERINGUE COOKIES

1 cup sugar
3 egg whites
⅛ teaspoon salt

1 teaspoon vanilla
1¼ cups shredded coconut

Sift sugar. Add salt to egg whites and beat until stiff. Add sugar slowly, beating constantly. Fold in vanilla and coconut. Drop batter from teaspoon onto greased and well-floured baking pan. Bake at 300° for about 30 minutes.

Makes 50 cookies.

Ginger Snaps

2 cups sugar	3¾ cups flour
2 well beaten eggs	1½ teaspoons baking soda
½ cup molasses	2 to 3 teaspoon ground ginger
2 teaspoons vinegar	½ teaspoon ground cinnamon
¾ cup butter	¼ teaspoon ground cloves

Cream butter and sugar. Stir in eggs, molasses, and vinegar. Sift and add dry ingredients. Mix all until blended. Form dough into ¾-inch balls. Bake on greased cookie sheet for about 12 minutes at 325°. (As the ball melts down during baking, the cookie develops a characteristic crinkle.)

Makes about 10 dozen 2-inch cookies.

The Filipinos are a wonderfully warm and welcoming people, and they had a special place in their hearts for Cliff Forster, whom they were welcoming home. Cliff had been born in Manila, grew up there, and was interned there during World War II by the Japanese. Davao residents had greeted the young American official as a *compadre* and urged us to carry on the family with a Davao-born baby. "Eat durian," they advised, certain that the huge, prickly, smelly fruit of the equatorial tropics would help mother nature. When I protested—I wasn't put off by the smell as much as some Westerners, but I didn't like the taste—they brought me durian ice cream. When we departed, childless, after two years, we received warm farewells, but sensed a tinge of reproach. We had let our Filipino friends down by remaining childless.

3

Chopsticks

AFTER OUR TOUR OF duty in the Philippines, Cliff was assigned to a year of intensive Japanese language and area studies at Yale University. The Peace Treaty with Japan had recently been signed. American libraries, established by the U. S. military occupation forces to introduce democratic ideas and practices to Japan, were being turned over to civilian officers from the Department of State. American speakers of Japanese were needed to serve as directors in what would become USIS Culture and Information Centers in small cities scattered throughout the Japanese Archipelago.

While Cliff struggled day and night to conquer complex grammar patterns and to memorize ideographic plus phonetic symbols, I worked as a secretary in the university graduate school. As a spouse I wasn't eligible for the language training, but I wanted to learn enough Japanese to function in the economy and associate with the Japanese people. My boss permitted a long lunch hour twice a week, during which I met privately with one of the Japanese tutors. In addition to giving me a basic toolkit of words and sentences, she took her job of acculturating me very seriously.

"Today our class will be devoted to the etiquette of eating with chopsticks," she said one day as we settled down for our lesson in a basement classroom. She opened a paper bag and took out two paper napkins—placing one in front of each of us—followed by two pairs of chopsticks and a box of Rice Krispies.

"You will learn to hold and use your chopsticks properly. Now let us eat the Rice Krispies with our chopsticks."

She had to be kidding! Cooked rice might be possible, because it holds together and can be picked up in chunks. Round kernels of dry cereal were an unfair challenge. We struggled through the lesson; lots of cereal ended up in my lap and on the carpet. However, by the end of the lesson I would never again be intimidated by chopsticks and would be able to approach Japanese dining with confidence and with pleasure.

Five months later, in Fukuoka, a group of Japanese university professors' wives organized a series of luncheon meetings with three of us American women living in their city. We exchanged cooking lessons. One week we prepared an American meal for them at one of our houses; the next week they showed us how to cook basic Japanese family fare. My Yale University training in chopstick etiquette, as well as Japanese conversation, was ideal preparation for these gatherings.

First Lessons in Japanese Cooking

Okonomiyaki (savory pancakes)
Vegetable fried rice
Sukiyaki
Ponzu and goma dare sauces
Sunomono (lightly picked cucumbers)

OKONOMIYAKI

1 tablespoon each flour and water	3 tablespoons finely diced chicken
1 egg	or ham
½ to 1 cup chopped cabbage	Oil for cooking
1 tablespoon chopped scallion	Soy or tonkatsu sauce
1 tablespoon chopped pickled	Mayonnaise, ketchup, hot
(red) ginger	mustard

Preheat skillet or grill to 400°. Combine water and flour in small bowl; beat in egg; stir in cabbage, scallion, ginger, and meat. Rub skillet lightly with oiled paper. Spoon in batter and press down with spatula. Cook about 5 minutes, turn, brush with soy or tonkatsu sauce and cook until brown. Serve with soy or tonkatsu sauce, mayonnaise, ketchup, and/or mustard, as desired.

Serves 1.

Note: Tonkatsu sauce can be found in the ethnic food section of some markets.

VEGETABLE FRIED RICE

¼ cup chopped onion	1 teaspoon chopped ginger
¼ cup shredded carrots	Oil for cooking
¼ cup mung bean sprouts	2 cups cooked rice
¼ cup snow peas	¼ cup chicken broth
1 clove chopped garlic	2 beaten eggs

Stir fry vegetables, garlic, and ginger in oil. Remove when they are crisp tender; set aside. Add more oil to pan and stir fry rice until it is lightly browned in spots. Return vegetables to pan. Add chicken broth to moisten the rice and season with soy. Push rice and vegetables to one side of pan. Pour beaten eggs into pan and stir fry into soft curds, then toss with rice mixture and cook a few minutes longer.

Serves 2.

SUKIYAKI

½ cup soy sauce
⅓ cup sake
¼ cup sugar
⅔ cup beef broth
1 tablespoon oil
2 pounds beef steak sliced very
   thin
8 dried mushrooms, soaked in
   water and sliced

2 large onions, sliced
1 bunch green onions, cut in
   2-inch pieces
2 cups sliced Chinese cabbage
1 bunch fresh spinach, washed
   and trimmed
1 block of tofu, cut in 1-inch
   cubes
Hot cooked rice

Combine soy sauce, sake, sugar, and broth to make sauce. Heat electric frying pan at table and add oil. Sauté meat, onions, and mushrooms, keeping each separate, until meat is seared. Sprinkle with sauce. Add vegetables and tofu (keeping them separated), pour the remaining sauce over them, cover, and cook until vegetables wilt. The traditional way of serving is for each person to beat one raw egg in a bowl, with chopsticks, take bites of meat and vegetables from cooking pan, and dip into egg before eating with rice. Other vegetables may be added or substituted. An alternative to the egg could be ponzu or goma dare sauce.

   Serves 6 to 8.

PONZU

½ cup soy sauce
½ cup fresh lime juice
2 tablespoons grated fresh ginger

2 tablespoons chopped green
   onion
½ to 1 teaspoon mustard powder
Several dashes Tabasco

Combine all ingredients. May be used as an alternative dip for sukiyaki and for salad dressing.

   Makes 1¼ cups.

GOMA DARE

½ cup sesame seeds
⅓ cup soy sauce

2 tablespoons mirin, sherry,
or sake
1 tablespoons sugar

Toast sesame seeds in ungreased heavy frying pan, turning and stirring until brown. Transfer to food processor and grind, then slowly add soy sauce and process until well mixed. Stir in mirin and sugar. May be used as dip for sukiyaki.

Makes 1 cup.

Note: I especially like goma dare as a dressing over fresh spinach that has been cooked, cooled, and squeezed dry, then formed into a 6- to 8-inch cylinder and sliced into 1-inch pinwheels. Place the pinwheels on a rimmed plate, pour over the goma dare, and place in the refrigerator to marinate for at least 1 hour.

SUNOMONO

2 cucumbers, preferably
Japanese, unpeeled, thinly
sliced
1 or 2 onions, thinly sliced

1 tablespoon salt
¼ cup rice vinegar
2 tablespoons sugar

Combine cucumbers and onions in a colander and toss with salt. Let marinate and lightly pickle for 1 to 2 hours. Rinse cucumbers and onions, drain, and place in a bowl. Add vinegar mixed with sugar and chill until serving. (Optional addition: black sesame seeds.)

Serves 4 to 6.

4

In the Shadow of
Matsuyama Castle

BEFORE MOVING IN THE fall to Fukuoka, we spent the summer of 1953 in Matsuyama, on the island of Shikoku across the Sea from Hiroshima. The cities along the Inland Sea were still recovering from heavy wartime damage. In Matsuyama, there were not enough residences to house the local population, let alone foreigners, so Cliff and I moved with our government-issued furniture into the newly constructed American Cultural Center. Located inside the castle moat, at the foot of one of the most beautiful and well-preserved feudal castles of Japan, the USIS Center—with an Olympic size sports facility and concert hall next door, all being built by the local government—symbolized the new Japan that was rising from the ashes of war.

We created an "apartment" by moving the bookshelves in the upstairs reading room away from the wall. Behind those shelves were our bed, two chairs, and a lamp; a table, a small refrigerator,

an electric hot plate, and a roaster oven functioned as kitchen. Our dining room was an open-air porch off this space; it had the best view in town of the castle, which was illuminated at night. There was a half-bathroom downstairs, which we shared with the public. Cliff shaved before the library opened in the morning. He usually had the company of Kiyo, the resident janitor's four-year-old daughter, who taught him her favorite Japanese children's songs. There was another sink in Cliff's first floor office, behind his desk. After we finished lunch upstairs, I would carry a pan of dirty dishes through the upstairs reading room, down the wide staircase in full view of all library patrons, and through the downstairs reading room to his office—to wash up as unobtrusively as possible. Frequently, Cliff had a visitor at the time and was trying to create an impression of dignity as the U.S. diplomatic representative in the area.

The summer fruits and vegetables were displayed like works of art in the small shops that lined the main street of town. These and the American canned and packaged goods shipped every two weeks by interisland steamers from the U.S. military commissary in Kobe were my raw materials. A small collection of cooking utensils, the hot plate, and the electric roaster oven were my tools.

On the outskirts of town was a small holdover from the days of U.S. Occupation—a "bachelor quarters" housing an Army major, a sergeant, and a private. They had a more elaborate kitchen plus a hired cook, and many nights we joined them for dinner and conversation in English. The only other English-speakers in Matsuyama, besides a few members of the USIS staff, were an American missionary couple who had been there prewar, and a Japanese college instructor who was born in California and lived there until he was ten. After dinner the sergeant (who had assumed the role of indulgent uncle to the kids in the neighborhood) would take a tray of homemade popsicles out of the freezer and distribute them to his gang. He spoke no Japanese, and their English vocabulary was limited to "Hello" and "Bye-bye," but they communicated effectively with smiles and gestures in the lingering twilight.

HOT PLATE COOKING IN THE AMERICAN LIBRARY

Cabbage skillet salad
Salmon and tomato salad
Ham and mushroom pasta

CABBAGE SKILLET SALAD

4 slices bacon
¼ cup vinegar
1 tablespoon brown sugar
1 teaspoon salt

1 tablespoon finely chopped
  onion
4 cups (medium head) chopped
  cabbage
½ cup chopped parsley

Cook bacon until crisp; remove from skillet and crumble. Add vinegar, sugar, salt, and onion to fat in skillet and cook until onion is soft. Add crumbled bacon. Remove from heat and toss cabbage and parsley in hot dressing.

Serves 6.

SALMON AND TOMATO SALAD

1 (16-ounce) can salmon,
  drained
1 tablespoon lemon juice
2 teaspoons chopped onions
1 cup diced unpeeled cucumber

3 hard-boiled eggs, sliced
¼ teaspoon salt
Dash pepper
6 large tomatoes

In mixing bowl, combine all ingredients except tomatoes. Starting at top, cut each tomato into quarters, without cutting all the way through. Place on serving plate and spread wedges open. Fill with salmon mix and serve with mayonnaise.

Serves 6.

Ham and Mushroom Pasta

6 to 8 ounces spaghetti	¼ cup tomato juice
3 tablespoons butter	¼ teaspoon rubbed sage
½ pound mushrooms, thinly sliced	⅛ teaspoon ground nutmeg
	⅓ cup cream
1 pound thinly sliced ham, cut into thin strips	¼ cup chopped parsley
	½ cup grated Parmesan cheese

In large frying pan, melt butter. Add mushrooms and cook, stirring occasionally, until juice evaporates and mushrooms are lightly browned. Add ham, tomato juice, sage, nutmeg, cream. Boil uncovered over high heat, stirring occasionally, until liquid is reduced to about half. Stir in parsley and 1 tablespoon cheese. Meanwhile, cook spaghetti until tender, then drain. Pour sauce over spaghetti and mix together until well blended. Serve with remaining cheese.

Serves 4.

The new sports stadium was completed during the summer, and a touring baseball team from Hawaii was invited to Matsuyama to play an exhibition game. The best seats from which to see all the action were on our second-story porch dining room. We invited the governor, the mayor, the press, and the heads of civic and sports organizations to be our guests. After the game we offered refreshments to them and all the ball players. The most popular items on our food table were the peanut butter and jam sandwiches that I had put together for the visitors from Hawaii, thinking they might be homesick for something other than rice and fish.

Reception for a Visiting Baseball Team

Peanut butter and jam sandwiches
Egg salad sandwiches
Sliced canned ham with rolls, mustard, and mayonnaise
Sweet potato salad
Fruit salad in watermelon shell
Butterscotch brownies
Cokes, beer, lemonade

Sweet Potato Salad

2 cans sweet potatoes or yams
4 finely cut green onions
1½ cups finely cut celery
4 mashed hard-boiled eggs

½ cup mayonnaise
½ cup cooked dressing (page 13)
½ teaspoon salt
Lettuce or watercress

Drain liquid from sweet potatoes. Mash potatoes and combine with remaining ingredients. This may be done a day ahead and kept covered in refrigerator. Serve with lettuce or watercress.

Serves 8.

Fruit Salad in Watermelon Shell

1 large watermelon
1 to 2 cans mandarin oranges
1 to 2 cups seedless grapes

1 to 2 cups sliced peaches
1 to 3 cups sliced apples
3 to 4 sliced bananas

Cut top off watermelon, creating an opening large enough for shell to serve as a bowl. Scoop out red flesh, remove seeds, and cut into bite-size pieces. Combine watermelon flesh with other fruit, making substitutions according to what is in season. Put the fruit salad in the watermelon shell.

Serves 12 to 20, depending on size of melon and amount of other fruit used.

BUTTERSCOTCH BROWNIES

¼ cup butter
1 cup brown sugar
1 egg
1 teaspoon vanilla
½ cup flour

1 teaspoon baking powder
½ teaspoon salt
2 cups finely chopped nuts or ¾
    cup grated coconut

Melt butter in saucepan and stir in brown sugar. Cool, then beat in egg and vanilla. Sift, then measure dry ingredients. Stir into butter mixture. Add nuts or coconut. Pour batter into well-greased and floured 9x9-inch pan. Bake for 20 to 25 minutes. Cut into bars when cool.

Makes about 16 thin, 2½-inch squares.

THE END OF SUMMER in Matsuyama was celebrated by a state fair for the surrounding prefecture's farmers. Shiny new farm machines were for sale, prize produce and livestock were on display, and booths offered games of chance and skill as well as publications for farmers. Much of this looked like an American event, with a distinctly Japanese flavor. We had watched the vibrant green rice fields turn to gold. As the stalks became heavy with plump grains, scarecrows made their appearance in the fields. During the fair, a scarecrow contest was held along Okaido, the main shopping street of Matsuyama. Their duties done in the now-harvested fields, these whimsical figures were propped up against the lamp posts with a ballot box available at each post, and shoppers were invited to select the most imaginative for a series of prizes.

Like the uprooted scarecrows, we too were being moved to another site for interaction with a new public, from the island of Shikoku to Fukuoka on the southern island of Kyushu.

Recipes for a Harvest Supper

Professor Kleinpell's tamale pie
Chicken vegetable casserole
Tomato pudding
Green beans with water chestnuts
Ozark pie with hard sauce

Professor Kleinpell's Tamale Pie

This was one of the first recipes in my collection. Professor Kleinpell had been in the same Japanese internment camp as Cliff in the Philippines, then returned to resume teaching at Berkeley. He and his wife entertained us when we were Stanford students and fed us tamale pie.

1½ pounds ground beef
1 large onion, chopped
1 (13-ounce) can tomatoes
1 (12-ounce) can corn
2½ teaspoons salt
¼ teaspoon pepper
4 to 6 teaspoons chili
1 clove garlic, minced

1½ cups cornmeal
1 cup water
1 cup pitted black olives
1¼ cups milk
2 tablespoons butter
1 cup grated cheddar cheese
2 beaten eggs.

Sauté meat. Stir in vegetables, 2 teaspoons salt, pepper, chili, garlic, and 1 cup cornmeal mixed with 1 cup water. Simmer 10 minutes. Add olives. Turn into casserole. To make topping, scald together milk, ½ teaspoon salt, and butter, then add ½ cup cornmeal, cheese, and eggs. Spoon topping over meat mixture and bake 40 minutes at 375°.

Serves 8.

Chicken Vegetable Casserole

2 strips bacon	2 stalks celery
3 to 4 pounds chicken pieces	4 small onions
1 teaspoon salt	12 mushroom caps
¼ teaspoon pepper	3 tomatoes
4 small potatoes	2 bay leaves
4 carrots	1 teaspoon rosemary
1 green pepper	¼ cup sherry

Lay bacon on bottom of large casserole. Cover with chicken and sprinkle with salt and pepper. Top with cut-up vegetables, bay leaves, and rosemary. Pour sherry over all. Cover and bake 1½ hours at 375°.

Serves 4 to 6.

Tomato Pudding

1 (32-ounce) can tomatoes	¾ cup boiling water
1 cup brown sugar	3 cups white bread cubes
1 teaspoon salt	½ cup melted butter

Strain tomatoes through sieve into a saucepan, crushing pulp thoroughly. Add brown sugar and salt; stir well. Add boiling water and let bubble on stove 5 minutes. Cut bread into ½-inch cubes and put in medium casserole. Pour melted butter over cubes; add boiling tomato mixture; stir again. Bake 50 minutes at 375°.

Serves 6 to 8.

Green Beans with Water Chestnuts

2 pounds green beans	1 teaspoon sugar
1 (5-ounce) can sliced water chestnuts	1 teaspoon salt
	1 teaspoon vinegar
2 tablespoons butter	Dash pepper
½ cup finely chopped onion	1 cup sour cream or yogurt

Cook beans until tender. Add water chestnuts and heat through; drain and put in bowl. In another pan, melt butter and cook onions until tender, not brown. Combine remaining ingredients with onions. Heat but do not boil. Pour sauce over beans and water chestnuts.

Serves 8.

Ozark Pie

2 large eggs, beaten	1 cup chopped walnuts and/or
1 to 1½ cups sugar	raisins
6 tablespoons flour	1½ cups raw apples, chopped
½ teaspoon salt	1 teaspoon vanilla
2 teaspoons baking powder	

Mix eggs and sugar. Sift dry ingredients and add. Stir in remaining ingredients. Pour into greased pie pan or 9x13-inch dish and bake about 45 minutes at 350°. Serve with hard sauce.

Serves 8 to 10.

Hard Sauce

½ cup butter	1 teaspoon vanilla, rum, sherry,
1½ cups sifted powdered sugar	or brandy
1 egg	

Work softened butter against bowl until light and creamy. Add sugar gradually, beating smooth. Fold in slightly beaten egg white and flavoring. Chill before using.

5

Parties in Fukuoka

B Y THE TIME WE reached Fukuoka in the fall of 1953, I had
a collection of tried-and-true recipes, and we were ready to
face a much more demanding schedule of receptions and formal
dinner parties. We were no longer the only U.S. official family in
town. As members of an American diplomatic team assigned to the
U.S. Consulate for the island of Kyushu, we had a support system
of colleagues with whom we could consult—and we could and did
help each other out. It was here that I became involved in giving
"American cooking lessons," something I would be requested to
repeat as we moved to other cities in Asia.

This was a wonderful time to be in Japan. With the years of bitter-
ness and battle behind us, we and the Japanese were discovering each
other as real people, trying to understand the complexities of each
other's culture and social habits, and enjoying the learning process.

The Japanese hesitated to invite foreigners into their homes,
embarrassed because their small living spaces were "too humble."
Wives were not expected to accompany husbands when they came
to our parties, or when the Japanese entertained in public places.
But after we got to know the women in our cooking-exchange
class, those women insisted on coming with their husbands (who
were university professors, doctors, journalists, and government

officials) to our dinner parties. We had broken down one formi-
dable cultural barrier.

Another exception to the "women belong at home" rule was the
Asahi Beer Club. That club embraced all the top business, civic,
and government leaders of Fukuoka, including the two men of the
U.S. Consulate. It had one purpose: for the men to get together after work Friday evenings and drink all the beer they could consume
from the time the starting gong was hit until the ending gong re-
sounded, about ninety minutes. A few times a year, the club hosted
gatherings for the wives.

On one occasion, a luncheon for the ladies was held in the
newly opened branch of Tokyo's Nikkatsu Hotel. This was the first
Western-style hotel in Fukuoka. Betty Martin (the Consul's wife)
and I arrived a bit late and found all the Japanese ladies were seated
at tables for four, which were set for a formal European-style dinner. The Master of Ceremonies, who regularly presided over the
beer club's men's meetings, met us at the door and escorted us to
a table for two right in the center of the room. Then he started
proceedings:

"Ladies," he announced to all who were present, "there are two
foreign women sitting at the table in the center of the room." All
heads turned towards us. "You will see that there are many spoons
and knives and forks in front of you. Please watch the two foreign
ladies to see which ones they use for each course. Then do exactly
as they do."

I have never seen a table with so many implements. Betty and I
looked at each other, shrugged, and agreed that we would simply
start from the outside and work in as course followed course, and
we would hope it all came out even. It did. When the luncheon
party ended, each of the kimono-clad ladies was sent home carrying a six-pack of Asahi beer.

When Joe DiMaggio brought his bride, Marilyn Monroe, to
Fukuoka where he was invited to spend a week as visiting coach

for the Nishitetsu Lions baseball team, they stayed at the Nikkatsu Hotel. Their first night they came to our American Cultural Center, where Joe gave an orientation lecture to Fukuoka's baseball elite. Cliff was left sitting next to Marilyn when Joe went to the front of the hall to make his presentation. How does one start a conversation with America's number-one sex goddess, who has just married a baseball hero? Cliff made a brave attempt: "Mrs. DiMaggio, do you enjoy baseball?" She responded candidly that the game bored her.

Marilyn left Fukuoka the next day, despite a nasty sore throat, to do a pre-Thanksgiving show for the GIs who were still stationed in Korea. A memorable photo of her performance in a snowstorm before thousands of homesick American boys, clad in what looked like a black slip, appeared on the cover of *LIFE* magazine. Marilyn, the trooper, went on with the show, undaunted by her own discomfort, feeling more at home performing than as an accessory to baseball.

Evenings such as that with the DiMaggios at the Center called for a reception to follow. We hosted receptions and/or dinners to celebrate concerts by visiting American musicians, speeches by American scholars, seminars led by poets, inspections by officials from Washington D.C. and the Tokyo American Embassy. Christmas, Thanksgiving, Halloween, Easter, and July Fourth all called for their own ceremonial hospitality. It was busy and it was fun.

CEREMONIAL HOSPITALITY—EVENING RECEPTION

Fish house punch
Holiday wine punch
Cheese wafers
Roquefort meatballs
Danish liver pate and bread or cucumber slices
Assorted raw vegetables
Deviled eggs

FISH HOUSE PUNCH

1½ gallons strong black tea
5 pounds sugar
3 pints lemon juice
3 pints brandy

6 quarts bourbon
3 pints rum
6 quarts soda water

Add sugar to hot tea. Cool. Add lemon juice, brandy, bourbon, and rum. Mix well. (Best to do this several days ahead.) Add soda just before serving.

Serves 75.

HOLIDAY WINE PUNCH

1 cup sugar
1 cup water
2 cups grapefruit juice
½ cup each lemon, lime, and
    orange juice
2 cups chilled club soda

1½ quart white wine (or ginger ale)
Thin slices of orange, lemon,
    and lime
Ice blocks (freeze ahead in plastic
    containers)

In 1- to 2-quart pan bring sugar and water to boil, stirring until sugar is dissolved. Let syrup cool, then chill in refrigerator. Add fruit juices to syrup. To serve, pour juice mixture into 5- to 6-quart punch bowl. Add club soda and wine (or ginger ale). Add ice and fruit slices. Ladle punch into cups to serve.

Makes 3¼ quarts, enough for 18 servings of about ¾ cup each.

Cheese Wafers

¼ pound sharp cheese
¼ pound butter
1 cup flour

2 teaspoons salt
1 teaspoon Worcestershire sauce
Dash cayenne

Grate cheese; add other ingredients and mix together until solid mass is formed. Shape into roll. Wrap in wax paper and refrigerate 24 hours. Slice thin and bake 8 to 10 minutes at 400°.

Makes about 60 wafers.

Roquefort Meatballs

1½ pounds ground beef
3 ounces Roquefort cheese, crumbled
¾ teaspoon salt

⅛ teaspoon pepper
¼ cup butter or oil
½ cup Burgundy or other red wine

Combine beef, cheese, salt and pepper. Form into 1-inch meatballs. Brown in butter or oil. Add wine and cook 3 to 5 minutes.

Makes about 50 meatballs.

Danish Liver Pate

1½ pounds chicken livers
1 cup butter
2 medium onions, chopped
2 cloves garlic, minced

½ teaspoon thyme
2 tablespoons cognac
¼ teaspoon ground allspice
Salt and pepper

Quarter the livers. In large frying pan, melt half the butter. Add onions, garlic, and thyme and cook over moderate heat until onions are soft but not brown. Add livers and sauté over moderately high heat until just cooked. Do not overcook. The appearance of red juices usually indicates that livers are done. Transfer contents of pan to blender and add cognac. Melt remaining butter and pour into blender. Process at high speed until completely smooth. Season with allspice, salt, and pepper. Pour into crock or other serving bowl and cover with plastic wrap. Store in refrigerator. Serve on cucumber slices or dark bread.

Makes about 1 quart.

CEREMONIAL HOSPITALITY—AFTERNOON TEA

Silver service tea and coffee
Virginia Sally Lunn bread
Cranberry tea bread
Date nut squares
Ribbon cookies
Cherry pie supreme
Blender pecan pie
Danish rum cake with rum sauce

VIRGINIA SALLY LUNN BREAD

5 eggs
2 cups milk
6 cups flour
1 cup shortening

1 package yeast dissolved in ¼ cup
  warm water
2 tablespoons sugar
2 teaspoons salt

Break eggs; add milk and beat together. Cream flour and shortening and add to egg mixture. Beat well. Add dissolved yeast, sugar, and salt. Let rise 4 hours. Beat down, then place in greased tube pan to rise for 1 hour or more. Bake 45 minutes at 350°.

CRANBERRY TEA BREAD

¾ cup butter
1½ cups packed brown sugar
4 eggs
3 cups flour
2 teaspoons baking powder
2 teaspoons baking soda

2 teaspoons ground cinnamon
½ teaspoon ground cloves
1 (1-pound) can whole-berry
    cranberry sauce
⅔ cup chopped walnuts
⅔ cup golden raisins

In large mixing bowl, beat butter and sugar together until creamy, then beat in eggs one at a time, beating well after each addition. Sift together flour, baking powder, baking soda, cinnamon, and cloves. Add to creamed mixture and stir until blended. Mix in cranberry sauce, nuts, and raisins. Spoon batter into two greased and floured 9x5-inch loaf pans. Bake at 350° for 1 hour or until done. Cool bread in pans 10 minutes, then turn out on wire rack to cool completely.

Makes two loaves.

DATE NUT SQUARES

2 eggs
½ cup sugar
½ teaspoon vanilla
½ cup sifted flour

½ teaspoon baking powder
½ teaspoon salt
1 cup chopped walnuts
2 cups finely cut dates

Beat eggs until foamy. Beat in sugar and vanilla. Sift and stir in flour, baking powder, and salt. Mix in walnuts and dates. Spread in well-greased 8-inch square pan. Bake at 325° until there is a dull crust (25 to 30 minutes). Cut into squares while warm. Cool, then remove from pan. Dip in powdered sugar if desired.

Makes 16 2-inch squares.

RIBBON COOKIES

2½ cups sifted flour
1½ teaspoons baking powder
½ teaspoon salt
1 cup soft butter or margerine
1¼ cups sugar
1 egg, unbeaten

1 teaspoon vanilla
¼ cup snipped candied cherries, drained
1 square unsweetened chocolate, melted
2 tablespoons poppy seeds

Sift flour with baking powder and salt. Cream shortening until light and fluffy, gradually adding sugar. Stir in egg and vanilla; beat well. Blend in flour mixture. Divide dough into three parts: add cherries to one, melted chocolate to second, poppy seeds to third. Into bottom of wax-paper-lined 9x5-inch loaf pan, pack cherry mixture evenly. Next pack in chocolate, then poppy seed layer. Cover with waxed paper and refrigerate at least 24 hours. To bake, remove dough from pan. Cut in half lengthwise, then crosswise into ¼-inch slices. Bake 8 minutes or until very light brown at 400°.

Makes 6 to 7 dozen cookies.

CHERRY PIE SUPREME

9-inch unbaked pie crust
1 can cherry pie filling
4 (3-ounce) packages soft cream cheese

2 eggs
½ teaspoon vanilla
1 cup sour cream

Prepare pie crust. Spread half of cherry pie filling in bottom; set rest aside. Bake at 400° for 15 minutes, or just until crust is golden. Remove from oven. Reduce temperature to 350°. Meanwhile, in small bowl, beat cheese with sugar, eggs, and vanilla until smooth. Pour over hot cherry pie filling. Bake about 25 minutes. Filling will be slightly soft in center. Cool completely on wire rack. To serve, spoon sour cream around edge of pie. Fill center with remaining pie filling.

Serves 8.

Blender Pecan Pie

9-inch unbaked pie crust
2 eggs
⅔ cup sugar
½ teaspoon salt
½ cup light corn syrup

2 tablespoons butter, melted
1 teaspoon vanilla
1 cup pecans
12 pecan halves for garnish

Prepare pie crust. Place eggs, sugar, salt, syrup, butter, vanilla in blender and process until mixed. Add pecans and run machine just long enough to chop pecans, not too small. Pour into pie crust. Arrange pecan halves on top and bake 15 minutes at 450°. Reduce heat to 350° and cook 30 minutes longer.

Serves 6 to 8.

Danish Rum Cake

1 cup butter
1 cup sugar
Grated rind of 2 oranges
  and 1 lemon
2 eggs
2½ cups sifted flour

2 teaspoons baking powder
1 teaspoon baking soda
½ teaspoon salt
1 cup buttermilk
1 cup finely chopped walnuts
1 cup chopped dates

Cream butter, add sugar gradually, and beat until light and fluffy. Add grated rinds. Add eggs and beat until light. Sift together flour, baking powder, baking soda, and salt. Add to creamed mixture alternately with buttermilk. Fold in nuts and dates. Pour into greased 9- or 10-inch tube pan. Bake at 350° about 1 hour. When done, pour rum sauce slowly over cake in pan. Cool in pan and store for a day or two before serving. If desired, serve with whipped cream.

Serves 8.

RUM SAUCE

Juice of 2 oranges	1 cup sugar
Juice of 1 lemon	2 tablespoons rum

Strain orange and lemon juices. Mix with sugar and rum and boil to dissolve sugar.

Makes 1 cup.

IN 1954, OUR FIRST son was born in a military hospital. Formerly a Japanese postal insurance company headquarters, it had been turned into a U.S. Army rear-lines hospital for casualties from the battles in Korea. We told Tom later, "Dear, you came to us by special delivery in the post office!"

Before Tom's birth, we had been living in Dazaifu, a beautiful and historic town outside of Fukuoka. It was in this area that Chinese writing and Buddhism were first introduced to Japan via the Korean peninsula, and here the thirteenth-century Mongol invasion of Japan was thwarted by a *kamikaze* ("divine wind," in this case an unseasonal typhoon). Our home was the guest house of a traditional Japanese inn, with its own classical garden, nestled at the foot of a holy mountain. It was beautiful and charming. And hard work. All water that came into the house had to be hand pumped—my job, which was even more challenging on wintry mornings, when a layer of ice formed on the pump. Setting fire to newspapers wrapped around the shaft was the only way to get the handle working. We bathed in an *ofuro,* a wooden tub with a wood-burning stove below it, into which logs were hand-fed from outside to heat the water. We had no central heating, just a kerosene space heater in the living room and a portable heater that we carried from room to room as we moved about the house. Both heaters often belched clouds of soot and heated little more than a three-foot radius. We cooked on the portable oven and hot plate we had used in the Matsuyama library. Any hot water for the kitchen had to be heated on that hot plate.

So, as my pregnancy advanced, we sought a house in town and found one that was more conveniently located. Though we still heated with space heaters, we had running water and—more significantly—we found two Japanese women who became our resident maids and coped efficiently with all the complexities of a non-Western house.

The entire island of Kyushu was the diplomatic domain of the Fukuoka Consulate. Cliff and I set off on a reconnaissance tour of our territory with Betty and Jim Martin (the Consul). We rode in a USIS van, with a Japanese driver and Cliff's senior Japanese assistant. No good highways existed in those days, and potholes were so endemic that we punctured at least one tire daily. Betty and I tried to time our picnic lunches with the tire-changing stop. Alternatively, we stopped at a village food stand for a quick and tasty hot lunch. It took us fourteen days to make the circuit; high school students running an endurance race about the same time did the distance in ten days. It was faster to run than to drive around the island!

Lunch on the Road

Oyako domburi (chicken and egg on rice)
Zaru soba (cold noodles with dipping sauce)
Miso soup (bean paste soup)
Chirashi sushi (cold rice salad)

DASHI

Dashi is a crucial ingredient in many Japanese recipes, including those below. A clear fish stock, it is used for soups, simmered dishes, and marinades. Packets of instant dashi are available in many oriental markets.

6 cups water
2-inch square kombu (dried kelp)

3 tablespoons katsuobushi (dried flaked bonito)

Bring water to boil. Wash kombu under cold tap water and add to boiling water. Stir and let boil 3 minutes, then remove kelp and add bonito. Bring to boil again and remove from heat immediately. Leave for a few minutes until flakes settle, then strain and use as needed.

Makes 6 cups.

OYAKO DOMBURI

1 large boneless, skinless chicken breast
2 cups chicken broth or dashi
3 tablespoons mirin or dry sherry

5 tablespoons soy sauce
6 eggs
¼ teaspoon salt
6 green onions, thinly sliced
Cooked short-grain rice

Cut chicken into small pieces. Heat chicken broth or dashi with mirin and soy sauce. When boiling, add chicken, return to boil, cover, and simmer 8 minutes. Meanwhile, beat eggs slightly, adding salt. Add eggs and ¾ of green onions to simmering broth. Without stirring, let mixture return to boil, then turn heat very low, cover, and cook 3 to 4 minutes until eggs are set but still soft. Spoon rice into individual ceramic serving bowls, then pour chicken and egg mixture over the rice. Garnish with remaining onions.

Serves 6.

ZARU SOBA

7 ounces soba (buckwheat
    noodles)
2 cups chicken broth or dashi
½ cup mirin or dry sherry
½ cup soy sauce

2 teaspoons sugar and/or
    ¼ teaspoon salt (optional)
1 sheet nori (dried seaweed)
1 tablespoon grated fresh ginger
3 green onions, thinly sliced

Bring large saucepan of water to boil and add noodles. When water boils again, add 1 cup cold water. Boil again and cook until noodles are just tender (about 2 minutes). Drain and rinse with cold water until they are cold. Drain well. Make a dipping sauce by combining broth or dashi, mirin or sherry, and soy sauce in a small pan. Bring to boil, remove from heat, and cool. Add salt and/or sugar to taste, and divide into 4 individual cups. Toast nori over gas or electric burner, or under grill in oven, until crisp. Divide noodles among 4 plates and crumble nori on top. Mix ginger with green onions and put portion on each plate. Each person stirs ginger mixture into sauce, then dips noodles into sauce before eating.

    Serves 4.

MISO SOUP

5 cups dashi or chicken broth
2 teaspoons red miso (bean
    paste)

1 cup cubed tofu (¼-inch cubes)
2 green onions, sliced diagonally
2 mushrooms, sliced

Bring dashi or broth to boil. Mix some of the hot liquid with bean paste in small bowl, stirring until smooth. Pour mixture back into dashi, stir well, add tofu and onions, and return to boil. Simmer only a few seconds. Ladle into bowls and garnish each with slices of mushroom.

    Serves 4.

CHIRASHI SUSHI

1 batch sushi rice (page 137)
4 dried shitake mushrooms
1 tablespoon soy sauce
1 tablespoon sugar
2 eggs
Pinch salt
Vegetable oil
½ cup cooked crab or shrimp

½ cup finely sliced cooked or
    raw fish
½ cup shredded bamboo shoot
½ cup cooked green peas
1 piece canned lotus root, sliced
1 tablespoon takuan (pickled
    Japanese radish), thinly sliced
1 tablespoon beni shoga (pickled
    red ginger) for garnish

Pour boiling water over mushrooms and soak 30 minutes. Remove and discard stems; slice caps thinly. In a medium pan, heat ½ cup of water used for soaking, add mushrooms, soy sauce, and sugar, then simmer 10 minutes. Beat eggs slightly, season with salt, and cook in lightly oiled pan to make a thin omelet, taking care not to let it brown. Cool, then cut into thin shreds. Toss prepared sushi rice gently with egg strips, simmered mushrooms, and all remaining ingredients, reserving a few of the most colorful for garnish, and serve cold.

Serves 6.

ON OUR TRIP AROUND the island, we called on governors and mayors and university presidents and newspaper editors. En route we stopped at ancient Korean-style burial mounds and Shinto shrines on the edge of the sea and at the foot of holy mountains which were revered as the origins of Japan's imperial history and the dynasty which has ruled from the seventh century BCE until today. In Kagoshima Prefecture, we traced the footsteps of the samurai warriors and feudal lords who were founders of modern Japan. In Nagasaki, we continued our journey through history with visits to the alleged home of Madame Butterfly, to Baishinji Temple where the last Czar of Russia stayed when he was a youth serving in the Imperial Navy (the Vladivostok-based fleet came to warmer Japanese waters for the winter), and to the peace statue commemorating the second atomic bomb explosion of the Second World War.

The only other American diplomatic post on Kyushu was in the center of Nagasaki. The American Cultural Center here was housed in two buildings, one serving as library and the other with a theater for film showings and rooms for meetings. The buildings were separated by a soy sauce factory, and permeated by the strong odor of beans being transformed into seasoning for Japanese cuisine.

COOKING WITH SOY

Beef teriyaki
Nabeyaki udon (hearty noodle soup)
Kakejiru (broth for hot noodles)

BEEF TERIYAKI

6 slices beef fillet	6 tablespoons mirin or sherry
1 clove garlic	2 tablespoons oil
½ cup plus 2 teaspoons sugar	2 teaspoons sugar
½ teaspoon grated ginger	4 tablespoons water or dashi
6 tablespoons soy sauce	1 tablespoon cornstarch mixed with cold water

Trim fat off beef. Crush garlic with ½ cup sugar and mix with ginger, soy sauce, and mirin. Marinate steaks in mixture for about 30 minutes, coating each side. Heat heavy griddle or frying pan and spread oil over surface. When hot, put steaks on griddle for 1 minute; turn to brown other side; reduce heat and continue cooking until done. In a small pan, combine remaining marinade, 2 teaspoons sugar, and water or dashi. Bring to boil, and stir in cornstarch. Stir until mixture boils and become clear, then pour over steaks.
Serves 8.

NABEYAKI UDON

6 dried shitake mushrooms
1 pound udon (thick wheat
   noodles)
1 can kamaboku (fish cakes—
   optional)

1 large chicken breast
2 green onions
6 cups kakejiru (below)

Soak mushrooms in hot water 30 minutes. Remove stems and slice caps thinly. Bring large saucepan of water to boil and add noodles. When water returns to boil, add 1 cup cold water. Bring to boil again and cook until noodles are just tender. Drain well. Slice fish cakes. Cut chicken breast into thin slices. Cut green onion into thin diagonal slices. Bring kakejiru to boil, add mushrooms and chicken, and simmer 4 minutes. Add noodles, heat through, then garnish with fish cakes and green onions.

   Serves 6.

KAKEJIRU

6 cups dashi (page 53) or
   chicken broth

½ cup mirin or sherry
½ cup soy sauce

Combine ingredients in saucepan and bring to boil. Reduce heat, cover, and simmer 10 minutes. Taste and add salt if necessary.

   Makes about 7 cups.

ONE OF THE "TARGET AUDIENCES" for the USIS program was university students. Being a student during the years when Japan was trying to recover from the physical and psychological scars of the Pacific War was not easy. The young people had no surplus cash, their classrooms had no central heating to soften the winter chills, and they were expected to stick to the business of studying and preparing to rebuild their nation, with no frivolities on the side. The USIS library was a favorite gathering place for university students. It was warm, welcoming, and had a good collection of books and periodicals—which were available to all on open shelves rather than locked up and restricted to the elite.

The USIS facilities shared a building with the American Consulate, at the dead end of a short, wide street, where the City Hall and the Prefectural Capitol were also located. A perfect place for political demonstrations, since the major institutions one would wish to protest against were on this street. One Saturday, the protest was against the "Rhee Line," which had been proclaimed by the president of Korea to keep Japanese fishermen out of what the Koreans claimed were their waters. At the head of the chanting, banner-waving crowd was a group of students from Kyushu University carrying an effigy of the U. S. Secretary of State, John Foster Dulles, the designated villain behind this unpopular demarcation. As they snake-danced through the carport of the U.S. building, the effigy hit the light fixture, breaking light bulbs. No further damage. The demonstration ended and participants went home.

Monday morning, three young men in their student uniforms asked to meet with the USIS director. One was carrying what looked like a shoebox, which he shifted nervously from hand to hand. "Please, come on into my office," said Cliff.

One of the young men explained their mission: "We like your library and want to continue to be able to use it. We were in the demonstration on Saturday and, regrettably, two of your light bulbs were broken. We are sorry, and we have brought you new bulbs to replace them."

Those were kinder, gentler days. Today a group of nervous young men carrying an unidentified package would not be readily welcomed into a U.S. diplomatic establishment abroad.

TASTES OF KOREA

Bulgogi (fiery beef) with dipping sauce
Kim chee (pickled cabbage)

BULGOGI

2 pounds lean beef	1 teaspoon grated fresh ginger
½ cup soy sauce	1 tablespoon sugar
½ cup water	½ teaspoon ground black pepper
4 tablespoons finely chopped green onions	2 tablespoons roasted, crushed sesame seeds
2 teaspoons minced garlic	

Cut beef into very thin slices. Beat them flat and cut into 1- to 2-inch squares. Prepare a marinade of the remaining ingredients and soak meat 3 hours or longer in refrigerator. When ready to serve, grill briefly over hot coals. Serve with Korean dipping sauce in individual bowls.

Serves 10 to 12 as an appetizer, 6 to 8 as a main dish accompanied by hot rice.

KOREAN DIPPING SAUCE

3 tablespoons soy sauce
2 teaspoons sesame oil
2 tablespoons water
2 tablespoons sake or sherry
1 tablespoon toasted, ground
    sesame seeds

2 teaspoons finely chopped green
    onion
½ to 1 teaspoon hot pepper sauce
    (optional)
1 small clove garlic, crushed
1 teaspoon sugar
Salt to taste

Combine soy sauce and sesame oil in a small bowl. Stir in water, wine, sesame seeds, onion, and pepper sauce. Crush garlic with salt and sugar to a fine paste and stir into the sauce.

Makes ½ cup.

KIM CHEE

1 large white Chinese cabbage
Salt (not iodized)
Cayenne pepper
6 green onions, finely chopped
6 cloves garlic, finely chopped
2 fresh red chilies, finely
    chopped

3 teaspoons fresh ginger, finely
    chopped
2 cups dashi or broth
2 tablespoons light soy sauce
Pinch monosodium glutamate
    (optional)

Cut base off cabbage, then slice lengthwise into 6 segments. Dry in the sun for half a day, then cut each segment in half crossways. Place in unglazed earthenware pot alternately with handfuls of salt and sprinkling of cayenne pepper, making several layers. Cover with wooden lid just small enough to fit inside the pot so that it rests directly on the cabbage. Weigh it down with a heavy stone and leave for a week. Rinse cabbage thoroughly under cold running water. Squeeze out as much liquid as possible. Slice into 1-inch sections and put into the pot, which has been rinsed out. This time, layer cabbage with onions, garlic, chilies and ginger. Fill pot with dashi or broth mixed with soy and monosodium glutamate. Cover with wax paper, return lid to top, and refrigerate. After 4 to 5 days, kim chee is ready for eating. Serve as condiment with hot rice and dashi or soy sauce. In cold weather, kim chee does not need refrigeration, but in warm weather store in refrigerator up to 3 weeks.

Makes approximately 1 quart.

6

In Japan's Cultural Heartland

I N EARLY 1956, WE moved again, this time to Kobe. At that time it was one of the busiest seaports in the world, a cosmopolitan and prosperous city, proud that it was one of the first in Japan to welcome resident foreign businessmen. With a large and socially active diplomatic community and Cliff's expanded role as the regional supervisor of American centers in Kobe, Osaka, Kyoto, Hiroshima, and Takamatsu on Shikoku, we were busy at home and on the road.

Our house was in a suburb, Ashiya, on a hilltop that overlooked a valley dotted with rice fields. It was a massive stucco residence with high ceilings and spacious rooms. The yard was a miniature pine forest sprinkled with azalea bushes that burst into a purple-and-white fairyland in the spring. It was a wonderful house in late spring, summer, and early fall. But with no central heating, it was frigid in the cool months. In winter we huddled around space heaters, dressed in layers of woolen clothing. If we entertained, we would invite a crowd, counting on the body heat to raise the room temperature.

I was invited to teach a series of cooking classes at a nearby farmers' cooperative headquarters. The members' wives wanted to know what Americans ate for breakfast, lunch, and dinner, and how to prepare some of the dishes. We progressed together through the basic "mom's home cooking" routine, from scrambled eggs and French toast to meatloaf and apple pie.

At the same time, Cliff and I were acquiring a taste for the Japanese breakfasts we were served at inns on our travels: rice, soup, fish, pickles, a raw egg, and green tea. Our son Tom, now age three, ate Japanese food with our two maids when we went out for the evening. One night as we were getting ready to leave, we heard loud complaints (in Japanese, the language he used more than English) coming out of the kitchen: "You didn't give me any seaweed! How can I eat my rice without seaweed?"

Tom attended a Japanese preschool. In his class of three-year-olds there were two other foreign children; everyone else in the school was Japanese. They all wore uniforms—black shorts or skirts, white shirts, black berets, regulation tennis shoes—and they carried white wicker lunch baskets. In late November the entire school went on an excursion into the woods to hunt for chestnuts. Mothers were invited to come along. It was an instructive lesson for me in how Japanese children are taught from an early age to share, how individual competitiveness may be tempered in favor of the group. The children were released, their lunch baskets in hand, to scramble for nuts under the trees. At the sound of the head teacher's whistle, every child ran back to where his or her class teacher sat at the edge of a blanket on the ground. Some children, like our aggressive Tom, had full baskets while some shy ones had just a few chestnuts. Teachers instructed the children to empty their baskets into a pile on the blanket, then proceeded to count out equal numbers of nuts for each child to take home.

Chestnut Recipes

Blanched, shelled chestnuts
Roasted chestnuts
Cream of chestnut soup
Holiday turkey stuffing
Mont Blanc (chestnut pudding)

BLANCHED, SHELLED CHESTNUTS

Cut a ½-inch crisscross gash on the flat side of each nut with a sharp vegetable knife. Cover with boiling water and bring to boiling point. Take nuts out of the water one at a time. Remove shell and inner skin with a sharp pointed knife.

ROASTED CHESTNUTS

Cut crisscross gash on each nut as above. Put nuts in shallow pan and add 1 teaspoon butter or oil for each cup of nuts. Bake about 20 minutes at 450°. Stir nuts occasionally so they will be coated. Serve warm as a snack.

CREAM OF CHESTNUT SOUP

1 quart chicken broth
1 cup blanched, shelled
   chestnuts

1½ cups cream or milk, heated
½ teaspoon salt
⅛ teaspoon paprika

Bring broth to boiling point. Add chestnuts and simmer until soft. Whirl in blender. Add heated cream or milk and seasonings.
   Serves 6 to 8.

HOLIDAY TURKEY STUFFING

Fill neck cavity of holiday turkey with shelled chestnuts. Use regular bread stuffing for larger cavity. (If chestnuts are not available, I use canned water chestnuts instead.)

MONT BLANC

1 pound blanched, shelled chestnuts	½ teaspoon salt
	1 teaspoon vanilla
Milk	2 tablespoons brandy or rum
1 cup powdered sugar	Baked pastry or meringue shells

Place chestnuts in saucepan, cover with milk, and cook until soft. Drain and mash with a fork. Sweeten to taste with sugar; add salt, vanilla, and liquor. Puree in food processor. To serve, pile lightly on 3-inch rounds of baked pastry or meringue shells. To create a snow-capped mountain, mound the puree on a serving dish and decorate with whipped cream.

Serves 6.

SINCE VISITING OUR HOUSE involved a trip of up to an hour for Japanese guests from the cities of Kobe, Osaka, or Kyoto, we tried to provide them with a full meal—if not a seated dinner at least a hearty "cocktail buffet." I was now searching for recipes that could be made in large quantities and preferably prepared ahead of time, since I did most of the cooking.

One of my favorite desserts was a recipe shared by the wife of another officer in the Kobe American Consulate. The first time Helen Redding served us her almond icebox dessert was the night our watchdog was being fed another kind of dessert, Morinaga Caramels. The sticky candies kept him from barking while two clever burglars waited for us to come home. They entered the house after we were asleep and helped themselves to silver and fine linen from the dining room, and cameras and wallets from our bedroom and that of our houseguest. I woke up seeing a burglar in our bedroom, scrutinizing the objects on top of the bureau by the light of a match. I screamed, and he fled with his cohort, taking along several bundles of treasure. They had cut our phone lines with kitchen knives, which were laid out on the dining table; Cliff had to go in person down the hill to the neighborhood police box to report the intrusion.

Feeding a Crowd

Chicken with apricots
Monterey turkey casserole
Beef Stroganoff
Carbonnade de boeuf
New Orleans broccoli mold
Chicken salad
Green pea salad
Tomato sour cream ring
Almond ice box dessert
Coupe Melba
Mint mousse

Chicken with Apricots

8 chicken breasts
1½ cups flour
Salt and pepper
1 teaspoon ground ginger
12 tablespoons butter or
  margarine
¾ cup water

¼ cup chopped onion
1 (1-pound) can apricot halves
Chicken stock
2 tablespoons cornstarch
¼ cup Cointreau or orange
  liqueur

Mix flour, salt, pepper, and ginger in paper bag and shake chicken to coat. Sauté in 4 tablespoons butter. Remove to large casserole. Add water and remaining butter, melted. Bake 30 minutes at 375°, basting frequently. Sauté onion in chicken browning butter. Drain apricots, saving juice. Add chicken stock to juice to make 2 cups. Blend in cornstarch. Add to onion and bring to boil. Add apricots and liqueur. Pour sauce over chicken.

Serves 4 to 6.

Monterey Turkey Casserole

2½ pounds frozen boneless
  turkey roast
4 tablespoons butter
6 tablespoons flour
2 cups milk

4 large or 6 medium potatoes
Milk, butter and salt
1½ cups shredded Monterey
  cheese
Paprika

Cook turkey roast and allow to cool overnight. To prepare sauce, melt butter, stir in flour, then gradually add milk, cooking until thick. Cook, peel, and mash potatoes, adding milk, butter, and salt as needed. Spread half of sauce on bottom of 9x13-inch baking dish. Top with thinly sliced turkey. Sprinkle with cheese. Top with remaining sauce. Dust generously with paprika. Spoon potato puffs around edge of casserole. Heat at 450° for 20 to 30 minutes.

  Serves 8.

Beef Stroganoff

2 medium onions
¼ cup oil
½ pound mushrooms
1 pound round steak
3 to 4 ripe tomatoes

2 tablespoons flour
1½ teaspoons salt
½ teaspoon Worcestershire sauce
1 cup sour cream or yogurt
Hot cooked rice or noodles

Slice onions thin and cook slowly in oil. Slice mushrooms and add to onions. Cook 5 minutes. Remove onions and mushrooms from pan. Brown steak, which has been sliced into ¼-inch strips. Sprinkle flour over browned meat. Stir in chopped tomatoes and their juice, salt, pepper, and Worcestershire. Cover and cook 30 minutes. Add onions, mushrooms, and sour cream. Cook slowly, covered, 30 minutes more. Serve over rice or noodles.

  Serves 4.

Carbonnade de Boeuf

4 pounds beef chuck or bottom   2 cans beer
   round   2 (10-ounce) cans consommé
4 large onions

Cut beef into bite-sized pieces. Brown beef, then the onions. Layer beef and onions in a casserole. Pour over consommé and beer. Cook 4 hours at 350° or simmer on top of stove in a Dutch oven.
   Serves 8 to 10.

New Orleans Broccoli Mold

3 tablespoons gelatin   ½ teaspoon salt
1 (10-ounce) can consommé   ½ cup mayonnaise
2 (10-ounce) packages frozen   3 hard-boiled eggs, chopped
   chopped broccoli   Boston lettuce
2 tablespoons lemon juice   Spiced crab apples
1 teaspoon Tabasco

Soak gelatin in ½ cup cold consommé for 5 minutes. Heat remaining consommé. Add and dissolve gelatin. Cool. Pour ½ cup consommé mixture in bottom of 6-cup mold. Let set in refrigerator. Cook and drain broccoli. Chop more thoroughly if necessary. Combine with remaining ingredients, including consommé mixture. Pour into ring mold over congealed gelatin. Chill until firm. Unmold on serving platter. Fill center with chicken salad. Surround with Boston lettuce and garnish with spiced crab apples.
   Serves 8.

Chicken Salad

6 chicken boneless, skinless
  breasts and 4 thighs
2 carrots
2 small onions
2 teaspoons salt
2 bay leaves

¼ teaspoon ground ginger
1 lemon
½ cup mayonnaise
½ cup sour cream or yogurt
1 teaspoon ground dill
¼ cup browned slivered almonds

Simmer chicken with carrots, onions, salt, bay leaves, and ginger for 2 hours. Cool chicken overnight on paper towels, covered with foil. Cut into bite-sized pieces and place in bowl. Pour juice of 1 lemon over chicken and let stand 1 hour. Toss with mixture of mayonnaise, sour cream, and dill. Sprinkle with almonds.

Serves 8 with broccoli mold, or 4 by itself.

Green Pea Salad

6 (10-ounce) packages frozen
  peas
⅔ cup salad oil.
⅓ cup red wine vinegar
1½ teaspoons salt

2 teaspoons crumbled mint
1 cup finely diced celery
½ cup yogurt or sour cream
4 tomatoes
Lettuce

Cook peas in small amount of water until just heated. Drain and reserve ½ cup cooking liquid. Add to this oil, vinegar, salt, and mint. Pour over peas, cover, and chill. Just before serving, mix in celery and yogurt. Spoon onto large lettuce-lined serving tray or bowl. Border with tomato wedges.

Serves 12 to 14.

TOMATO SOUR CREAM RING

1¼ cups tomato juice
1 cup water
2 packages lemon-flavored
  gelatin
1 cup sour cream
1 cup mayonnaise
3 tablespoons prepared
  horseradish

¼ teaspoon salt
4 drops Tabasco
2 cucumbers, sliced
1 small onion, sliced
1 cup vinegar
¼ cup sugar
Salad greens

Heat tomato juice and water to boiling. Pour over gelatin and stir until gelatin is dissolved. Cool until syrupy but do not allow to set. Mix together sour cream, mayonnaise, horseradish, salt, and Tabasco. Add these to tomato gelatin mixture and beat until smooth. Pour into 5 cup ring mold. Chill until firm. Combine cucumbers, onions, vinegar, and sugar and marinate 20 minutes or longer. Unmold ring mold on salad greens. Fill center with cucumber mixture. (For luncheon dish, may circle with chicken salad.)

Serves 6.

ALMOND ICE BOX DESSERT

1 cup almonds
½ cup butter or margarine
3 cups powdered sugar

6 eggs
1 box vanilla wafers

Toast almonds. Cream butter and 1½ cups sugar. (If margarine is used, add ½ teaspoon vanilla.) Separate eggs, beat yolks, and add to mixture. Beat well. Add remaining sugar. Add almonds. Beat egg whites and fold in. Crush wafers very fine. Place half in 9x13-inch pan. Pour mixture on them. Sprinkle remaining crumbs on top and decorate with whole almonds. Refrigerate 48 hours.

Serves 12.

COUPE MELBA

1 can peach halves
1 pint vanilla ice cream
1 package frozen raspberries, pureed

1 pint heavy cream, whipped
¼ cup toasted almonds

Layer in individual serving dishes: peach half, ice cream, berries, whipped cream. Decorate with almonds. (Meringue shells may be used instead of peaches.)

Serves 4 to 6

MINT MOUSSE

2 (2-ounce) packages lime gelatin
1½ cups boiling water
1 cup cold water

½ cup green crème de menthe
1 cup whipping cream
1 chocolate bar, for shavings

Add boiling water to gelatin. Stir until dissolved. Add cold water and crème de menthe. Chill until slightly thick. Whip cream until stiff and fold into gelatin. Pour into 10x5-inch loaf pan and refrigerate until set. To remove from pan, immerse bottom and sides in hot water for 5 seconds. Decorate with rosettes of whipped cream and chocolate shavings.

Serves 8.

WHEN WE LIVED IN Fukuoka, I discovered Japanese traditional pottery. As we traveled around the island of Kyushu, we visited local kilns. Many of the potters traced their ancestry back to the 1500s, when Japanese invaders of Korea brought craftsmen home as war booty. We explored many more kilns after we moved north to Kobe on the island of Honshu, and my pleasure in cooking was enhanced when I presented my culinary creations on beautiful ceramic dishes that reflected a long history of loving artistry.

Japan's ancient imperial capital of Kyoto was an hour and a half away from Kobe by fast train or by car. As the center of political power for many centuries, the city also attracted artists who catered to court tastes. Kyoto has remained a cultural capital. We spent many days there visiting castles, temples, and gardens and browsing through elegant shops. At the end of the day we would often go into the ancient Gion geisha quarters, climb polished stairs in an old wooden house, and sit down on the floor at low tables to eat one of our favorite Japanese meals. It was served on dishes made by potters who were designated "living national treasures." The restaurant was called Zuynidanya, "the house of the twelve steps," and their specialty was "shabu-shabu," named for the sound made by swishing paper-thin slices of beef and vegetables through a hot pot of bubbling water.

HOT POT RECIPES

Beef shabu shabu
Chicken mizutake

HOT POT COOKING

A traditional hot pot is a ring-shaped pan with a chimney that rises from the middle. It is placed in the center of the table, within reach of all guests. At serving time, the chimney is filled with glowing charcoal and hot water or broth is poured into the pan surrounding it. Each guest cooks his or own meal, holding or placing ingredients in the hot liquid with chopsticks, often dipping in a sauce before eating. The broth is kept simmering throughout the meal, with more added as needed. An electric pan or other tabletop cooker may be used as an alternative to the hot pot.

Beef Shabu Shabu

2 pounds beef fillet	4 tablespoons sesame seeds
1 head Chinese cabbage	2 tablespoons rice vinegar
1 bunch spinach	¼ cup soy sauce
12 green onions	2 tablespoons chopped green
2 to 3 carrots	onion tops
1 pound button mushrooms	2 tablespoons chopped fresh
1 package rice sticks (thin	ginger
noodles)	Sansho (Japanese pepper mixture)
8 to 9 cups chicken broth	Hot cooked rice

Cut beef into very thin slices. (More easily done if meat is placed in freezer and sliced while partially frozen.) Cut cabbage and spinach into 2-inch lengths. Cut carrots and green onions into sticks, chopping and reserving 2 tablespoons of the onion tops. Trim mushroom ends and cut in halves unless they are very small. Arrange meat, vegetables, and rice sticks decoratively on a large platter. Refrigerate if prepared ahead. Make sauce by combining sesame seeds, vinegar, and soy. Set each place with a bowl, chopsticks, and a smaller bowl for sauce. Ingredients (starting with meat and ending with rice sticks) are picked up with chopsticks and held in the boiling broth of the hot pot (see above) until barely cooked, then transferred to individual bowls, dipped into sauce (to which chopped onion tops, ginger, and sansho have been added to taste) and eaten with rice. When all the meat and vegetables are eaten, the stock is served as a soup. Hot sake, beer, and/or Japanese tea should accompany the meal.

Serves 8.

Chicken Mizutake

1½ pounds ground chicken
2 egg whites plus 1 egg
¼ cup sake
2 tablespoons plus ½ cup soy
  sauce
1 tablespoon grated ginger
2 tablespoons sugar
1½ teaspoons salt
2 bunches spinach

1 bunch green onions
1 head cauliflower
8 to10 cups hot broth
1 cup lemon juice
2 tablespoons chopped green
  onion tops
2 tablespoons chopped ginger
Sansho (Japanese pepper mixture)
Hot cooked rice

Mix chicken with eggs, sake, 2 tablespoons soy sauce, ginger, sugar, and salt. Place in food processor or blender and chop fine. Form chicken mixture into meatballs. Cut vegetables into 2-inch lengths. Use hot pot filled with hot broth (see above) to cook chicken and vegetables. Combine remaining ½ cup soy sauce with lemon juice, then divide this sauce into six bowls. Season each bowl with green onion, ginger, and sansho and use as dipping sauce for mizutake. Serve with rice. Hot sake, beer, and/or Japanese tea should accompany the meal.

Serves 6.

Cindy's arrival in 1957 had been an exciting adventure. Our daughter was born in a hospital established by Canadian missionaries to serve a very poor neighborhood on the outskirts of Osaka. In the best of times, it was a forty-five-minute ride from our house to the hospital. The day Cindy was born, a hurricane had flooded most of the roads under the railroad lines—the roads that were our direct route to the hospital. We were forced to detour all the way into the center of Osaka, Japan's second largest city after Tokyo, and then back out again, doubling our driving time. And when we arrived we found the entire area blacked out—the power lines had been downed by the storm. Fortunately, the hospital had an emergency generator for surgery and delivery rooms, and our little girl was safely delivered ten minutes after we reached the hospital.

In spring, when the azaleas were in full bloom in our garden, we had Sunday afternoon picnics—for the local branch of the Stanford University Alumni Club; for the Japanese and American staff members of USIS centers in Kobe, Osaka, and Kyoto; and for the visiting dancers of the New York City Ballet. This was the first American ballet troupe to perform in Japan, and their exuberance and artistry enchanted audiences at the Osaka Festival. The dancers let off steam after a hectic week of daily performances, enjoyed the country air and home cooking, and cavorted among our trees, playing with a toy new to the American scene—the Frisbee.

Spring Picnic among the Azaleas

Grilled hot dogs and/or hamburgers with buns and condiments
(*or* Sliced ham and turkey)
Meat and spinach loaf
Potato salad
Shredded cabbage toss
Deep chocolate upside down cake
Ginger cake with lemon custard sauce

Meat and Spinach Loaf

1¼ pounds ground meat
1 (10-ounce) package frozen
  spinach
½ cup bread crumbs
Salt and pepper
¼ teaspoon ground nutmeg
½ cup chopped celery

½ cup chopped parsley
¼ cup milk
1 clove garlic, minced
1 tablespoon butter
½ cup chopped onion
2 eggs, lightly beaten
3 slices bacon

Mix meat with chopped spinach, bread crumbs, salt, pepper, and nutmeg. Blend celery, parsley, milk, and garlic and add to meat. Cook onion in butter and add. Blend in eggs and shape to fit loaf pan. Cover with bacon and cook at 350° for 1¼ to 1½ hours. Pour off fat and let cool before slicing.

Serves 6 to 8.

Potato Salad

6 large or 4 medium potatoes
½ cup chopped onions
¼ cup diced pimentos
¼ cup diced dill pickles
¼ cup grated carrot
½ cup sliced radishes
½ cup sliced celery

¼ cup olive oil
¼ cup vinegar
1 teaspoon salt
Pepper
Mayonnaise to taste
2 hard-boiled eggs, chopped
¼ cup chopped parsley

Boil potatoes in skins until tender. Cool, peel, and cut into about ½-inch dice. Put into a large bowl and add onions, pimentos, pickles, carrot, radishes, and celery. Stir in oil, vinegar, salt, and pepper. Add mayonnaise to taste. Garnish with eggs and parsley.

Serves 8 to 10.

Shredded Cabbage Toss

2 cups shredded cabbage	3 tablespoons sugar
¼ to ½ cup chopped parsley	1 teaspoon salt
1 medium onion	3 tablespoons vinegar
1 green bell pepper, sliced into rings	2 tablespoons salad oil

Combine vegetables. Combine other ingredients, stirring to dissolve sugar. Pour dressing on vegetables and toss.

Serves 6.

Deep Chocolate Upside Down Cake

½ cup butter	1 (3-ounce) can flaked coconut
¼ cup water	1 package Duncan Hines Deep Chocolate Deluxe cake mix
1 cup brown sugar	
1 cup chopped nuts	Whipped cream (optional)

Melt butter in 9x13-inch pan. Add water and brown sugar. Mix in nuts and coconut; spread evenly on bottom of pan. Mix cake at medium speed of electric mixer for 2 minutes, as directed on package. Pour batter over mixture in pan. Bake at 350° for 40 minutes. Let stand 5 minutes until topping begins to set. Turn upside down onto large platter or cookie sheet. Serve with whipped cream, if desired.

Serves 6 to 8.

Ginger Cake

½ cup butter	Scant ½ teaspoon ground cloves
½ cup sugar	½ teaspoon ground ginger
1 egg	½ teaspoon salt
1 cup molasses	1½ teaspoons baking soda
2½ cup flour	1 cup hot water or hot strong coffee
1 teaspoon cinnamon	

Cream butter and sugar until smooth. In large bowl, beat egg into molasses and add creamed mixture. Sift together dry ingredients, except baking soda. Fold dry ingredients into molasses mixture. Dissolve baking soda in water or coffee and add to batter. Beat vigorously for several minutes. Spoon batter into greased 8x8-inch pan. Bake at 350° for 45 minutes to 1 hour, until a knife inserted in center comes out clean. Serve with lemon custard sauce.

Serves 6 to 8.

Lemon Custard Sauce

1 cup sugar	2 cups warm water
3 tablespoons cornstarch	4 egg yolks, beaten
1/8 teaspoon ground nutmeg	4 tablespoons melted butter
Pinch of salt	1/4 cup lemon juice

Mix sugar, cornstarch, nutmeg, and salt in saucepan. Slowly stir in water. Heat, stirring constantly, on medium high heat until sauce thickens. Beat 1 cup of hot sauce into beaten egg yolks. Stir warmed yolk mixture back into saucepan and cook for 1 minute more, stirring constantly. Remove from heat and blend in butter and lemon juice. Chill.

Makes 3 cups.

When we left Japan in June of 1958, our children were leaving the only home they really knew. We all headed, after a short home leave in the United States where they could meet their grandparents, to a new home in an unknown land—Burma.

7

Orchestrating Menus in Burma

OUR TWO YEARS IN Burma—1958 to 1960—were extraordinary in many ways. It was a charmed period in the country's post World War II history; there was a new caretaker government in charge, an optimism in the air, camaraderie between the diverse elements of Burmese society (which embraced those of us in the diplomatic community), and relative freedom for foreign residents to explore this beautiful and fascinating country.

We took time to study language, history, and customs. We traveled to the Burmese borders with China, Thailand, and Bangladesh. Everywhere, the countryside was dotted with pagodas and wooden structures with intricately carved adornment. In the interior we visited the holy and royal sites at Mandalay, the ancient city of Pagan with its Buddhist monuments spanning the eighth to eleventh centuries, the once wealthy rice-growing Irrawaddy River Delta, the confluence of rivers flowing out of Tibet north of Bhamo, the leg-rowers of Inle Lake who plied their boats between villages built on stilts out in the water. In the hill country we saw merchants from diverse tribal groups in distinctive costumes who had walked for days to carry their goods to markets that moved daily between towns. Some of these were elderly Chinese women who took mincing steps on their bound feet. Taking a lunch break in the local bazaar, they regained strength with Burma's favorite foods.

Burmese One-dish Meals

Mohinga (rice vermicelli with fish soup)
Kyaukswe (chicken curry with noodles)

Mohinga

1 pound fillets of strong flavored fish or 2 cans herring in tomato sauce
4 medium onions, coarsely chopped
6 cloves garlic, peeled
2 teaspoons chopped fresh ginger
1 teaspoon ground turmeric
½ teaspoon chili powder
2 tablespoons sesame oil
4 tablespoons vegetable oil
1 or 2 fresh chili peppers
4 cups thin coconut milk
1 (8-ounce) can bamboo shoots

1 teaspoon dried shrimp paste
1 tablespoon fish sauce
3 tablespoons chick pea flour or cornstarch
2 cups thick coconut milk
2 tablespoons lemon juice
Salt to taste
1 pound fine rice vermicelli or egg noodles
Condiments: green onions, white onions, coriander leaves, roasted chick peas, crisp fried noodles, lemon wedges, dried chilies, chili powder

Wash and scale the fish fillets and simmer for 5 minutes in water to cover. Reserve stock. Put onions, garlic, ginger, turmeric, and chili powder in blender and puree. Heat both oils in large saucepan and fry blended ingredients and fresh chilies. When golden brown and beginning to stick to pan, add water or stock as needed, thin coconut milk, and bamboo shoots. Dissolve dried shrimp paste in fish sauce and add to mixture. Mix chick pea flour with a little cold water and add to pan. Keep stirring until it comes to a boil. Simmer 5 minutes and add fish (including liquid if using canned fish). Add thick coconut milk and lemon juice. Stir as it comes to simmering point and season with salt if necessary. Cook noodles until just tender, drain well, and serve in large bowl next to soup. Prepare some or all of the following condiments and place in small bowls on table: finely sliced green onions including tops, white onions finely sliced or chopped and fried, chopped fresh coriander (cilantro) leaves, roasted chick peas finely ground in blender, crisp fried noodles (canned chow mein noodles), lemon wedges, dried chilies fried 3 to 4 seconds in oil, chili powder. Serve noodles in individual bowls. Ladle soup over top; guests add condiments.

Serves 6 to 8.

KYAUKSWE

¾ cup yellow split peas
1½ cups water
½ cup salad oil
¼ teaspoon ground turmeric
3 large onions, chopped
3 to 4 cloves garlic, minced
2 teaspoons finely chopped ginger
1 teaspoon cayenne
2 tablespoons curry powder
½ teaspoon ground cumin

8 whole chicken breasts, skinned and boned, cut into 3-inch by ½-inch strips
1 bay leaf
1 cinnamon stick
2 quarts chicken broth
1½ cups coconut milk
Fish sauce or salt
Cooked Chinese noodles or vermicelli
Condiments (see list opposite for mohinga)

Whirl split peas in blender until finely ground. Mix with water and set aside. Place oil in 8- to 10-quart pan and set over low heat. Add onions and garlic and cook until limp but not brown. Stir in turmeric, cayenne, curry, and cumin and cook about 1 minute, taking care not to burn the spices. Add chicken, bay leaf, and cinnamon. Stir chicken until it is coated with spice mixture. Add broth. Stir in split pea mixture and coconut milk. Bring to boil, cover, and simmer until broth thickens, about 30 minutes. Add fish sauce to taste. (Can be made a day ahead, cooled, covered and chilled. Reheat, covered, over low heat.) Serve over noodles, letting guests select condiments as for mohinga.

Serves 10 to 12.

CLIFF TRAVELED EXTENSIVELY WITH his colleagues, meeting with local officials, journalists, and teachers to discuss ways in which "democratic processes" might alleviate the burdens of ordinary citizens. He relished sharing hopes, dreams, and plans through a "people to people" kind of diplomacy; on one trip, he observed the collaboration between elephants and U.S. government-supplied tractors to haul teak logs out of the deepest jungle.

On separate trips, I joined Betty Lou Hummel and Lois Rollefson, two other embassy wives. We participated in teacher conferences with Fulbright scholars in remote towns, explored the ruby mines in Mogok and the jade mines in Mogaung, and rode the river boat down the long reach of the Irrawaddy and experienced the rhythms of a timeless society knit together by the rhythm of the river traffic. To pass the hours on the river, we set up our Scrabble set, much to the fascination of our fellow deck passengers who thought we had a new form of mahjong, which was their favored travel recreation.

When we took these trips into the hinterland we went with a full "kit" of supplies: bedroll and mosquito net to throw over wooden bed frames in Spartan government bungalows, medical supplies including anti-malarial medicine and a snakebite kit, purified drinking water, and basic food supplies we could prepare for ourselves, without reliance on refrigeration and/or stove.

We traveled in an open jeep, over dusty, bumpy roads, through heat-baked countryside and sleepy villages. Betty Lou's husband, Arthur, was an enthusiastic hunter, and shortly before we headed north to Mandalay he returned from an expedition with a barking deer, a small species native to South Asia. The Hummels' inventive cook prepared a box lunch for our first day—including sandwiches of sliced, roasted barking deer on homemade bread with mayonnaise and pickle relish—which we ate in the shade of a purple-blooming jacaranda tree at the edge of the road.

"Meals Ready to Eat" for the Road to Mandalay

Scotch whiskey, bottled soft drinks, and water
Canned spaghetti and meatballs, baked beans, tuna fish
Peanut butter and jam, crackers and cheese whiz
Hard-boiled eggs, powdered coffee, dry cereal
Barking-deer sandwiches

We lived in a Burmese-style house that rested on stilts at the edge of a small lake. When we entertained guests, the numbers were usually large—and unpredictable. The Burmese were relaxed about responding to invitations and, when they came, often brought others along. They loved a party and these were fun to plan and to host. But, because of the uncertainty of numbers, I learned quickly that buffet service rather than sit-down dinners was the way to avoid resetting the table at the last minute. My job was to plan and orchestrate. An Indian from Madras did our cooking, a household manager ("bearer") from Bengal carried all messages from me to the kitchen, and, in what was the norm for embassy families in that place and time, one Burmese woman cared for the children, another did the laundry, a Karen tribesman from the hill country took care of the garden, and another south Indian served as the "sweeper" (doing all the menial household chores). When we invited all our household servants and their immediate families for a Christmas party, there were thirty-seven men, women, and children!

As had been the case in Davao, healthy fresh foods were limited in supply and vegetables had to be cooked thoroughly. Planning menus was a continuing challenge to one's gastronomical creativity, but we managed to dine well and to entertain with gusto. There was more "gusto" than usual the night we decided to serve Singapore Gin Slings at a large party. We had recently traveled by a Dutch ship from Singapore to several Indonesian islands and persuaded the bartender to share his recipe with us. I used that recipe to make a concentrate—a syrup with flavorings and liquor that we would then use sparingly for individual servings, with a generous topping of soda water. Cliff did not realize the soda part, so he gave our guests glasses full of undiluted dynamite. Our guests celebrated this new drink—with compliments, requests for refills, and spirited conviviality.

Food and Drink for Convivial Parties

Singapore gin sling
Brandy (the favorite of Burmese journalists), whiskey, and gin
Iranian chicken and rice
Baked ham with hot and cold sauces
Sweet potato puree with lime
Fruit trifle
Vanilla custard sauce
Pound cake
Coffee dessert punch

Singapore Gin Sling

1 ounce gin	11 teaspoon grenadine syrup
½ ounce cherry brandy	1 teaspoon sugar
1 ounce Cointreau	Lemon slice
Juice of ½ lemon	Soda water

Combine first 6 ingredients, shake well with ice, add a slice of lemon, and fill glass with soda. For a crowd, make up a batch of concentrate, multiplying above ingredients by number of servings desired.

Serves 1.

IRANIAN CHICKEN AND RICE

2 chickens, cut up
Salt
½ cup butter
1¼ cups water
1 large orange
3 cups grated carrots

¼ cup slivered almonds
⅛ teaspoon saffron
1½ teaspoons sugar
2 tablespoons chopped pistachios
    or parsley
Cooked long-grain rice

Sprinkle chicken with salt and brown in ¼ cup butter. Add ½ cup water and simmer 45 minutes. Thinly pare orange zest, sliver, cook in boiling water 3 minutes, and drain. Melt remaining butter, add carrots, and cook 5 to 8 minutes. Add orange zest, almonds, ½ teaspoon salt, saffron, and sugar. Add ¾ cup water; cook rapidly until water evaporates. Meanwhile cook rice. Add carrot mix and salt, if needed, to rice. Spoon rice into center of large casserole, with chicken around the sides. Bake 20 minutes if warm, 40 if cold. Garnish with pistachio nuts or parsley.

Serves 6 to 8.

HOT SAUCE FOR BAKED HAM

1 jar currant jelly
Grated rind and juice of 1
    orange
¼ teaspoon ground nutmeg

¼ teaspoon ground cinnamon
⅛ teaspoon ground ginger
2 tablespoons port wine

Combine all ingredients except wine. Heat in top of double boiler. Add port and remove from heat.

COLD SAUCE FOR BAKED HAM

2 cucumbers	4 teaspoons prepared mustard
1 cup mayonnaise or yogurt	1 teaspoon salt
5 tablespoons prepared horseradish	Dash of pepper

Peel, seed, and grate cucumbers. Combine all ingredients and chill.

SWEET POTATO PUREE WITH LIME

4 medium-sized sweet potatoes	4 tablespoons butter or yogurt, to taste
2 tablespoons fresh lime juice	Salt

Prick sweet potatoes and roast on a foil-lined baking sheet in middle of oven at 350° for 1 hour or until very soft. Cool potatoes until they can be handled, and scoop flesh into food processor. Puree potatoes until smooth. Add lime juice, butter or yogurt, and salt to taste and puree until well combined. May be kept up to 2 days, covered, in refrigerator. Warm before serving.

    Serves 4.

FRUIT TRIFLE

2 cups fresh and/or canned fruit	2 cups vanilla custard sauce (below)
5 to 6 cups leftover pound cake (below), broken into chunks	2 cups heavy cream
1 cup liquor (brandy, sherry, or rum)	½ teaspoon vanilla
	Sugar to taste
	Slivered toasted almonds

Prepare fruit (peaches, oranges, cherries, berries, bananas, etc.). Using a large bowl (glass shows off the layers of the dessert), arrange a layer of pound cake chunks on bottom. Pour over some of the liquor and allow it to soak in. Spoon over a custard layer, then sprinkle on fruit layer. Repeat layers, using all ingredients. Top with cream whipped with vanilla and sugar to taste. Decorate with almonds and/or more fruit.

Serves 16.

VANILLA CUSTARD SAUCE

2 cups milk
¼ cup sugar

4 eggs
1 teaspoon vanilla

In a heavy saucepan, heat milk and sugar almost to a boil. Break eggs into a blender and whirl, slowly adding milk to cook eggs. Add vanilla. This should cook the mixture sufficiently to coat a spoon. If not, pour it back into pan and cook gently, stirring until it thickens. If custard should overcook and become lumpy, return it to blender to whirl it smooth.

Makes 2 cups.

POUND CAKE

1 pound butter, softened
3 cups sugar
6 eggs
4 cups unbleached white flour

2 teaspoons baking powder
1 cup milk
2 teaspoons vanilla, almond, or
   lemon extract

Generously butter and flour a 10-inch Bundt pan. Cream butter and sugar and beat in eggs. Add 2 cups of flour and beat well. Mix in milk and extract. Combine baking powder and remaining flour and add to batter. Beat well. Pour batter into Bundt pan. Bake at 350° for about 1 hour until cake pulls away from sides of pan and knife inserted in center comes out clean. When done, turn cake upside down on a plate to cool. Leave pan on top of cake for about 20 minutes so cake will hold its shape.

COFFEE DESSERT PUNCH

4 quarts strong coffee	5 tablespoons granulated sugar
1 quart heavy or whipping cream	5 teaspoons vanilla extract
	2 quarts vanilla ice cream

Make, then refrigerate coffee. Just before serving, whip cream, adding sugar and vanilla. Spoon or slice ice cream into large punch bowl. Add whipped cream, pour coffee over. Stir to mix with ice cream. Can double as both desert and after-dinner coffee.

Serves 50 to 60 in small cups.

THE BURMA-AMERICA INSTITUTE, not far from Rangoon University, was built to serve as a center for cultural exchanges, lectures, exhibits, and classes. I was asked to do a series of cooking classes and repeated my Kobe formula: typical American meals from breakfast through dinner. (The typical Burmese meals were a hearty curry breakfast about 11:00 a.m. and dinner, again mostly curries, in the evening.)

One day, during one of my demonstrations, I mentioned to the mixed group of Burmese, Indian, and Pakistani women that it was relatively easy for people like me to learn to cook from the precise recipes we found in American magazines and cookbooks. It was a different situation trying to recreate non-American recipes obtained from women who had learned all their domestic skills by observing and working with their mothers. A "pinch" of this and "handful" of that, combined until it "looked right" and seasoned "to taste" was hard to replicate.

On the last day of our class we had a potluck luncheon at my house. Everyone brought a favorite traditional dish. My students produced a wonderful South and Southeastern Asian array, and then they went one step further. They had carefully measured all their ingredients, written down the processes step by step, and assembled their recipes together in an American-style cookbook, which they presented to me with great pride on their part and appreciation on mine.

BURMESE AND SOUTH ASIAN RECIPES

Garam masala (Indian spice mix)
Burmese pork curry
Burmese shrimp and bamboo shoot curry
Burmese beef and potato curry
Burmese mixed vegetable salad
Parsi pilau (spiced rice)
Kofta (meatball) curry
Curried chicken with cashews
Spiced lamb with saffron and almonds
Keema (ground meat) and split pea curry
Dhal (lentil puree)
Cucumber with yogurt
Tomato salad with mint and green onions
Spiced eggplant with yogurt
Mint coriander chutney

GARAM MASALA

Garam masala is an Indian spice mix used in many South Asian recipes, including those below. Prepared garam masala is available in many Asian markets.

4 tablespoons coriander seeds
2 tablespoons cumin seeds
1 tablespoon whole black peppercorns

2 teaspoons cardamom seeds
4 (3-inch) cinnamon sticks
1 teaspoon whole cloves
1 whole nutmeg

In a small pan, roast separately the coriander, cumin, pepper, cardamom, cinnamon, and cloves. As each one begins to smell fragrant, turn onto a plate to cool. Put all into electric blender and grind to a powder. Finely grate nutmeg and mix in. Store in glass jar with tight cover.

BURMESE PORK CURRY

3 pounds ham or fresh pork shoulder
1 large onion
12 to 15 cloves garlic
2-inch piece of ginger
8 shallots
2 tablespoons white vinegar

½ cup peanut oil
2 tablespoons sesame oil
1½ teaspoons salt
2 fresh chilies, finely chopped
1 teaspoon turmeric
1 teaspoon shrimp paste
Hot cooked rice

Cut pork into cubes and place in a dish. Peel onion and grate it finely. Pour onion liquid over pork, saving pulp. Crush 2 to 3 cloves garlic and finely grate half the ginger. Add this to pork with finely chopped shallots. Add vinegar and mix well. Marinate 2 hours, stirring occasionally. Heat half the oils in saucepan and fry pork about 5 minutes, until lightly colored. Add salt and enough water to cover generously. Bring to boil and simmer 1½ hours, skimming surface occasionally. Finely chop remaining garlic and ginger. Heat remaining oil and fry onion pulp, garlic, ginger, and chilies for about 4 minutes over medium heat. Add turmeric and shrimp paste and fry another 3 to 4 minutes, adding water to pan if needed to prevent sticking. Add this mixture to pork and cook 8 to 10 minutes until meat is completely tender. Serve with rice.

Serves 6 to 8.

BURMESE SHRIMP AND BAMBOO SHOOT CURRY

2 pounds fresh unpeeled medium shrimp	3 tablespoons vegetable or peanut oil
Salt	1½ teaspoons ground turmeric
Cornstarch	1½ teaspoons dried chili flakes
12 ounces peeled fresh or canned young bamboo shoots	1 cup fish stock or water
2 medium onions	1½ cups thick coconut milk
8 cloves garlic	Fish sauce
2-inch piece fresh ginger	Hot cooked rice

Peel and de-vein the shrimp. Rinse with cold water, rubbing with a little salt and cornstarch to remove fishy smell and keep them white. If using fresh bamboo shoots, boil them in lightly salted water until they are tender enough to pierce easily. Drain shoots and slice thinly, or cut into small cubes. Peel and thinly slice onions and garlic. Shred ginger. Heat oil in saucepan and fry onions, garlic, and ginger about 4 minutes until softened and lightly colored. Add turmeric and chili flakes and continue frying until onions are well colored. Add about 2 tablespoons cold water and simmer until liquid has evaporated. Add fish stock or water and bring to boil. Simmer 2 to 3 minutes, add shrimp, coconut milk, and bamboo shoots, and bring almost to a boil. Cook gently 5 minutes until mixture is well heated. Do not boil. Add fish sauce to taste and serve with rice.

Serves 6.

BURMESE BEEF AND POTATO CURRY

1½ pounds beef	1 teaspoon chili powder
¾ pound potatoes	½ cup light sesame oil or corn oil
2 large onions	½ teaspoon ground cumin
5 large cloves garlic	½ teaspoon ground coriander
2 teaspoons chopped fresh ginger	1½ teaspoons salt, or to taste
1 teaspoon ground turmeric	2 cups water
	Hot cooked rice

Cut beef into large squares. Peel and cut potatoes into quarters. Puree onion, garlic, ginger, turmeric, and chili in blender, then fry in hot oil until sizzling. Add cumin and coriander and mix well, still cooking, then add meat and stir until coated and brown. Add salt to taste, water, and potatoes. Simmer slowly until meat is tender and potatoes are cooked. Serve with rice.

Serves 4 to 6.

BURMESE MIXED VEGETABLE SALAD

3 cups sliced vegetables (beans, cabbage, cauliflower, okra, carrots, bamboo shoots, green onions, bean sprouts, and/or zucchini)

Salt	2 large onions, thinly sliced
½ cup vegetable oil	4 cloves garlic, thinly sliced
1 tablespoon sesame oil	2 tablespoons white vinegar
½ teaspoon ground turmeric	3 tablespoons sesame seeds

Cut vegetables into bite-size strips and boil 1 to 2 minutes in lightly salted water, until tender but still crisp. Drain and rinse with cold water in colander to prevent overcooking. Heat two oils in frying pan, add turmeric, onions, and garlic and fry over medium heat, stirring constantly. When onion and garlic start to brown, remove from heat and continue stirring until they are brown and crisp.

When cool, pour a little of the cooking oil over the vegetables, add onion and garlic, and toss lightly but thoroughly. Add extra salt and vinegar to taste. In dry pan, roast sesame seeds over medium heat until golden brown. Turn onto a plate to cool, then sprinkle over the vegetables.

Serves 6.

Parsi Pilau

2 tablespoons oil	½ teaspoon saffron strands, soaked
4 cardamom pods, bruised	in 2 tablespoons boiling water
1 small cinnamon stick	Rind of 1 orange, finely grated
4 whole cloves	2 tablespoons raisins
10 black peppercorns	2 tablespoons blanched sliced
2½ cups long grain rice	almonds
4 cups water	2 tablespoons blanched halved
2½ teaspoons salt	pistachios

Heat oil in heavy saucepan and gently fry cardamom, cinnamon, cloves, and peppercorns for 2 minutes. Add rice and continue stirring for 2 to 3 minutes. Add water, salt, soaked saffron strands and liquid, and orange rind. Stir well and bring to boil, then turn heat very low, cover, and cook 20 minutes. Scatter raisins over surface of rice, replace lid, and cook 5 minutes longer. Serve garnished with almonds and pistachios.

Serves 5 to 6.

KOFTA CURRY

½ pound ground meat
2 chopped onions, plus juice
  of ½ onion
½ teaspoon cinnamon
¼ teaspoon coriander powder
Pinch chili powder
2 tablespoons oil
2 sliced cloves

2 tablespoons ground coconut
1 teaspoon minced garlic
1 teaspoon poppy seeds
1 teaspoon coriander
¼ teaspoon turmeric
4 tomatoes, chopped
1 cup water

Combine meat, 1 chopped onion, onion juice, cinnamon, coriander, and chili powder. Shape into meatballs and fry in oil until brown. Remove from pan and set aside. Brown second onion, add remaining spices, and fry 5 minutes. Add meatballs, tomatoes, and water and cook over low heat ½ hour.

Serves 4.

CURRIED CHICKEN WITH CASHEWS

3 tablespoons oil
2 large onions, finely chopped
2 cloves minced garlic
1½ teaspoons grated fresh ginger
3 tablespoons curry powder
1 teaspoon chili powder or
  paprika (less hot)
3 teaspoons salt
3 tomatoes, peeled and chopped

2 tablespoons chopped fresh
  coriander (cilantro) or mint
1 chicken, cut into small pieces
2 teaspoons garam masala or curry
  powder
½ cup yogurt
½ cup raw cashews, finely ground
Chapatis or hot cooked rice

Heat oil in large saucepan and slowly fry onion, garlic and ginger until soft and golden, stirring occasionally. Add curry powder and chili or paprika and stir for 1 minute. Add salt, tomatoes, chopped leaves, and cook to a pulp, stirring with wooden spoon. Add chicken and stir well to coat it with spice mixture. Cover tightly and simmer on very low heat 45 minutes or until chicken is tender. Stir with wooden spoon every 15 minutes and scrape bottom of pan to prevent spices from sticking. Stir in garam masala and yogurt and simmer, uncovered, 5 minutes. Stir in cashews and heat through. Curry may be garnished with extra chopped coriander or mint leaves before serving with chapatis or rice.

Serves 6.

SPICED LAMB WITH SAFFRON AND ALMONDS

½ teaspoon saffron strands	1 onion, chopped
2 tablespoons boiling water	4 minced cloves garlic
1 tablespoon salt	2 teaspoons grated fresh ginger
1 cup yogurt	2 teaspoons ground cumin
3- to 4-pound leg of lamb, boned and cubed	2 tablespoon ground almonds or 25 whole blanched almonds
4 tablespoons oil	½ cup water
1 stick cinnamon	1 tablespoons chopped fresh mint
6 cardamom pods, bruised	Hot cooked rice or parsi pilau
4 whole cloves	

Soak saffron in boiling water until soft, about 10 minutes, then press strands between fingers to diffuse as much color and fragrance as possible. Stir saffron and salt into yogurt in large bowl, add lamb, and mix well. Cover and let stand at room temperature while preparing other ingredients. Heat oil in heavy saucepan with a well-fitting lid. When hot, add cinnamon, cardamom, and cloves and fry over medium heat 1 to 2 minutes. Add onion, garlic, and ginger and continue frying and stirring until onion is soft and golden, about 10 minutes. Add cumin and fry another minute. Drain lamb from yogurt marinade and add to pan, turning pieces as they come in contact with heat on all sides. Add ground almonds to marinade in bowl. (If ground almonds are not available, soak whole almonds in ½ cup boiling water for several minutes, then pulverize in blender.) Stir ½ cup water into marinade and add to pan. Stir well. Reduce heat to low, cover, and cook 1 hour until lamb is tender and gravy thick. Stir occasionally with wooden spoon to prevent sticking. Sprinkle with mint, cover, and cook additional 10 minutes, then serve hot with rice or parsi pilau (page 95).

Serves 6 to 8.

KEEMA AND SPLIT PEA CURRY

½ cup split peas
2 tablespoons oil
2 medium onions, chopped
2 minced cloves garlic
1 teaspoon grated fresh ginger
1 teaspoon turmeric
½ teaspoon chili powder

1 tablespoon chopped fresh
  coriander (cilantro) or mint
4 small ripe tomatoes, chopped
2 teaspoons salt
1 pound ground meat
2 teaspoons garam masala or
  curry powder

Wash split peas and soak for one hour. Heat oil and gently fry onions, garlic, and ginger until soft. Add turmeric, chili powder, chopped leaves, tomatoes, and salt. Stir over medium heat several minutes, then add meat and drained split peas. Stir until well mixed, then cover tightly and cook 40 minutes or until meat and peas are tender. Stir occasionally and add hot water if liquid evaporates. Add garam masala and cook until all liquid evaporates. Stir frequently to prevent burning. Serve this dry curry with Indian bread and other accompaniments, such as vegetable preparations and chutneys (below).

Serves 4 to 6.

DAHL

½ pound red lentils
1½ teaspoons oil
1 large onion, finely sliced
2 cloves garlic, minced
1 teaspoon grated ginger

½ teaspoon turmeric
3 cups hot water
1 teaspoon salt, to taste
½ teaspoon garam masala

Wash lentils thoroughly, removing those that float on surface of water. (Any type of lentils may be used, but others need overnight soaking.) Drain well. Heat oil and fry onion, garlic, and ginger until onion is golden brown. Add turmeric and stir well. Add drained lentils and fry 1 to 2 minutes, then add hot water. Bring to boil then reduce heat to simmer. Cover and cook 15 to 20 minutes, until lentils are half cooked. Add salt and garam masala, mix well, and continue cooking until lentils are soft, similar to consistency of porridge. If too much liquid, cook without lid on pan. Serve dahl plain or garnished with sliced onions that have been fried until deep golden. Eat with hot rice, Indian breads, or as a light meal by itself.

Serves 4 to 6.

CUCUMBER WITH YOGURT

2 large cucumbers
2 teaspoons salt
1 clove garlic, minced

¼ teaspoon grated ginger
1 cup yogurt
Lemon juice to taste

Peel and slice cucumbers very thinly. Put in bowl, sprinkle with salt, and chill about 1 hour. Pour off liquid, pressing out as much as possible. Mix garlic and ginger into yogurt, then stir in cucumbers and combine thoroughly. Taste and add more salt if necessary. Add lemon juice to taste. Serve chilled.

Serves 6.

TOMATO SALAD WITH MINT AND GREEN ONIONS

4 firm ripe tomatoes
6 green onions
½ cup fresh mint leaves
3 tablespoons lemon juice

½ teaspoon salt, to taste
2 teaspoons sugar
½ teaspoon chili powder
   (optional)

Peel tomatoes and cut into thin wedges. Finely slice green onions and chop mint leaves. Add to tomatoes. Mix lemon juice, salt, sugar, and chili powder, stirring until sugar dissolves. Pour over tomatoes and mix gently but thoroughly. Cover and chill until serving time.

Serves 4 to 6.

Spiced Eggplant with Yogurt

3 tablespoons oil
1 teaspoon black mustard seeds
1 medium onion, finely chopped
2 fresh green chilies, peeled and
    sliced
1 medium eggplant, peeled and
    diced
1 small ripe tomato, diced

1 teaspoon salt
1 teaspoon garam masala
½ teaspoon chili powder
    (optional)
¼ cup water
1 cup yogurt
2 tablespoons chopped coriander
    (cilantro) leaves

In saucepan heat oil and fry mustard seeds until they pop. Add onion and chilies and fry until onion is soft. Add eggplant and fry for several minutes, stirring, then add tomato, salt, garam masala, and chili powder. Stir well, add water, cover, and cook until eggplant and tomato are very soft. Mash into a puree, cool, then stir in yogurt and half the coriander leaves. Serve garnished with remaining leaves.

Serves 4 to 6.

Mint Coriander Chutney

1½ cups fresh mint leaves
1½ cups fresh coriander
    (cilantro) leaves
1-inch piece peeled ginger
1 green chili pepper

1 medium onion, cut into chunks
1 teaspoon sugar
½ teaspoon salt
2 teaspoons lime juice

Combine all ingredients in a blender and process to a fine paste, adding enough water to make a thick sauce. Chill.

Makes 1½ cups.

ONE OF THE MORE dramatic political events during our stay in Burma was the defection of Cliff's counterpart in the Soviet Embassy, their diplomat in charge of cultural and media relations with the Burmese. Alexander Kaznacheev walked into the USIS Library and told the American librarian that he had become disenchanted with his own government and would like to seek asylum in the United States. He had become very fond of the Burmese people, admired their independent ways, and came to believe he could find similar independence with the Americans.

Kaznacheev was staying in the U.S. Embassy, incognito, for several days. Our children and I were upset with Cliff when he did not get home in time to attend two-year-old Cindy's birthday party. When we learned the reason for Dad's delay, we wrapped up a package of birthday cookies—which our cook had cut out in the shape of rabbits—and sent them to Kaznacheev as a gesture of neighborliness.

Meanwhile, the Soviet Embassy was looking for their missing member and accused the Americans of kidnapping him. To put the record straight, the American diplomats decided to host a public press conference in the embassy and let their guest speak for himself. Cliff's team fanned out across the city, delivering invitations to the dozens of local newspapers large and small, as well as members of the foreign press corps. The questions asked and answers given at that forum made it clear that Mr. Kaznacheev had made a personal decision to opt out of the Soviet system.

"Communism is evil, it deprives the individual of pride and self-respect," was the headline in the major Burmese paper on June 27, 1959. The paper printed a transcript of the letter which Kaznacheev had brought with him to the American Embassy three days earlier.

> I have decided on my own free will to leave my former life
> and responsibilities. I desire a life of freedom... Since I have
> been in Burma, I have been forced by my superiors in the
> Soviet Embassy to spy on my fellow Russians as well as on

my Burmese friends. I love the Russian people but I hate
the government of the Soviet Union and its cruel police and
intelligence services which oppress the Russian people.

Following the press conference, Kaznacheev headed for the
U.S.A. on an American airplane. Cindy and Tom wondered, did
the bunny-rabbit cookies serve as a happy introduction to his new
life of freedom?

SUGAR COOKIES

½ cup soft butter   ½ teaspoon lemon extract
½ cup sugar   1½ cups flour
1 egg or 2 egg yolks   1 teaspoon cream of tartar
1 tablespoon milk or cream   ½ teaspoon baking soda
½ teaspoon vanilla   ¼ teaspoon salt

Cream sugar and butter; add remaining ingredients. Chill dough.
Roll out very thin. Cut into fancy shapes with cookie cutters.
Sprinkle with colored sugar and bake at 400° on greased cookie
sheets until very lightly browned, 5 to 6 minutes. Watch carefully
to keep from over-browning.

Makes about 80 small cookies.

8

Inside the Beltway

IN 1961, AFTER ELEVEN years of living overseas, it was time for an assignment to the home office in Washington D.C. The change from keeping house with a staff of servants to being my own domestic-of-all-trades was a reverse culture shock for me, but it was also a relief to have our home to ourselves. We were no longer carrying the burden of "representing" our country twenty-four hours a day. This was the first opportunity since our wedding to establish our own household in the U.S.

The day we found our dream house in a Maryland suburb, President Kennedy was being inaugurated. Young men and women our age were proclaiming a "New Frontier" for the United States. We were in the midst of the excitement that permeated the air of Washington, part of the dreams and hard work of those new leaders.

Cliff spent the first months of 1961 in New York, as a member of Ambassador Adlai Stevenson's team at the United Nations. Cuba was center stage during this UN session; there was the debacle of the "Bay of Pigs" in the spring and, in the fall, the fearful tension during the Cuban Missile Crisis. I had several Cuban recipes in my collection, and it seemed fitting to try them out now.

Dining with a Cuban Accent

Picadillo (seasoned ground beef)
Arroz con pollo (chicken and rice)
Lime and cilantro chicken breasts with tomato salsa
Black beans with peppers and tomatoes

Picadillo

3 tablespoons olive oil
1 pound ground beef
1 onion, chopped fine
1 large clove garlic, minced
1 tart apple, peeled, cored, and chopped
1 pound tomatoes, chopped fresh or canned
1 to 2 canned jalapeño or Serrano chilies

¼ cup raisins, soaked in warm water 10 minutes and drained
13 small pimento-stuffed olives, halved
⅛ teaspoon thyme
⅛ teaspoon oregano
Salt and pepper to taste
Hot cooked rice
¼ cup slivered toasted almonds

In large heavy skillet, heat oil until it is hot and sauté ground beef until it is no longer pink. Add onion and garlic and cook over moderate heat, stirring, for 5 minutes. Add apple, tomatoes, chilies, raisins, olives, thyme, oregano, salt, and pepper. Simmer mixture, stirring occasionally, for 15 minutes. Serve over rice and garnish with almonds.

Serves 4 to 6.

ARROZ CON POLLO

¼ teaspoon saffron threads
¼ cup olive oil
3½ pounds chicken pieces
2 onions, chopped
2 small green peppers, chopped
¾ pound Roma tomatoes (about 6) chopped
2 cloves garlic, minced

4 teaspoons paprika
3 cups short grain rice
6 cups chicken broth
½ cup sliced or chopped pimiento
1 cup thawed frozen peas
¼ cup minced fresh parsley (optional)

Dissolve saffron in hot water, drain, and crumble. In large heavy skillet, heat oil until hot but not smoking and reduce heat to moderately low. Cook chicken, which has been patted dry, in batches in oil, turning to brown each side, for 15 to 18 minutes until cooked through. Transfer to a bowl. Pour off all but 3 tablespoons fat and cook onions and green peppers until vegetables are softened. Add tomatoes, garlic, paprika, and saffron and cook, stirring, 1 minute. Add rice and cook, stirring, 3 minutes. Add heated broth and simmer, stirring occasionally, for 7 minutes. Transfer the mixture to a shallow 5-quart baking dish and top with chicken. Bake in middle of 325° oven for 15 minutes; spread pimiento and peas over top and bake 5 to 10 minutes more until liquid is absorbed and rice is al dente. Sprinkle with parsley.

Serves 8.

LIME AND CILANTRO CHICKEN BREASTS WITH TOMATO SALSA

4 skinless boneless chicken breasts
1 clove garlic, minced
3 green onions, thinly sliced
1 tablespoon fresh lime juice
Freshly ground pepper
2 tablespoons chopped cilantro, plus extra for garnish

1 avocado, peeled, pitted, quartered
3 jalapeño peppers, seeded and quartered
2 large tomatoes, quartered
2 green onions, quartered
1 teaspoon wine or cider vinegar

Place chicken breasts around outer rim of 10-inch glass pie plate, leaving center open. Sprinkle with garlic, green onions, and lime juice. Cover with wax paper and microwave on high for 3 minutes or until cooked through. Let stand 3 minutes. Cut each avocado quarter into 4 to 6 long thin slices and fan them beside a chicken breast on individual plates. Garnish with cilantro. To make salsa, combine ingredients and pulse in blender. Spoon salsa on plate.

Serves 4.

BLACK BEANS WITH PEPPERS AND TOMATOES

½ cup oil-packed dried tomatoes, drained
1 tablespoon oil from dried tomatoes
1 small chopped red onion
½ cup pimiento, cut into thin strips

2 (15-ounce) cans black beans, rinsed and drained
¼ cup minced cilantro
Fresh cilantro sprigs
Lime wedges
Sour cream

Cut up tomatoes and set aside. Combine tomato oil and onion in skillet and cook, stirring often, until onion is soft. Add tomatoes and pimiento strips and cook, stirring, until hot. Add beans and cilantro and cook until heated through. Pour into bowl and garnish with cilantro sprigs. Add juice from lime wedges and sour cream to taste.

Serves 4 to 6.

WHEN CLIFF CAME BACK from New York to Washington to take over the Japan/Korea Desk at the U.S. Information Agency, we often gathered together with Foreign Service colleagues who, like ourselves, had come home for a Washington assignment. We entertained Japanese and Korean diplomats and Japanese newspapermen and their wives. They became lifelong friends whom we met again on our later assignments to Japan. Casseroles—make-ahead meals—were the dinner fare of choice.

RECIPES FROM FOREIGN SERVICE WIVES

Betty Martin's Georgia country captain
Ele Nickel's beef Burgundy
Ele's molded cucumber and cottage cheese salad
Franny Nichols' charcoal grilled beef

BETTY MARTIN'S GEORGIA COUNTRY CAPTAIN

⅓ cup oil	½ cup chopped celery
1 clove garlic, minced	1 green pepper, chopped
2 medium onions, sliced	3½ cups canned tomatoes
½ cup flour	1 cup raw rice
1 teaspoon salt	¼ cup currants
Pepper to taste	2 tablespoons butter
1 pound chicken, cut up	⅓ cup almonds
2 teaspoons curry powder	Snipped parsley

In hot oil, fry garlic and onion until limp; remove from oil. Combine flour, salt, and pepper in paper bag. Shake chicken pieces with flour mix to coat. Brown in oil, then add curry powder, celery, pepper, and tomatoes. Cover and simmer 45 minutes until chicken is tender. Meanwhile, cook rice. Once cooked, add currants to the rice and toss. Brown almonds in butter. Garnish chicken with almonds and parsley and serve with rice.

Serves 4 to 6.

Ele Nickel's Beef Burgundy

1¼ cups diced salt pork
¼ cup cognac
½ cup parsley
½ teaspoon pepper
½ cup flour
1½ teaspoons salt
3 pounds bottom round beef,
   cut into 1¼-inch pieces
¼ pound butter

4 large onions, chopped
½ teaspoon thyme
½ teaspoon marjoram
1½ cups red wine
2 cups beef broth
¼ pound mushrooms
14 pearl onions
Salt, pepper, and cayenne to taste

Marinate salt pork in cognac with ¼ cup parsley and ¼ teaspoon pepper. Mix flour, salt, and remaining pepper; dredge the beef with this. Melt half the butter in a Dutch oven; brown the meat and remove it from the pan. Add chopped onions and brown them. Fry the salt pork, having drained and reserved the cognac. Transfer beef to casserole and add pork, with fat removed. Deglaze pan with cognac. Add to beef. Add thyme, marjoram, wine, and broth. Cover and cook in 375° oven 1½ hours. Brown mushrooms and pearl onions in remaining butter and add to beef. Cook covered 1 hour more and correct seasonings.

   Serves 8 to 10.

Ele's Molded Cucumber and Cottage Cheese Salad

1 package lemon Jell-O
1 cup hot water
1 cup mayonnaise
1 pint cottage cheese
½ cup finely chopped celery
1 large cucumber, peeled and
   diced

Salt, pepper, and cayenne to taste
½ cup parsley
1 small onion, minced
1 teaspoon salt
1 tablespoon vinegar
½ cup blanched almonds
Lettuce leaves as garnish

Soften Jell-O in hot water and let cool until syrupy but not set. Stir in remaining ingredients. Turn mixture into mold. Let chill overnight or until firm. Unmold on plate and garnish with crisp lettuce leaves.

Serves 8.

FRANNY NICHOLS' CHARCOAL GRILLED BEEF

3 pounds beef chuck roast or   ¼ cup soy sauce
   shoulder   ¼ cup water
½ cup bourbon whiskey

Combine bourbon, soy sauce, and water and marinate beef 6 hours or overnight, turning occasionally. Cook over charcoal 30 minutes on each side.

Serves 6 to 8.

DOUG WAS BORN THE week before Christmas, 1961. This time it was a first-class birthing experience. My doctor was the partner of Jackie Kennedy's obstetrician and the delivery was at Georgetown University Hospital. In early December, the ladies of our neighborhood gave me a baby shower. The most memorable gift was brought by a wise grandmother who focused on the older siblings rather than the new baby. She created for Tom and Cindy a mobile, from which hung assorted cookie cutters—for gingerbread men, stars, Christmas trees, and bells—and a tiny book with Christmas cookie recipes. Every Forster Christmas season since 1961, thanks to Ann Johnstone, has started with a full day of making gingerbread men and sugar cookies to pack in boxes as gifts, hang on our tree, and hand out to visitors during the holiday season.

Christmas Sweetmeats for Family and Friends

Sugar cookies (page 102)
Gingerbread men
Christmas cake cookies
Meringue stars
Sugar coated walnuts

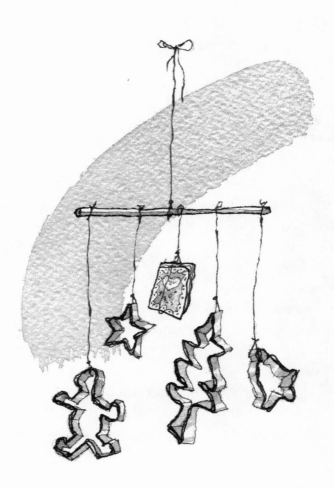

GINGERBREAD MEN

½ cup shortening
½ cup sugar
½ cup light molasses
½ teaspoon vinegar
1 beaten egg

3 cups flour
¼ teaspoon salt
½ teaspoon baking soda
½ teaspoon ground cinnamon
½ teaspoon ground ginger

Bring shortening, sugar, molasses, and vinegar to a boil. Cool, then add egg. Add sifted dry ingredients and mix well. Chill. Roll out on lightly floured surface. Use cookie cutters for gingerbread men or any other desired shapes. Bake on greased cookie sheets at 375° for 6 minutes or until lightly browned.

Makes 30 cookies or 15 gingerbread men.

CHRISTMAS CAKE COOKIES

2 pounds dates
½ pound candied cherries
½ pound candied pineapple
½ pound shelled almonds
½ pound shelled Brazil nuts
2½ cups sifted flour

1 teaspoon baking soda
1 teaspoon salt
1 teaspoon cinnamon
1 cup butter
1½ cups sugar
2 eggs

Discard date pits and cut dates in chunks; cut candied cherries in quarters; slice pineapple into thin slivers; blanch almonds, chop, and toast until golden; chop Brazil nuts. Sift flour, baking soda, salt, and cinnamon together. Preheat oven to 400°. Work butter until soft and creamy. Add sugar gradually and continue working until quite smooth. Beat in eggs thoroughly, then stir in sifted flour combination and all the fruits and nuts. Drop batter from a teaspoon onto ungreased cookie sheets and bake 10 minutes. Don't over bake, as cookies are nicer when soft. Remove from oven. Cool slightly and remove from cookie sheets.

Makes 150 small cookies, which keep extremely well.

Meringue Stars

1 cup soft butter	2 tablespoons sherry
½ cup granulated sugar	2 egg whites
1 egg yolk	2 tablespoons powdered sugar
3 cups flour	⅓ to ½ cup finely chopped nuts

Combine first five ingredients. Chill. Roll out between ⅛ and ¼ inch thick. Cut into star shapes with cookie cutter. Place on slightly greased cookie sheets. Beat egg whites until stiff and fold in powdered sugar. Heap this meringue in center of each star. Sprinkle nuts on meringue and bake at 325° for 25 to 30 minutes.

Makes 60 to 70 small stars, 36 to 40 larger ones.

Sugar Coated Walnuts

2½ cups walnut halves	1 teaspoon cinnamon
1 cup sugar	1 teaspoon salt
½ cup water	1½ teaspoons vanilla extract

Place walnut halves in shallow pan and heat in 375° oven about 15 minutes. Stir frequently. Remove nuts from oven. Cook together sugar, water, cinnamon, and salt to soft-ball stage (235°) without stirring. Remove from heat and add vanilla and nuts. Stir gently until nuts are well coated and mixture becomes creamy. Turn out on a greased platter, separating the nuts as they cool.

Makes 3 cups.

When Doug was a few months old, I decided I needed to prepare and certify myself for a proper career, as a teacher in the field that had been my Stanford major and which continued to be my first love—history. To become certified in Maryland as a high-school history/social studies teacher, I needed to return to college and take a number of courses, most of them in education, including a nine-week practicum as student teacher. Summer school was easy for me to manage. I could take daytime classes, hiring as babysitters two teenage girls who lived down the street and were happy to earn some money during their vacation. An evening class in the fall also worked out—Cliff could man the home front while I went downtown to attend lectures.

My practicum at nearby Walt Whitman High School was more of a problem. Finding babysitters to take care of Doug every day was a constant challenge, and on a number of mornings, in desperation, I had to leave my wee one with a neighbor. One day a week I knew I could count on Irene Moran. She was a widowed and retired government worker who was one of our favorite sitters. On one of her days at the house, she wrote down a recipe she thought we would enjoy using when we entertained, a version of Spanish paella that had no shellfish. She knew that Cliff and I were both allergic to shrimp, crab, lobster, and all their crustacean relatives; those who do not share this allergy can of course add seafood to the recipe. When I serve paella I usually make a citrus salad and serve red-wine sangria. The food section of the *Washington Post* was a splendid source of inspiration, and there I found one of my favorite dessert recipes.

A WASHINGTON MENU FOR COMPANY

Irene Moran's paella
Citrus salad with sweet sesame dressing
Sangria
Washington Post cream of the crop

Irene Moran's Paella

15 to 20 chicken pieces
¼ cup oil
½ teaspoon salt
¼ teaspoon ground pepper
3 garlic cloves
2 to 3 medium onions, sliced
2¼ cups raw long grain rice
1 can tomatoes
6 cups water or chicken broth

½ teaspoon saffron or 1 teaspoon turmeric
1 Italian sausage (hot or mild)
1 large green pepper, diced
1 to 2 jars artichoke hearts
1 (4-ounce) jar pimientos, sliced
1 package frozen peas
½ cup chopped parsley

Brown chicken in oil. Sprinkle with salt and pepper. Divide into 2 large casseroles. With garlic press, squeeze garlic over chicken. Add browned onions. Combine rice, tomatoes, broth, and saffron or turmeric and pour over chicken. Slice sausage and add. Cover and bake at 375° for 45 minutes. Remove cover and add green pepper, artichoke hearts, pimiento, peas, and parsley. Cover and bake 30 minutes more, until rice is cooked.

Serves 10 to 12.

Citrus Salad

2 bunches lettuce (head, Boston, and/or romaine)
1 bunch watercress

1 can grapefruit sections
2 cans mandarin orange sections
Sweet sesame dressing

Combine all ingredients in a large bowl.

Serves 10.

SWEET SESAME DRESSING

½ cup sugar
1 teaspoon paprika
1 teaspoon salt
1 teaspoon Worcestershire sauce
½ cup dry mustard

2 tablespoons finely chopped
   onion
2 cups salad oil
1 cup vinegar
½ cup lightly toasted sesame seeds

Combine all ingredients in a quart jar with a lid and shake well.
   Makes about 1 quart and keeps well.

SANGRIA

Peel of ½ medium-sized orange
2 cups orange juice
1 bottle dry red wine

½ cup Cointreau or brandy
¼ cup sugar (optional)

With vegetable peeler, cut the peel off the orange. In bowl, using a
spoon, bruise the peel with sugar to release oils; then stir in orange
juice, wine, Cointreau or brandy, and sugar if desired. Cover and
chill. After 15 minutes remove orange peel and transfer to pitcher
or bowl with ladle.
   Serves 6.

WASHINGTON POST CREAM OF THE CROP

1 cup cream
¾ cup sugar
1 tablespoon (envelope) gelatin
½ cup milk

1 cup sour cream or yogurt
1 teaspoon vanilla
1 package frozen raspberries in
   syrup

Heat cream and sugar together. Sprinkle gelatin over milk to soften,
then stir into hot cream. Cool. Fold in sour cream and vanilla.
Turn into mold that has been rinsed with cold water. Chill until
firm. Unmold and offer thawed frozen raspberries as a sauce.
   Serves 6.

The "practice teaching" was a wonderful experience professionally, the most valuable class of my postgraduate education. My mentor teacher, George Kohut, taught five sections of senior world history. He read my resume, concluded that I came with more professional background than the usual student teacher, and readjusted his course schedule to cover the chapter on Asia during my nine weeks. He gave me one week to visit all the other history and social studies teachers' classes so I could observe their various instructional styles. Then he turned over all his classes to me, taking advantage of my presence to spend full time on his role as assistant coach of the football team.

On the last day of my classes, November 22, 1963, the students presented me with a twelve-foot-long illustrated scroll—a timeline including all the events I had emphasized and stories I had shared during my sessions with them. As the final class of my final day was about to end, we were interrupted by an announcement over the school's speaker system: President Kennedy had been shot in Dallas and might not survive. From contemplating the history of Asia through the centuries, we were catapulted into a contemporary flash point of local and world history as we waited for the rest of the news from Dallas.

Three days later, when the assassinated president was buried, our family stood among the crowds on Pennsylvania Avenue, shocked and grieving.

9

In the Shadow of Mount Fuji

OUR SECOND TOUR OF duty in Japan, from 1964 to 1970, was framed by two major events that symbolized Japan's rebirth from the ashes of war and its emergence on the world scene as a modern, powerful, and self-confident nation. We arrived just before the 1964 Tokyo Olympics. This was a massive celebration, a stylish party put on by the Japanese, who invited the world to come see what they had wrought. Tokyo sparkled with new buildings and sunny October skies. Potted chrysanthemums adorned streets and lined the Olympic swimming pool and basketball court. People were transported elegantly and efficiently on new Tokyo subways, automobile expressways, and the super-fast "bullet trains" between Tokyo and the cities of central Japan. This was national "show and tell" designed to impress the visitors.

We left Japan in the summer of 1970, just after another huge party—the Osaka International Exposition. By then, the Japanese had come so far they no longer needed to impress outsiders; this celebration was for the insiders, the family, with the rest of the world welcome to join in. Young people swarmed to the exposition, not the ultra-serious, no-frills youths we had seen in the fifties, but a new generation who stood tall (their postwar diet of milk and meat had produced longer legs than those of their fathers and grandfathers) and who found the time, despite their rigorous studies, to enjoy themselves. Busloads of Japanese senior citizens, led by flag-bearing tour guides, came from the hinterland. Theirs was the generation that had been too engulfed in the long Pacific War to indulge in travel abroad for pleasure. Now they experienced a veritable world tour—the industrial marvels of the Soviet Union, the moon rocks and modern art of the United states, Czech theater and glass, Canadian lumberjacks, Indonesian exotica, and glittering exhibits from places like Abu Dhabi, which the Japanese (and most others) had never heard of before.

During those years in Tokyo, we lived in a Japanese neighborhood in a house that was mostly Western in design, with one room preserved as a historic Japanese site. It was in this room, at the end of the Sino-Japanese War of 1894-85, that Japanese leaders met to establish the terms they would demand of the defeated Chinese. The spoils of that war were the beginning of Japan's overseas empire.

It was a cozy house for living and entertaining and we specialized in small dinner parties. Ambassador Reischauer was the star of the evening when we invited Japanese professors and journalists to come for informal conversation with the scholar-diplomat who had acquired Japanese fluency as a child of missionaries living in Japan. Our son, Tom, quickly recalling enough of his Japanese to make friends in the neighborhood, brought his Japanese pals home for cookies and Coca-Cola. I presided over ladies' luncheons and committee meetings.

When Marjorie Coleman visited Tokyo, I gathered a group of Japanese ladies to meet her at lunch. Marjorie had known Cliff since he was a child in the Philippines; he and her daughter Barbara had grown up together, and Barbara was now married to Dick Moore, the USIS information officer at the embassy. At our luncheon, everyone commented on how tasty the casserole was and wanted to know its name. "Chicken casserole," I said.

"That isn't imaginative enough," Marjorie said. "Let's give it a better name. What's the name of this area where you live?" I told her we were in the Takanawa District of Tokyo. "Good! We're eating 'Chicken Takanawa.'"

Takanawa Luncheon for the Ladies

Chicken Takanawa
Asian cabbage salad with oranges
(or Lime cardamom fruit salad)
Pears fandango

Chicken Takanawa

¾ cup sliced cooked chicken
1 cup sliced celery
2 teaspoons chopped onion
½ cup walnuts
2 cups cooked rice
1 can cream of chicken soup
½ teaspoon salt
¼ teaspoon pepper
1 tablespoon lemon juice
¾ cup mayonnaise
¼ cup water
3 hard-boiled eggs, sliced
2 cups crushed potato chips

In a large bowl, combine all ingredients listed through the lemon juice. Mix water and mayonnaise and add. Stir in eggs. Turn into casserole and top with potato chips. Bake 20 to 25 minutes at 425°.
Serves 6.

Asian Cabbage Salad with Oranges

3 medium-sized oranges
10 cups thinly shredded Chinese cabbage
1 (8-ounce) can sliced water chestnuts, drained

⅓ cup unseasoned rice vinegar   2 tablespoons soy sauce
2 tablespoons minced fresh   1 tablespoon salad oil
  ginger   3 green onions, sliced

Cut rind and white membrane from oranges and slice into ¼-inch rounds. Mix slices with cabbage and water chestnuts. Whisk vinegar with ginger, soy sauce, and oil. Pour dressing over cabbage mixture; gently mix to coat. Sprinkle onions over salad.

   Serves 8.

Lime Cardamom Fruit Salad

⅓ cup fresh lime juice
½ teaspoon ground cardamom
¼ teaspoon salt
⅛ teaspoon white pepper
2 large bananas

1 (20-ounce) can lychees, drained and chilled
1 (11-ounce) can mandarin oranges, drained
1 cup seedless grapes
2 tablespoons chopped fresh mint

Mix first 4 ingredients in large bowl. Slice bananas into mixture. Add remaining ingredients and toss to coat with juice. Chill and garnish with mint leaves.

Serves 6 to 8.

Pears Fandango

4 large, ripe pears
1 tablespoon butter or margarine
¼ cup firmly packed light brown sugar

¼ cup rum or Cointreau
1 teaspoon grated lemon peel
3 tablespoons lemon juice
1 pint to 1 quart vanilla ice cream

Peel, core, and thinly slice pears. In a 10- to 12-inch pan over medium high heat, melt butter. Add pears and cook until slices are lightly browned, about 20 minutes. Add sugar, rum, lemon peel, and juice. Boil on high heat until sauce is thick enough to cling lightly to fruit, 2 to 3 minutes. Keep warm. Divide ice cream among individual serving bowls, spoon sauce over, and serve immediately.

Serves 6 to 10.

The Japanese staff of the USIS Information Section considered their boss and his wife—Dick and Barbara Moore—special friends. They also wanted to honor Barbara's visiting mother. Cliff and I were invited along for the party at a yakitori restaurant on the Ginza, Tokyo's fashionable shopping hub. The food was wonderful, grilled on skewers, washed down by tumblers of sake (no small cups for the heated rice wine in this robust eatery), and seasoned with good conversation and much laughter. As a grand finale we were served the house specialty: a small bird, quail-like, flattened, speared, roasted, and ceremoniously served to each individual's plate. The feathers were gone, but the beak and bones were all there. Dick, Barbara, Marjorie, and I were dutiful guests and chewed our way through from beak to leg. Cliff was seated next to the wall where our coats hung on hooks. Marjorie caught him eyeing the nearest coat pocket and loudly exclaimed, "Not in my coat pocket, Cliff Forster!" All eyes were on him. His plan to jettison his portion was foiled and we gleefully watched, and listened, as he chewed on the bones.

Yakitori on the Ginza

Yakitori sauce
Yakitori chicken balls with quail eggs
Yakitori of chicken, onion, and peppers

Yakitori refers to Japanese dishes—often chicken—that are skewered on bamboo skewers then grilled with a special sauce until delicately cooked.

YAKITORI SAUCE

½ cup sake	¼ cup mirin (or sherry)
½ cup dark soy sauce	2 tablespoons sugar
¼ cup light soy sauce	Sansho (Japanese pepper mixture)

Mix all ingredients except sansho in saucepan and bring to boil. Remove immediately from heat. Let cool. Grill yakitori skewers (see following recipes) over glowing coals, turning frequently, until half cooked. Brush with yakitori sauce and return to heat. Continue to grill and baste with sauce until all are done. Do not overcook. Arrange on a platter and sprinkle lightly with sansho.

Serves 6.

YAKITORI CHICKEN BALLS WITH QUAIL EGGS

2 pounds ground chicken meat	1 tablespoon sugar
1 egg	10 quail eggs (or whole water
2 tablespoons soy sauce	chestnuts), drained
2 teaspoons minced ginger	Bamboo skewers
1 teaspoon salt	

Process in food grinder all ingredients except quail eggs (or water chestnuts) until very smooth. Use wet hands to form mixture into walnut-sized balls. Thread meatballs onto bamboo skewers, 3 to 4 at a time. Thread eggs or chestnuts similarly and set aside, or thread eggs and chicken balls alternately on same skewer. Grill with yakitori sauce, as described above.

Serves 5.

YAKITORI OF CHICKEN, ONION, AND PEPPERS

1½ pounds boneless	4 green or red peppers
chicken meat	6 leeks or green onions
Salt	Bamboo skewers

Cut skinned, boned chicken into long strips or bite-sized cubes. Sprinkle lightly with salt. Seed peppers and cut into eighths. Trim leek or onion and cut into 1-inch lengths. Pleat chicken strips and thread these (or chicken cubes) onto other skewers, alternating with onion or leek slices. Thread several pieces of pepper onto additional skewers. Grill with yakitori sauce, as described above.

Serves 6.

WITH MY NEWLY MINTED credentials as a secondary-school history teacher, I was hired to teach junior-high social studies at Nishimachi International School. This unique institution was founded by Tane Matsukata, a granddaughter of two nineteenth-century founders of modern Japanese business and government. Tane was the beneficiary of an international education in her Tokyo home and abroad before the war. Postwar, her friends asked her to provide a similar education for their children, and she started a kindergarten in the old family residence, teaching the youngsters in English. By the time those original students were in third grade, Americans living in Tokyo heard about the school and asked Tane to open her doors to their children, providing instruction in Japanese. Thus, a bilingual school through grade nine was conceived. Nishimachi graduates, representing many different countries as the school grew, were prepared to move into a Japanese senior high school or an English-speaking one. Those who spent several years at Nishimachi had the gift of fluency in both languages.

My sister Cindy and her husband, Jim Hawkins, were both teachers and came to Tokyo to teach at Nishimachi. Their dog, Sadie, a big black Labrador, came with them and gave her name to another of our favorite family recipes. We planned to gather for New Year's at the guest house built by Tom and Maggie McVeigh (members of the American business community) on a bluff overlooking Sagami Bay southwest of Tokyo. Each of us cooked up hearty fare for the first days of the New Year, which our now extended family would celebrate with the McVeighs and other friends. Japanese stores would be closed, and it was essential to plan ahead. Cindy made a huge pot of her quick, easy, and tasty chili and left it out on her kitchen table to cool while she and Jim went to a party. When they returned, Sadie had sampled the pot deeply, and the dish became famous as "Sadie Hawkins Chili."

COOKING FOR THE NEW YEAR'S HOLIDAY AT MIURA BEACH

Sadie Hawkins chili
Maggie's easy Scotch casserole
Zurich cheese fondue
Russian beet salad
Green bean salad
Chilled marinated potatoes
Stuffed baked apples
Melon in rum lime sauce

Sadie Hawkins Chili

1 pound lean ground beef   1 (12-ounce) can tomatoes
1 package onion soup mix   1 tablespoon chili powder
1 can kidney beans, rinsed and
   drained

In Dutch oven, brown beef and stir in onion soup mix. Add remaining ingredients and simmer 30 minutes. Multiply amounts to serve a crowd.

   Serves 4.

Maggie's Easy Scotch Casserole

8 ounces macaroni   ¼ cup chopped onion
1 can corned beef, chopped   Dash garlic salt
¼ cup sharp cheese, diced   ¾ cup bread crumbs
1 cup milk   Butter
1 can mushroom soup

Cook macaroni. Mix with corned beef and cheese. To make sauce, blend milk and soup and add onion and garlic salt. Fill casserole with alternating layers of macaroni mixture and sauce. Top with crumbs and dot with butter. Bake uncovered at 350° for 45 minutes.

   Serves 6.

ZURICH CHEESE FONDUE

1 pound Swiss cheese (may mix with Emmentaler)	White wine
1 clove garlic	4 to 6 tablespoons cornstarch
Salt and pepper	2 tablespoons kirsch or vodka
	1 loaf French bread, cut into cubes

Grate cheese. Rub garlic around sides and bottom of cooking dish (preferably an electric fondue pot). Put cheese, salt, and pepper into dish and almost cover with white wine.   Cook over medium heat, stirring constantly, until cheese melts, but no longer. Mix cornstarch and kirsch into a smooth paste and stir into melted cheese. Cook 2 to 3 minutes until fondue is the consistency of a thin white sauce. Place pot in center of table. Serve with cubes of French bread, which diners dip on forks into the fondue.

Serves 4 to 6.

RUSSIAN BEET SALAD

8 fresh beets	1 cucumber, seeded and chopped
½ cup cider vinegar	2 hard-boiled eggs, chopped
1 clove garlic, minced	2 tablespoons fresh dill or
2 teaspoons honey	1 teaspoon dried dill
½ cup red onion, finely chopped	2 cups yogurt
1 scallion, thinly sliced	Salt and pepper

Boil beets 20 to 30 minutes. Rinse under cold water. Rub off skin. Cut into ½-inch cubes. Marinate in mixture of vinegar, garlic, and honey for at least 30 minutes. Add remaining ingredients, mix well, and refrigerate.

Serves 4 to 6.

Green Bean Salad

1½ pounds fresh green beans
5 tablespoons lemon juice
2 large cloves garlic, minced
½ cup olive oil
1 tablespoon red wine vinegar
½ teaspoon dried tarragon
½ teaspoon dried dill

Salt and pepper to taste
2 teaspoons Dijon mustard
½ cup minced parsley
½ cup chopped green olives
½ cup thinly sliced green and/or
   red pepper
½ cup toasted slivered almonds

Steam beans until barely tender, remove from heat, and rinse in cold water. In serving bowl, combine next 9 ingredients (lemon juice through parsley) to make dressing. Add beans and mix well. Cover tightly and marinate 2 to 3 hours, stirring occasionally. Add olives and peppers. Mix and marinate overnight. Serve topped with almonds.

Serves 4 to 6.

Chilled Marinated Potatoes

6 medium potatoes
⅔ cup olive oil
¾ cup red wine vinegar
¼ teaspoon fresh black pepper
1½ teaspoons salt

3 green onions, thinly sliced
1 small bell pepper, very thinly
   sliced
¼ cup minced parsley
Chunks of ripe, red tomato

Peel, cut into cubes, and cook potatoes. Drain and let cool. Add remaining ingredients, mix, and chill.

Serves 8 to 10.

STUFFED BAKED APPLES

4 tart cooking apples
¼ cup Grape-Nuts cereal
¼ cup minced walnuts
¼ teaspoon ground cinnamon
Handful of raisins or currants
2 tablespoons honey

Core and seed apples. Combine remaining ingredients and fill each apple. Place stuffed apples in a shallow baking dish and add ¼ inch of water. Bake at 375°, uncovered, 40 minutes. Serve hot, cold, or at room temperature. May be garnished with a wedge of cheddar cheese, yogurt, or vanilla ice cream.

Serves 4.

MELON IN RUM LIME SAUCE

1 cantaloupe
1 small honeydew melon
⅛ watermelon
1 cup blueberries
⅔ cup sugar
⅓ cup water
1 teaspoon grated lime rind
½ cup lime juice
½ cup light rum

Scoop out melon flesh with a melon baler, or cut into cubes. Combine all the fruit (substitutions may be made according to season) in serving bowl. Heat together sugar, water, and lime rind until all sugar dissolves; add lime juice and rum. Cool and pour over fruit. Refrigerate.

Serves 8.

WE HAD A WONDERFUL household helper during those years in Tokyo, Yoneko-san. She was barely four feet tall, but she was a giant when it came to efficiency and determination. Though our children were rapidly surpassing her in height, they meekly submitted to her commands. She ran the household and managed the kids when Cliff and I were at work or at the endless round of diplomatic affairs. She studied my recipes and cooked great meals for us. She kept the house and our clothing immaculate. But the numbers were stacked against her, three kids to one Yoneko-san, and occasionally they outsmarted her. They would find where she hid the newly baked cookies, for instance, then hide them in their own secret hideaway.

One night when we were out and Yoneko-san and the children were eating together, two policemen came to the door. They brought a warning and an apology. There had been a major robbery at the estate of the Japanese business tycoon next door. The robbers had established their lookout, their operations center, in a crudely built tree house. This, the police were sorry to report, was located on a steep slope outside our kitchen door. The policemen wanted our family to know that we had been exposed to danger. They formally apologized for the trouble the problem was causing to a distinguished diplomatic family.

Tom, Cindy, and Doug burst into gales of laughter. "That's no robbers' hideaway," said Tom. "It's our secret tree house!"

The Very Favorite Cookies

Vienna crescents
Yoneko-san's chocolate chip cookies

Vienna Crescents

½ cup butter
⅔ cup granulated sugar
⅔ cup chopped almonds (or
  walnuts or pecans)

¼ teaspoon salt
1⅔ cups all-purpose flour
Powdered sugar

Mix first 4 ingredients thoroughly, then work flour into mixture with hands. Chill dough. Pull off small pieces of chilled dough and work with hands until pliable but not sticky. Roll between palms into pencil-thick strips and shape into small crescents on ungreased cookie sheet. Bake at 375° until set, not brown. Dredge cookies in powdered sugar when cool.

Makes 75 cookies.

Yoneko-san's Chocolate Chip Cookies

½ cup butter
½ cup brown sugar
½ cup white sugar
1 egg
½ teaspoon vanilla

1 cup plus 2 tablespoons sifted
  flour
½ teaspoon salt
½ teaspoon baking soda
½ cup chopped nuts
1 cup semi-sweet chocolate chips

Cream butter and add sugars, beating until creamy. Beat in egg and vanilla. Sift and add dry ingredients. Stir in nuts and chocolate. Drop teaspoons of batter, well apart, on a greased cookie sheet. Bake 20 minutes at 375°.

Makes about 45 2-inch cookies.

Leon Picon, a student of Egyptian hieroglyphics who had been among those who broke the Japanese codes during the war, was ending a long and effective stint as Cultural Officer with the embassy. We gave him a farewell party, inviting Japanese and foreign guests from his list of favorite people, a stellar group indeed. This was an occasion for something stellar on the table, and *Sunset Magazine* came to my rescue. Their recently published recipe for a dessert called "Meringue Mountain" was made to order. I customized it to create the ultimate symbol of Japan for our departing friends, "Mount Fuji Dessert."

Recipes for a Farewell Dinner

Lamb curry
Garden salad with sour cream dressing
Mount Fuji Dessert with chocolate sauce

Lamb Curry

2 pounds boneless, lean lamb
2 tablespoons butter
1 medium onion, finely chopped
½ green pepper, seeded and chopped
1 stalk celery, chopped
1 teaspoon curry powder
1 teaspoon salt
Dash pepper

¼ teaspoon ground ginger
¼ teaspoon ground turmeric
1½ cups chicken stock
2 tablespoons flour
¼ cup water
¼ cup yogurt or sour cream
¼ teaspoon paprika
Hot cooked rice

Cut lamb into 1-inch cubes. Heat butter in large frying pan; add lamb and brown thoroughly. Add onion, green pepper, and celery and cook about 5 minutes. Stir in seasonings and stock. Simmer, covered, until meat is tender, about 45 minutes. Dissolve flour in water, blend into meat mixture, and continue cooking about 15 minutes, stirring often. Remove from heat; stir in yogurt or sour cream and paprika. Serve over rice with condiments. (See recipe for chicken curry, page 12, for suggested condiments.)

Serves 6 to 8.

GARDEN SALAD WITH SOUR CREAM DRESSING

3 envelopes unflavored gelatin
1¾ cups cold water
1 cup boiling water
½ cup sugar
¾ cup cider vinegar or rice
  vinegar
2 teaspoons salt
2 bunches radishes, sliced thin

2 medium cucumbers, peeled and
  sliced
¼ cup green onions, sliced
1 teaspoon dill
Lettuce and watercress
Olives
Tomato wedges

Soften gelatin in ½ cup cold water, adding boiling water and sugar; stir until gelatin is dissolved. Blend in remaining cold water (1¼ cups), vinegar, and salt and chill until mixture begins to thicken. Fold in radishes, cucumbers, onions, and dill. Pour into 1½ quart mold and chill 5 hours or overnight. Unmold salad, garnish with greens, olives, and tomato, and serve with sour cream dressing (recipe below).

Serves 10.

SOUR CREAM DRESSING

1½ cups sour cream (or yogurt)   2 teaspoons sugar
½ teaspoon salt   2 teaspoons vinegar

Combine all ingredients and blend well.

MOUNT FUJI DESSERT

6 egg whites   Chocolate sauce
½ teaspoon cream of tartar   ½ cup slivered almonds, toasted
2 cups sugar   1 cup heavy cream, whipped

Beat egg whites and cream of tartar until frothy, add sugar, and continue beating until stiff. Drop meringue into puffs, ¼ cup each, on cookie sheets covered with brown paper. Bake at 250° for three hours. Turn off oven and leave meringues inside for several hours or overnight. To assemble mountain: Arrange 6 meringues on a serving platter to create a circular base. Drizzle with warm chocolate sauce (recipe below) and sprinkle with almonds. Add continuing layers, each smaller, to create a volcanic cone, drizzling each layer with chocolate and garnishing with almonds. Cover with whipped cream and serve with remaining sauce, heated. (Each person removes a meringue with serving tools and helps self to sauce.)
Serves 10 to 12.

CHOCOLATE SAUCE

½ cup sugar   12 ounces semisweet chocolate
1 cup corn syrup   bits
1 cup half and half   2 tablespoons water
⅛ teaspoon salt   2 teaspoons vanilla

Combine sugar, syrup, cream, and salt and heat to boiling point, stirring constantly. In a separate pan, heat chocolate and water until chocolate has melted. Add vanilla, then add chocolate to sugar mixture. Keep warm while assembling Mount Fuji. Warm remaining sauce before serving.

Makes 3½ cups.

ONE OF THE MOST amazing hosting assignments we had in Tokyo came after we had moved from the rented Takanawa house to a larger embassy-owned residence. This house lacked coziness but offered modern conveniences and space to entertain on a grander scale. When the Los Angeles Philharmonic Orchestra came to Tokyo under the sponsorship of our embassy—specifically Cliff's section of the embassy—it fell to us to provide an opening-night reception for performers and selected members of Japan's cultural elite. Conductor Zubin Mehta was the star of the evening, along with his beautiful wife. Guests began arriving at 11:00 p.m., after the concert ended and people had traveled across Tokyo from the performance hall. The musicians were famished and headed immediately for the buffet table with its precarved turkey and ham, one of them picking up a whole turkey leg and chewing ravenously.

Also in town was Bozo the Clown, performing for a different clientele, but welcomed at our reception as a representative of American culture. Luckily, it was a balmy night in May so the two-hundred-plus guests could flow out of our living room onto the adjacent lawn. That was where Bozo headed. He enchanted the children of neighboring diplomats and our own brood, who had been allowed to have their mini-party in an upstairs bedroom so they could witness this cultural event from the windows. With Bozo on site, however, there was no keeping them confined to the second floor.

MENU FOR A BUFFET AFTER THE SYMPHONY

Roasted turkey, presliced and reassembled
Mustard, mayonnaise, butter
Breads, crackers
Stuffed eggs
Raw vegetables and dips
Platters with assorted sushi
Assorted cheeses
Full bar: hard and soft drinks

ONE OF MY CLOSEST Japanese friends was Hatsue Horikawa, whom I had met in Washington when her husband was assigned there as a newspaper reporter during the Kennedy years. In Tokyo we were both members of the College Women's Association and worked together on a committee that selected Japanese graduate students to receive scholarships to travel and study abroad. The funds for this effort were raised by holding an annual Japanese print show and sale, featuring artists who were creating an exciting new art form as heirs to the masters of the woodblock print, which had recorded scenes of feudal Japan.

During this time, Hatsue's father served as the Foreign Minister of Japan. Knowing that my favorite sushi was norimaki, a stuffed rice roll wrapped in a sheet of seaweed, Hatsue's mother invited me to the official ministerial residence, where mother and daughter gave me a cooking lesson and a set of sushi-making tools.

MAKING SUSHI

Sushi rice
Norimaki (sushi wrapped in seaweed)
Inari sushi (sushi in fried bean curd)
Nigiri sushi (sushi rice with raw fish)
Fukusa sushi (sushi wrapped in omelet)

SUSHI RICE

2½ cups short- or medium-grain
   white rice
2½ cups water
4 tablespoons rice vinegar

3 tablespoons sugar
1½ teaspoons salt
2 tablespoons mirin or dry sherry

Cook rice in water. Combine remaining ingredients in small bowl and mix until sugar dissolves. Pour dressing over cooked rice and mix gently but thoroughly. Cool to room temperature.

NORIMAKI

Sushi rice
4 dried mushrooms
2 tablespoons soy sauce
1 tablespoon sugar
2 eggs
¼ teaspoon salt
Few drops vegetable oil
1 cucumber

1 small piece takuan (pickled
   radish)
4 ounces raw tuna, bonito, or
   kingfish
1 teaspoon wasabi (Japanese
   horseradish)
6 sheets nori (dried seaweed)
Shaved pickled ginger
Additional soy sauce

Prepare sushi rice. While it cooks, soak mushrooms in hot water for 20 minutes. Cut off and discard stems; shred caps into very thin slices, and simmer in ½ cup of the soaking liquid, mixed with soy and sugar, until liquid is almost evaporated. Beat eggs with salt and cook in lightly oiled pan like a thin omelet. Cool, then cut in strips. Peel cucumber thinly, leaving trace of green. Cut lengthwise into pencil-sized strips. Drain takuan and cut likewise. Remove skin and bones from fish, cut in strips, and smear with wasabi. Toast nori sheets by holding each in tongs and passing them back and forth over a gas flame or electric stove element a few times. Divide prepared sushi rice into 6 portions. Put a sheet of nori on bamboo mat or linen napkin. Spread one portion of rice on nori sheet, covering ⅔ of the surface. In a row down the middle of the rice (lengthwise), place one or a combination of the vegetables and fish. Roll up the sushi in the mat (or napkin) keeping firm pressure on the rice so it becomes a neatly packed cylinder. Repeat with other 5 portions. Let rolls rest for 10 minutes before cutting into about 6 pieces each. Arrange on tray and decorate with tiny leaves. Add a mound of shaved pickled ginger and offer soy sauce for dipping. Serve cold.

Makes about 36 pieces.

INARI SUSHI

1 package aburage (sheets of fried bean curd)	Mirin or dry sherry
Soy sauce	Sushi rice

Use half as many sheets of aburage as the number of inari sushi desired. (Each sheet makes 2.) Place aburage in colander and pour 3 to 4 cups boiling water over to remove excess oil. Press out most of the water by rolling in paper towels. Sprinkle with a few drops of soy sauce and mirin. Cut each sheet in half across center and pull sides apart. Fill each half sheet three-quarters full with rice mixture, then fold cut ends over to enclose the filling. Place folded end down on serving tray.

3 sheets of aburage make 6 pieces.

NIGIRI SUSHI

1 cup sushi rice	2 teaspoons wasabi powder
2 tablespoons sushi rice dressing	2 tablespoons cold water
1 pound very fresh fillets of tuna, snapper, or bream	Shaved pickled ginger
	Soy sauce

Prepare rice for sushi and reserve 2 tablespoons of dressing. Skin fish and cut into very thin slices with a sharp knife. Refrigerate until needed. Mix reserved dressing with 2 tablespoons cold water and use it to moisten hands before shaping rice. Shape one rounded tablespoon of sushi rice at a time into a compact oval. These should be a bit smaller than the fish slices, so fish will completely cover one side of the rice. Spread each fish slice with a little wasabi dressing (made by mixing powder and cold water) and place it, dressing side down, on the rice oval. Press and mold into neat shape. Arrange on tray, garnish, and serve with a few pieces of shaved ginger and soy sauce for dipping.

Makes about 24.

FUKUSA SUSHI

½ quantity chirashi sushi (page 55)	½ teaspoon salt
4 eggs	Few drops vegetable oil
2 tablespoons cold water	Thin strips nori (seaweed)

Press chirashi sushi into a square or rectangular cake pan to depth of 1 inch. Weigh down and leave while cooking egg wrappers. Beat eggs lightly, add water and salt, and cook on low heat in small lightly oiled pan to make 8 or 9 very thin omelets. Do not let eggs brown. Cut pressed chirashi into 8 or 9 pieces about 2 inches square. Put each square in the center of an omelet and fold up to enclose rice. Wrap a thin strip of nori around the parcel and place on serving plate with omelet fold on bottom. Repeat with remaining sushi and omelets. Serve cold.

Makes 8 or 9 pieces.

WHEN WE FIRST ARRIVED in Tokyo, friends whom we had known in Fukuoka introduced us to their favorite restaurant, Tonki's Tonkatsu, which was adjacent to the Meguro train station. The menu consisted of only one dish—tonkatsu, Japan's version of pork cutlets. It was produced by an assembly line of family members from Northern Honshu, and served to a standing-room-only clientele at a wood counter. The matron in charge commanded all the assembly labor, seated customers in order of their entry through the split curtains over the door, and enthusiastically greeted repeat customers. She even recognized us when we returned after a several-year absence from Japan and wanted an update on where we had been.

TONKI'S TONKATSU

4 pork cutlets	Vegetable oil for frying
½ teaspoon salt	Hot cooked rice
¼ teaspoon pepper	Shredded cabbage
¼ cup flour	Tonkatsu sauce
2 eggs, beaten	Hot mustard
½ cup panko (Japanese bread crumbs)	Lemon wedges

Trim fat from cutlets, make shallow incisions in each one, and pound gently to tenderize. (Do not make them too thin.) Dredge cutlets in mixture of salt, pepper, and flour. Shake off excess flour and dip into eggs, coating each side. Dredge in panko, coating each side. Deep fry in very hot oil until brown. Turn cutlets over and fry a few more minutes. Remove from oil and drain on paper towels. Slice each cutlet into 5 or 6 pieces and place on serving plate with rice and shredded cabbage. Serve with tonkatsu sauce, hot mustard, and lemon wedges.

Serves 4.

Note: Tonkatsu sauce and panko are available in many supermarkets.

10

Imperial Entertainments

As mid-level diplomats, we were on the guest list for the various functions hosted by the Imperial Family and the Japanese government during the year. On New Year's Day, the emperor received the diplomatic corps in his palace. In spring, the prime minister hosted a garden party in one of Tokyo's largest public garden parks. One fall, there was a duck-netting party at an imperial game preserve.

The dress and protocol for the January First reception at the Imperial Palace were very formal. The American Embassy ladies invited to attend were given lessons in how to curtsy. We were told that our gowns were to be floor length, with long sleeves and high necklines; colors to be avoided were red (reserved for the imperial family), black (mourning in the West), and white (mourning in the East). We were to wear hats. Our husbands were to wear full-dress white tie; those who did not own the attire (the majority) had to rent it (and take a chance on having trousers that drooped over their shoes or ended at mid-calf).

When we entered the palace, we were ushered into a huge waiting room, where a chamberlain of the Imperial Household explained exactly what was expected of us, using a pointer and a chart of the reception hall. Each diplomatic couple would enter the hall separately, in order of seniority. We would walk slowly to the middle of room (spot indicated on the chart) and stop in front of the lineup of Imperial Highnesses. The gentleman would bow deeply, the lady would curtsy, then both would slowly walk backwards to a door on the other side of the room.

The first time we did this, I was in terror that I would trip over my gown during the backward-stepping exit. But I encountered another problem. My "hat" for this occasion was a big artificial rose mounted on a small velvet pillbox, which I anchored to my hair with bobby pins. When the time came for our formal presentation, Cliff went into a deep bow that put his head at waist level. As I made my curtsy, I sought to lower my head to the same level as his. As I bent forward, I could feel the hat slipping forward. My dilemma: do I keep my head higher than Cliff's, indicating I am not as respectful as he and thus earmarking me as rude, or do I deepen my bow and risk having the hat tumble across the floor and land at the feet of the Empress? I opted for the first choice.

Outside the hall, we were nourished with a cup of sake and an individually boxed assortment of New Year's delicacies.

NEW YEAR'S AT THE IMPERIAL PALACE

Sake
Sweet red beans
Cooked lotus root slices
Pounded rice cake (mochi)
Marinated cooked fish fillet
Marinated root vegetables

THE FOOD WAS BEAUTIFULLY ARRANGED in lacquer boxes, but we barely had time to sample each delicacy before the next wave of dignitaries arrived. At a chamberlain's signal, we wrapped up our boxes and the white porcelain sake cups which were decorated in gold with the sixteen-petal imperial chrysanthemum crest. They were ours to take home.

The Prime Minister's garden party was much less formal and an event we always looked forward to. It was held at a time when cherry trees and azaleas were in blossom. Business suits were the order of dress, and it was an opportunity to show off one's prettiest hat. (In those days, we still wore hats to church and other ceremonial occasions.) We were free to roam the gardens and talk with friends from various embassies. Cliff's colleagues were surprised when the Soviet Ambassador and his wife came up to talk with us. (These were the bitter cold war days.) They sought us out, not for diplomatic conversation, but in their role as parents of a girl who was my student at Nishimachi School.

The Crown Prince and Princess (who became the Emperor and Empress in 1989) were led among guests by their aides and introduced to selected individuals. We were impressed when the Crown Princess greeted us by name, recalling that she had met us when she cut the ribbon for one of the College Women's Association print shows.

There was lots of good food and we were urged to stay as long as we wished, and to enjoy the surroundings.

The food at a Japanese reception was always lavish and delicious, whether at the Prime Minister's garden party or a business reception in one of Tokyo's leading hotels. The Japanese foods were usually served at individual stalls and cooked on the spot. The Western items would be arranged along a buffet table, the roast beef sliced to order at the end of the table.

SERVED AT A LARGE JAPANESE RECEPTION

Sushi selections
Yakitori skewers
Hot Japanese noodles in broth
Assorted small canapés
Smoked salmon with condiments
Sliced roast beef with condiments
Beer, sake, wine, liquor

WHEN WE ATTENDED THE imperial duck-netting party, it was an excursion into another era. Arriving at the Imperial game preserve north of Tokyo, we were escorted into a wooden pavilion and seated in ancient wicker chairs. All the guests were shown a sepia-toned movie of bygone netting parties. The sepia gentlemen were wearing clothes reminiscent of the knickers my grandfather used to wear to play golf in the thirties.

After the film, we proceeded to the grounds of the preserve, where ducks were flushed from canals, and guests attempted to catch them mid-flight with long-handled nets. Our team included the Princess Chichibu (widowed sister-in-law of the Emperor) and a bachelor ambassador from Europe who threw his net on the ground in disgust when he failed, yet again, to net a bird. The Princess gracefully leaned down, retrieved the net, and placed it back in his hands.

Those (few) who caught ducks had their booty spirited away by servants, and their hands were free to try again. As we left the game preserve, a brace of dead ducks was presented to each couple to take home—an equal distribution that was reminiscent of Tom's nursery-school chestnut hunt! When I presented the ducks to Yoneko-san, she said de-feathering and cleaning game was beyond her capabilities. Perhaps, she suggested, I should present the challenge to the proprietor of the chicken shop up the street. He did a beautiful job and we feasted on imperial duck.

IMPERIAL DUCK FEAST

Roast duck
Apple and onion stuffing
Baked sweet potatoes in orange cups
Gravy and currant jelly
Green beans or Brussels sprouts
Banana soufflé

ROAST DUCK

    1 duck, cleaned and de-feathered
    1 handful of celery leaves
    1 recipe apple and onion stuffing

Place celery leaves in duck cavity. Bake stuffing in a separate pan so it will not absorb the fat from duck. Put duck on rack in an open roasting pan. Prick in several places so some of the fat will drain off. Roast at 325° until tender, about 30 minutes per pound. Do not baste. Turn often to brown evenly. Pour off fat as it accumulates.

    Serves 3 to 4.

APPLE AND ONION STUFFING

2 tablespoons bacon fat	½ cup dry bread crumbs
½ cup chopped onion	½ teaspoon ground nutmeg
½ cup chopped celery	½ teaspoon ground cinnamon
2 diced tart apples, unpeeled	Salt and pepper to taste
2 teaspoons sugar	

Cook onion and celery in fat for 2 minutes; add apple. Cook 5 minutes and add bread crumbs and seasonings. Heat in oven for 15 minutes at 325°.

    Makes about 2 cups.

BAKED SWEET POTATOES IN ORANGE CUPS

1 large or 2 medium sweet potatoes	Butter
2 oranges, halved and juiced	Sherry, Cointreau, or rum
	Brown sugar

Peel then boil sweet potatoes. Drain and mash. Moisten with juice from oranges. Season with salt, butter, and liquor if desired. Fill orange half shells with potato mixture and sprinkle with brown sugar. Bake at 350° until slightly glazed.

Serves 2 to 4.

BANANA SOUFFLÉ

4 egg whites	1 cup ripe bananas
Pinch of salt	Sugar to taste

Mash bananas. Beat egg whites until dry. Fold in salt and bananas, add sugar to taste, and turn into buttered casserole. Bake at 350° for about 45 minutes, until soufflé rises and browns.

Serves 4.

11

Tasting History in Israel

I N 1970-71 WE LIVED in Washington, where Cliff spent a sabbatical year as a member of the State Department's Senior Seminar,
learning more about the inner workings of the U.S. political, economic, and social fabric. The children and I were also integrated
into the domestic scene—they as students in elementary, junior,
and senior high school, and I as a substitute teacher at the junior-
high level. In the summer of 1971, we were on the road again, this
time to our first assignment outside of East Asia—Israel.

This was a country where we lived intensely. Current politics
and the continuing "war of attrition" with Israel's neighbors were
constant in conversations, and each person had strong opinions.
(Prime Minister Golda Meier said that Israel was an impossible
country to govern—everyone wanted to be the ruler. And a visiting
conductor of the Israel Symphony said the same—every musi-
cian wanted to lead.) Illuminating recent history were countless
personal stories of suffering, loss, displacement, and courage. At
the same time we (and the Israelis) lived with older history. The
men and women of the Hebrew Bible were introduced to us as
people with all the dynamism of today's neighbors. The stories of
the life of Jesus came alive as we walked in his footsteps in Galilee

and Jerusalem and celebrated Christmas Eve at the Church of the Nativity in Bethlehem. Weekend outings took us to medieval crusader castles and Roman and Byzantine ruins. Tom spent a summer excavating King Solomon's gates at the archaeological site of Gezer; Cindy spent time on a kibbutz in the Negev desert, where her work assignment was to shovel manure out of the chicken house. Together Tom and Cindy traveled into the interior of the Sinai peninsula with a Columbia University professor documenting the pre-Islamic poetry of Bedouin nomads.

Although Jerusalem was the capitol for the Israelis, most foreign governments—including ours—had their embassies in Tel Aviv rather than in the ancient and disputed city in the Judean hills. Cliff, as Public Affairs Officer, was now in charge of the entire USIS operation and was also spokesman for the embassy. This was a time when there were intense and often controversial negotiations between Israeli and American officials, and when the Israeli bureaucrats and journalists often got their news from inside sources in Washington just as soon as, if not before, the embassy did.

Our residence was in a suburb north of the city, and we entertained frequently, inviting journalists, professors, artists, and politicians to our house for informal and fruitful encounters—to learn more about their points of view as we in turn tried to explain ours. We didn't have the benefit of the servants who had eased the housekeeping and entertaining burden in our Asian posts, so our children—particularly fourteen-year-old Cindy—were dragged into service. Chopping onions. Greeting guests and taking coats. Passing canapés. Clearing and washing dishes. Cindy's reward was sitting at the table during intimate dinners when opera stars, nuclear physicists, syndicated columnists, and/or ranking government officials would swap stories and wrestle with complex ideas. Tom was away during the school year, studying in the United States.

When our guests were Israelis who observed religious dietary laws, it was an added challenge. The most fastidious told me,

"Don't try to cook for us. Your kitchen doesn't meet our standards for cleanliness." (For example, separate cooking and eating utensils for dairy and meat.) "Prepare hard-boiled eggs, which we will peel ourselves, and give us a can of tuna fish, which we will open and eat from paper plates with plastic forks."

Many Israelis were quite relaxed about what they ate, but I still made an effort to avoid the obvious taboos, like pork, and found it easy to avoid shellfish because of Cliff's and my allergy. I had prepared a dinner with extra care for a couple whom we were both becoming very fond of. He had formerly been assigned as a diplomat to San Francisco and was now attached to a prestigious scientific institute. The dinner's centerpiece was Cornish game hens that had been shipped from Northern Europe to our embassy commissary. As Cindy was passing the canapés and we were having a relaxed conversation, the wife wrinkled her nose and exclaimed, "Ahhh, I smell bacon!" (My favorite way of cooking game hens was to split them and lay a strip of bacon over each half before roasting.)

I was mortified. I apologized and headed for the kitchen to provide a substitute entrée. "Oh, don't make any changes," our guests urged. "We love bacon, and it's almost impossible to buy it here in Israel."

Game Hen Recipes

Cornish game hens basted with bacon
Cornish game hens with raisin almond rice

CORNISH GAME HENS BASTED WITH BACON

2 Cornish game hens, split   Cranberry sauce or chutney
4 slices bacon   Rice or baked potatoes
Salt and pepper

Arrange hens in banking dish, cut sides down. Place strip of bacon over each hen half. Bake at 400° for 45 to 60 minutes, until skin is brown and meat is tender when pierced with a fork. Salt and pepper to taste. Serve with cranberry sauce or chutney and rice or baked potatoes.

Serves 4.

CORNISH GAME HENS WITH RAISIN ALMOND RICE

3 Cornish game hens, split   1 cup white or brown rice
Salt and pepper   1½ cups water
Nutmeg   6 tablespoons raisins
5 tablespoons butter or   4 tablespoons slivered almonds
  margarine   Watercress
¾ cup white or rosé wine   Sliced oranges

Sprinkle cavities of birds with salt, pepper, and nutmeg to taste. Place birds on rack in shallow pan. Melt 4 tablespoons butter and stir in ¼ cup wine. Brush mixture over hens. Roast at 400° for 1 hour, basting frequently with butter mixture. Meanwhile, in saucepan, bring rice, water, remaining butter, remaining wine, and 1 teaspoon salt to boil. Reduce heat, cover pan tightly, and cook until all liquid is absorbed, about 20 minutes (longer for brown rice). Stir in raisins and almonds. Unmold rice onto hot platter. Surround with hens and garnish with watercress, oranges, and additional almonds and raisins, if desired.

Serves 4 to 6.

TAKING A PICNIC TO the beach was a favorite Sunday pastime, usually shared with embassy colleagues who had children the same ages as ours. Often we would drive north to Caesarea, the remains of the Roman capital built at the time of Caesar. Though it had been many years since his representatives governed Palestine and traded goods across the Mediterranean from this port, we could still find pieces of Roman glass and—on a lucky day—ancient coins in the sand. Looming over our chosen beach was the open-air amphitheater, renovated and fitted with a modern sound system, which was home to the mid-summer Israel Festival. Here we attended the opera *Sampson and Delilah,* with real pillars from antiquity and a real moon over the sea as part of the staging. Here we also attended performances featuring the American Theater of the Deaf, Theodorakis, Herbie Mann, Isaac Stern, and world-famous Israeli artists.

For our beach picnic fare we would bring typical dishes of the region, either from our own kitchen or the deli down the street. In the process, we discovered many new ways to enjoy eggplant.

A MEDITERRANEAN PICNIC

Hummus with tahini
Baba ganouj
Creamy ganouj
Mushroom ganouj
Spicy eggplant relish
Eggplant caviar
Tabouli
Raw vegetable sticks
Greek olives
Pita bread

TAHINI

Tahini is a sesame-seed paste used in many North African, Greek, Turkish, and Middle Eastern recipes. Prepared tahini is available in many Western markets.

½ cup finely ground sesame seeds   1 teaspoon oil
1½ tablespoons lime or lemon   6 tablespoons water
   juice

Grind sesame seeds in a spice or coffee grinder. Place juice, oil, and water in blender; add ground sesame seeds while blending. Continue blending until mixture is consistency of heavy cream.
   Makes ¾ cup.

HUMMUS WITH TAHINI

3 cups cooked garbanzo beans   3 cloves garlic, pressed
1 cup water or bean-cooking   1 teaspoon salt
   liquid   ⅛ teaspoon cayenne
4 to 5 tablespoons fresh lemon ¼ cup chopped parsley
   juice   1 to 2 tablespoons olive oil
½ cup tahini   (optional)

Blend garbanzo beans, ½ cup of the liquid, and the lemon juice in a food processor or blender. Add more liquid if needed, but do not over blend. Texture should be grainy. Add remaining ingredients and mix well. Hummus will keep several days in refrigerator and may be frozen. Serve as dip for vegetable sticks and pita wedges.
   Makes 4 cups.

BABA GANOUJ

3 medium eggplants	1 teaspoon salt, to taste
Juice of 1 large lemon	Freshly ground black pepper
½ cup tahini	¼ cup minced scallions (optional)
3 medium cloves garlic, crushed	1 tablespoon olive oil
½ cup finely chopped parsley	

Prick eggplant skin in several places with a fork and roast in 400°
oven until shriveled and soft, about 45 minutes. Remove from
oven and let cool. Scoop out insides and mash well. Combine with
other ingredients except oil. Chill. Drizzle oil over top just before
serving as a dip with vegetables and pita.

   Makes 4 cups.

CREAMY GANOUJ

1 cup yogurt or sour cream	Several dashes of cayenne
½ teaspoon ground cumin	Mayonnaise to taste (optional)

Add above ingredients to baba ganouj and chill.

MUSHROOM GANOUJ

1 cup finely minced onions	1 tablespoon olive oil
1 cup finely minced mushrooms	Salt to taste

Sauté onions and mushrooms in olive oil and add a little salt. Add
mixture to baba ganouj and chill.

Spicy Eggplant Relish

2 medium eggplants
1 green pepper, chopped
2 to 3 large onions, chopped
1 stalk celery, chopped
2 tablespoons chopped parsley
2 tablespoons olive oil

2½ teaspoons vinegar
2 cloves garlic, pressed
Salt and cayenne or black pepper
   to taste
Pita bread or crackers

Prick eggplant skin in several places with a fork and roast in 400° oven until shriveled and soft, about 45 minutes. Remove from oven and cool. Scoop out meat and chop finely. Add remaining ingredients and marinate at least 2 hours or overnight. Serve as a dip with pita or crackers.

Makes 3 cups.

Eggplant Caviar

1 large eggplant
2 large tomatoes, chopped
½ cup chopped onion
¼ cup chopped parsley

1 tablespoon lemon juice
1 tablespoon olive oil
Salt and pepper to taste
Pita bread

Prick eggplant skin in several places with a fork and roast in 400° oven until shriveled and soft, about 45 minutes. Remove from oven and cool. Scoop out meat and chop finely. Mix in a bowl with tomatoes, onion, parsley, lemon juice, oil, salt and pepper. Serve with pita wedges.

Makes 3 cups.

Tabouli

1 cup bulgur (cracked wheat)	4 large tomatoes, finely chopped
½ cup olive oil	Several celery stalks, finely chopped
½ cup lemon juice	2 small cucumbers, finely chopped
1 bunch green onions, chopped	Salt to taste
2 large bunches parsley, chopped	Romaine lettuce leaves

Layer ingredients in a large ceramic or glass bowl. Begin with bulgur. Add oil and lemon juice and stir. Next, layer chopped vegetables in order given, without stirring. Sprinkle salt over top. Cover loosely and refrigerate at least 24 hours. Before serving, toss all ingredients to mix well. Serve on a bed of lettuce or as individual servings to be scooped up and eaten by hand, wrapped in lettuce leaves.

Serves 6 to 8.

ANOTHER FAVORITE SUNDAY OUTING was to drive up the hills to Jerusalem and north to Ramallah, in the Palestinian West Bank, for a melt-in-your-mouth luncheon of roasted chicken, Palestine style. This was served at an open-air restaurant, under an arbor of grape leaves, in the company of multigenerational Arab families.

SUNDAY LUNCH AT THE RAMALLAH RESTAURANT

Palestinian mousakhan (roasted chicken)
Garlic cabbage slaw

PALESTINIAN MOUSAKHAN

½ cup extra virgin olive oil
5 large onions, coarsely chopped
Salt and freshly ground black
  pepper to taste
3 pounds bone-in chicken
  breasts (about 4)

2½ pounds chicken legs and
  thighs (about 4 each)
1 cup pine nuts (optional)
¼ cup ground sumac
1 teaspoon ground allspice
1 teaspoon ground cloves
8 small pita breads

Heat ¼ cup olive oil in large skillet over low heat. Add onions and cook 5 minutes, then sprinkle salt to taste. Continue cooking, stirring occasionally, until golden, about 15 minutes. Season chicken pieces with salt and pepper, rubbing well into skin. Transfer onions to 13x9-inch baking pan. Brown chicken pieces in oil (adding more if needed) and place on top of onions. Bake at 450°, uncovered, 5 minutes. Reduce heat to 375° and bake 15 minutes more. Drizzle a tablespoon or so of remaining oil into skillet. Heat, then add pine nuts, stirring frequently until pine nuts are brown, 10 minutes. Mix together sumac, allspice, cloves, and pine nuts in small bowl. Remove chicken from oven and sprinkle with sumac and pine-nut mixture. Drizzle remaining oil over top and return the dish to the oven. Continue baking until the chicken is cooked, 30 to 40 minutes. Serve chicken with onions and juices in pita bread, accompanied by garlic cabbage slaw.

Serves 8.

GARLIC CABBAGE SLAW

2 cups finely shredded cabbage	2 cloves garlic, pressed
¼ cup olive oil or salad oil	½ teaspoon salt
3 tablespoons lemon juice	¼ teaspoon pepper

Place cabbage in salad bowl. Stir together other ingredients. Pour over cabbage and mix well.

Serves 4 to 6.

AT THAT TIME, ISRAEL still occupied the entire Sinai Peninsula, their booty from the Six Day War of 1968. It was sparsely settled, with only an occasional military camp or a lean-to serving Arab coffee (today, returned to Egyptian rule, the pristine beaches have sprouted luxury hotels catering to sun-hungry northern Europeans). Sharm-el-sheik at the tip of the peninsula had a very rudimentary motel, without dining room. Our family and another embassy family, a total of four adults and six children, decided to drive to Sharm with all the trimmings on board for our Thanksgiving dinner. For our ancestral feast, we spread out blankets and beach chairs on a sand dune overlooking the Red Sea. A group of Arab youngsters emerged from the seeming emptiness and stood in a semicircle around us, watching in awe.

THANKSGIVING ON THE SINAI SAND

Cold roasted turkey
Stuffing
Jellied cranberry sauce
Celery and carrot sticks
Candied sweet potatoes
Israeli wine and fruit juice
Pumpkin or squash pie

Candied Sweet Potatoes

6 sweet potatoes
Salt and pepper
¾ cup brown sugar or ¼ cup maple syrup

½ teaspoon grated lemon rind
1½ teaspoons lemon juice
2 tablespoons butter

Boil potatoes until nearly cooked. Cool and peel. Slice and place in shallow greased baking dish. Sprinkle with sugar or syrup, lemon rind, and juice. Dot with butter. Bake uncovered at 350° for about 20 minutes.

Serves 6 to 8.

Pumpkin or Squash Pie

1 baked pie crust
1½ cups cooked pumpkin or squash
1½ cups undiluted evaporated milk
1 cup brown sugar
¼ cup white sugar
¼ teaspoon salt

1 teaspoon cinnamon
½ teaspoon ginger
⅛ teaspoon cloves
4 slightly beaten eggs
1 teaspoon vanilla or 2 tablespoons rum or brandy
¾ cup chopped walnuts (optional)

Combine all ingredients (except pie crust, vanilla, and walnuts) in top of a double boiler and cook over hot water until thick. Cool slightly and add vanilla and nuts. Pour into baked shell. Serve with whipped cream.

Serves to 6 to 8.

Refrigerating and then heating our portable larder was a real challenge. Especially when we were on the road for several days. We relied on ice chests, tinned and boxed foods, and canned heat. Most of the meal tasted just fine served at nature's temperature, but we wanted our instant coffee hot and it takes a long time to boil water over a can of Sterno.

On another trip into the Sinai with just our own family, we received some unexpected help from the Israeli army. Our third night, we set up a camp south of Eilat. The tent had been raised and a can of Sterno lit to start the long process of boiling water, when we were confronted by an angry Israeli officer with an Uzi rifle slung over his shoulder.

"This beach is a military security area and off limits for civilians. What do you think you're doing here?" he wanted to know. After we explained our innocent purposes, he mellowed and said he and his small detachment of men on the hillside overlooking our camp-site would make an exception and allow us to remain for this one night. He sneered at the feeble flame in our Sterno can and invited Cindy and Tom to climb up the hill with him to his camp, where he would give them proper desert fuel. They returned with a tablet about the size of an Alka-Seltzer tablet, which the Israelis stand on edge in the ground when on maneuvers, light with a match, and achieve instant and powerful flames. Cindy and Tom were also given a loaf of fresh bread to add to our dinner of canned beef stew, which tasted better than usual, thanks to having been heated by the Israel Army's fuel.

I taught in two schools during our Tel Aviv assignment. The first year, I drove the harrowing two-lane highway south twice a week to teach history to students in a boarding school for Jewish children who came from abroad to spend a year in the land of their ancestors. Their academic program, taught in English, followed the New York State Regents' curriculum and on weekends they went on trips to holy and historic sites. The Molly Goodman Academic

High School was on the campus of an Israeli agricultural high school in Ashkelon, the hometown of Sampson, and near the entrance to the Gaza Strip. The drive was harrowing because I shared the highway with truck drivers hauling massive loads of industrial products from Asia. This road was a land bridge that carried cargo off-loaded at Eilat on the Red Sea to Israel's Mediterranean ports. The Suez Canal was still closed to all shipping that had any connection with Israel. Those Israeli truckers, most of them tank drivers in the military reserve, were undaunted by oncoming traffic and had no intention of waiting to pass until the road was clear. My only recourse was to swerve off the highway. When I got home I needed a good stiff drink before cooking the family dinner. And when I was offered a job the following year at the International School, two blocks down the street from our house, I eagerly took it.

That put four of us on the same campus. Doug was in seventh grade and Cindy in eleventh. I was teaching juniors and seniors. All of those with Israeli citizenship (the majority) were slated for required military service immediately after graduation. These students paid close attention to their history lessons and had already formulated strong ideas about local politics and international relations.

The fourth Forster at school was our dog, Cao. A mixture of Irish setter, Labrador, and Collie, he was a skilled fence-jumper. The higher Cliff built the fence in our yard, the higher Cao jumped. He wanted to join the family at school. Doug's homeroom teacher eventually recognized a fait accompli and put the dog on the seventh-grade attendance list.

FAMILY DINING IN TEL AVIV

Khorake bademjan (eggplant and beef)
Honey glazed chicken 'n' biscuits

Khorake Bademjan

2 medium eggplants
2 large onions, chopped
2 tablespoons butter
1½ pounds ground beef
1 teaspoon ground nutmeg
1 teaspoon ground cinnamon

2 cloves garlic, minced
Salt and pepper to taste
3 medium tomatoes, sliced
Paprika
Yogurt or sour cream

Cut eggplants in half lengthwise, then into ½-inch slices. Place on baking sheet and brown under broiler, turning to brown second side. Cook onions in butter until soft. Crumble and brown beef in same pan. Add seasonings. In a large casserole, layer half of the eggplant, seasoned meat, sliced tomatoes, remaining eggplant, and onions. Sprinkle with paprika. Cover and bake at 375° for 30 minutes. Serve with yogurt or sour cream.

Serves 6.

Honey Glazed Chicken 'n' Biscuits

2 to 3 pounds chicken pieces
2 tablespoons butter, melted
1 teaspoon salt
¼ teaspoon pepper
⅔ cup honey
½ cup orange juice
2 tablespoons flour

1 tablespoon lime juice
1 teaspoon cinnamon
1 teaspoon Worcestershire sauce
1 (8-ounce) can refrigerated
   buttermilk biscuits
⅓ cup cornflakes, slightly crushed

Place chicken pieces in ungreased 13x9-inch baking dish, skin side up. Brush with melted butter. Sprinkle with salt and pepper. Bake for 50 to 55 minutes at 400°, until golden brown. Prepare glaze by combining next 6 ingredients. Drain excess fat from baking dish. Move chicken to one end of dish. Separate dough into 10 biscuits and place at other end of dish. Spoon glaze over chicken and biscuits and sprinkle cornflakes over biscuits. Continue baking 10 to 15 minutes longer until chicken is glazed and biscuits are golden brown.

Serves 4 to 6.

SOME OF THE BEST food we ate dining out was at Arab restaurants. One of our favorites in Jerusalem was also a favorite of Shimon Peres, who was then a cabinet minister, working hard to find a way to achieve peace in the Middle East. (He became president of Israel in 2007.) He introduced us to Jerusalem-style trout.

FAVORITE ARAB RECIPES

Jerusalem trout
Arab Potato Salad
Arab bean salad
Jerusalem style Turkish coffee

JERUSALEM TROUT

Trout, about 1 per person
Almonds
Raisins

Salt and pepper
Bacon (optional)

Use 1 small trout per person, a larger one for two. Have fish man clean and slit fish for stuffing. In the pocket place a mixture of almonds and raisins, about ¼ cup of each. Salt and pepper the fish to taste. Place on a baking sheet and cover each serving with a slice of bacon. Bake 1 hour at 350°.

Arab Potato Salad

3½ pounds new potatoes
⅓ cup olive oil
⅓ cup lemon juice
1 clove garlic, minced
½ cup finely chopped onion

½ teaspoon salt
¼ teaspoon pepper
1 teaspoon dill weed (more if
  fresh)
¼ cup chopped parsley

Cook potatoes in boiling salted water. Cool and peel. Cut into ¼-inch dice. There should be 6 cups. For dressing, combine remaining ingredients in bowl. Pour over potatoes and mix gently. Chill before serving. Add more salt, pepper, and lemon juice to taste if needed. Chill.

Serves 6 to 8.

Arab Bean Salad

2 to 3 pounds green beans
Dressing for Arab potato salad (above)

Trim ends and strings from beans; cut into 2-inch pieces. Cook until crisp-tender. Prepare dressing and pour over beans. Chill.

Serves 6 to 8.

Jerusalem Style Turkish Coffee

2 cups cold water
6 heaping tablespoons ground
  coffee

4 teaspoon sugar
Pinch of cardamom

Put all ingredients in pot. Bring to boil and turn off heat. Pour coffee into cups at once.

Makes 6 demitasses.

Though the embassy was in Tel Aviv, Cliff spent much of his working time in Jerusalem, since many of the people he needed to meet lived and worked there. When Marsh Clark, the correspondent for Time magazine, was sent to Ireland for a three-month assignment, he invited us to sublet his apartment on the Via Dolorosa in the heart of the old walled city. This became our weekend and vacation home for a marvelous period that coincided with the Christian Easter, the Islamic feast ending the holy month of Ramadan, Hebrew Passover, and spring vacation from our school.

The rooms of the apartment were built against a wall that abutted a mosque and cordoned off the Dome of the Rock, the third holiest site in the Islamic world. Off our living room was a library in an archway that led across the Via Dolorosa to the Church of Saint Ann, built on the site of the Roman fortress where tradition has it that Pontius Pilate washed his hands of the consequences of the execution of Jesus. "I give you the man—ecce homo," said Pilate. The Ecce Homo Arch marks the First Station of the Cross, the start of the Via Dolorosa pilgrimage route for Christians. A rooftop terrace above our living room overlooked the street and the arch. We often went up there to enjoy the view across sandstone domes to the various towers of the city.

We invited a group of Israeli and Arab friends and colleagues to join us on the terrace for a luncheon buffet on the Friday before Easter. It was the perfect vantage point from which to watch the gathering of worshippers from many lands—nuns from Asia, clergymen and their congregations from Germany, pilgrims from North and South America, black-robed men and women from Greece and Turkey.

Good Friday Luncheon on the Via Dolorosa

Mushroom pate
Egg and olive dome
Crackers and bread
Russian vegetable salad
Ratatouille (Mediterranean vegetable stew)
Mediterranean cucumber salad
Middle Eastern beef salad
My sister's chicken salad
Fresh fruit
Prune spice cake

Mushroom Pate

1 tablespoon vegetable oil
⅔ cup chopped scallions
1 celery stalk, chopped
5 cups sliced mushrooms
½ teaspoon dried basil
¼ teaspoon dried thyme
1 block of tofu, blanched and
   crumbled

1 cup whole-wheat bread crumbs
½ cup walnuts, chopped
¼ cup tahini
2 tablespoons soy sauce
⅛ teaspoon each black pepper
   and cayenne

Sauté scallions and celery in oil until scallions are soft. Add mushrooms, basil, and thyme and continue cooking on low heat until mushrooms are soft. To blanche tofu, put block or cubes in pan of boiling water, simmer about 5 minutes, and drain; this makes tofu firmer. Combine vegetables mixture, tofu, and remaining ingredients and blend in a food processor. Oil a medium loaf pan and line with waxed paper large enough to lap over sides of pan. Oil the paper. Spoon in the pate mixture. Fold waxed paper across the top and bake about 1½ hours at 400°, until a toothpick inserted in the middle comes out clean. Cool pate and fold back paper on top. Invert on serving platter and peel away the paper. Garnish platter with greens and small sweet pickles. Slice pate thinly and serve with bread or crackers.

Serves 6 generously.

Egg and Olive Dome

6 hard-boiled eggs, chopped	4 tablespoons soft butter
5 tablespoons chopped green, pimento-stuffed olives	¾ teaspoon salt, to taste
3 tablespoons chopped celery	Freshly ground black pepper
3 tablespoons chopped onion	Cayenne pepper, to taste
2 tablespoons chopped parsley	Garnishes

Combine all ingredients except garnishes. Put through a food processor to achieve smooth mixture. Taste and correct seasonings. Shape into a sooth dome on serving plate. Garnish with parsley, sliced pickles, radishes, thin slices red pepper, and/or sliced olives.

Serves 6.

Russian Vegetable Salad

3 large white-skinned potatoes	¼ cup olive oil
1 cup cooked peas	¼ cup wine vinegar
1 cup cooked diced carrots	1½ teaspoons salt
½ cup chopped pimiento peppers	Pepper to taste
½ cup minced onion	Mayonnaise to taste
	Garnishes

Boil potatoes in skins until tender. Cool, peel, and cut into ¼-inch dice. Place in large bowl and add other vegetables. Toss together with oil, vinegar, salt, and pepper. Taste and correct seasonings. Add a few spoons of mayonnaise to taste and toss again. Mound salad on an oval platter and smooth it with a wide knife or spatula. Spread mayonnaise over top into a smooth frosting. Decorate with garnishes such as parsley, carrot slices, slivers of pepper, chopped hard cooked egg. Refrigerate until serving.

Serves 8 to 10.

Ratatouille

¼ cup olive oil
4 cloves garlic, crushed
1 bay leaf
1 medium onion, chopped
2 teaspoons salt, to taste
2 small eggplant, cubed
3 tablespoons dry red wine
½ cup tomato juice
1 teaspoon basil
1 teaspoon marjoram
½ teaspoon oregano

Dash of ground rosemary
Black pepper, to taste
2 medium bell peppers, cut into squares
2 small or 1 medium zucchini, sliced
2 medium tomatoes, cut into eighths
2 tablespoons tomato paste
Chopped parsley

Heat oil in large cooking pot. Add garlic, bay leaf, onion, and some salt. Sauté over medium heat until onion is soft. Add eggplant, wine, and tomato juice. Add herbs. Stir to mix well; cover and simmer 10 to 15 minutes. Add salt, pepper, bell peppers, zucchini, tomatoes, tomato paste, and parsley and mix well. Continue cooking until all vegetables are tender. Serve hot or cold with French bread.

Serves 6.

Mediterranean Cucumber Salad

2 small cucumbers
1 cup yogurt
3 tablespoons monukka (or other) raisins
¼ cup chopped walnuts

1 onion, finely chopped
Salt to taste
Freshly ground pepper to taste
1 tablespoon chopped mint leaves

Peel cucumbers, slice lengthwise, and remove seeds. Dice cucumbers and place in bowl. Add remaining ingredients and mix well. Chill and serve very cold.

Serves 4.

MIDDLE EASTERN BEEF SALAD

1 pound lean ground beef
1 tablespoon safflower oil
 (optional)
¼ cup raisins, chopped
Salt and pepper to taste

1 small onion, finely chopped
⅓ cup watercress leaves
⅓ cup wheat germ
1 cup yogurt

Brown beef in skillet, in oil if desired. Drain all liquid. Add raisins, salt, and pepper and cook a few minutes longer. Combine onion, watercress, wheat germ, and yogurt in a bowl and add cooled beef. Chill thoroughly.

Serves 4.

MY SISTER'S CHICKEN SALAD

3 cups cubed cooked chicken
2 tablespoons salad oil
1 tablespoon lemon juice
1 (20-ounce) can pineapple
 chunks
½ cup chopped celery

½ cup sliced water chestnuts
¼ cup chopped green onions
⅔ cup mayonnaise
1½ to 2 teaspoons curry powder
¼ cup toasted sliced almonds.

Combine chicken with oil and lemon juice, stirring well. Drain pineapple and add along with celery, water chestnuts, and onion. Mix mayonnaise and curry; stir into chicken. Arrange on greens and sprinkle with almonds.

Serves 4.

PRUNE SPICE CAKE

½ cup prunes
¾ cup water
1 cup vegetable oil
1 cup honey or maple syrup
3½ teaspoons vanilla
3 eggs, beaten
1 cup buttermilk
2 cups flour

1 teaspoon cinnamon
½ teaspoon ground allspice
⅛ teaspoon ground cloves
⅛ teaspoon ground nutmeg
½ teaspoon salt
1 teaspoon baking soda
1½ cups pecans, chopped

Butter and flour a 10-inch Bundt pan or 9x13-inch baking pan. Cook prunes in water until soft. Pit them, if necessary, and puree in a blender with any remaining cooking water. In large bowl, beat together oil, honey or syrup, vanilla, eggs, buttermilk, and prune puree. Sift together dry ingredients and stir into wet ingredients. Mix well, then fold in pecans. Pour batter into pan. Bake at 350° for 30 to 45 minutes, until knife inserted in center of cake comes out clean.

Serves 6 to 8.

BY MISTAKE, OUR SKIS had been included in our household shipment to Israel. Much to our surprise, we had a chance to use them. The Golan Heights, like the Sinai, had been captured during the Six Day War. The high point—where Israel, Lebanon, and Syria meet—gets some snow during the winter and the Israelis had recently installed a ski lift. The weekend we decided to try out the slopes coincided with a series of Israeli military raids on southern Lebanese settlements, in response to the ambush and killing of a kibbutz family by infiltrators from Lebanon. As we rode up the lift for our first run of the day, we could see attack planes coming out of Galilee, heading north, and dropping their loads with resulting puffs of smoke. After skiing down (the snow quality left much to be desired!), we headed for the snack bar at the foot of the ski lift. Ahead of us in line for beef hot dogs and French fries were Israeli soldiers in full combat dress. They had been in land action north of the border and were on their lunch break before returning to battle in Lebanon.

One of our most memorable guests was Beverly Sills. Just before Christmas, the beloved American opera star came to Tel Aviv to perform a recital version of *Daughter of the Regiment*, and we invited Israeli musicians and art lovers to a reception at our house. Inside the front door we had a fully decorated Christmas tree, thanks to the Israeli Government, which made a habit of pruning its forests in December and delivering the cut trees to homes of foreign diplomats. Beverly and her daughter, Muffy, were amazed and delighted; they had not expected to see Christmas décor during their time in Israel. Both ladies radiated holiday spirit as they took it on themselves to assist with the hosting jobs—Muffy helped Cindy in the kitchen, and Beverly picked up trays of canapés to pass around to the guests gathered to honor her.

RECEPTION FOR BEVERLY SILLS

Embassy punch
Mulled red wine
Caviar mousse
Olive cheese snacks
Salt pickled vegetable crisps
Cheese cutouts
Frosted coffee bars
Almond butter cookies

Embassy Punch

This was the standard nonalcoholic punch served at the Ambassador's residence in Tel Aviv. Cindy liked it and asked his housekeeper for the recipe.

Mint leaves and cherries frozen in ice
2 cups sugar, boiled in 1 cup water

1 cup lemon juice
3 cups grapefruit juice
3 cups orange juice
2 cups soda

For the ice garnish: Lay mint leaves and maraschino cherries in a tube-shaped mold, top with a small amount of water, and freeze. When leaves and cherries are firmly in place, fill the mold with additional water and return to freezer. Chill all the other ingredients and combine just before serving in a glass punch bowl. Add ice ring.
Serves 20.

Mulled Red Wine

3 bottles dry red wine
1½ cups brandy
1½ cups sugar
3 cinnamon sticks

8 whole cloves
3 small lemons, zest scored lengthwise and sliced thin crosswise

In a large saucepan bring wine and brandy to a simmer with sugar, cinnamon, and cloves. Stir and cook, barely simmering, 2 minutes. To serve, stir in lemon slices and ladle into heatproof cups. Keep warm in chafing dish for self-service on buffet table.
Serves 24.

Caviar Mousse

6 ounces red caviar	1 cup heavy cream
¼ cup chopped parsley	1 envelope gelatin
1 teaspoon grated lemon rind	¼ cup water
1 pint sour cream	Freshly ground pepper

In a large bowl combine caviar, parsley, and lemon rind. Stir in sour cream. In separate bowl, whip heavy cream. Sprinkle gelatin over water in small saucepan and cook over low heat, stirring until dissolved. Stir into caviar mixture. Fold in whipped cream and add pepper. Spoon into mold and chill until set. Unmold and serve as an appetizer with crackers or small slices of pumpernickel bread. Caviar mousse can also be served as a first course, pouring mousse into 8 individual molds and unmolding onto lettuce.

Makes about 3 cups.

Olive Cheese Snacks

1 (5-ounce) jar bacon-cheese spread	Dash Tabasco
	Dash Worcestershire sauce
4 tablespoons butter or margarine	¾ cup sifted flour
	Small jar (about 30) stuffed olives

Blend cheese and butter until light and fluffy. Add Tabasco and Worcestershire; mix well. Stir in flour and mix to form a dough. Shape around the olives, using about 1 teaspoon dough for each. Place on ungreased cookie sheet. Bake at 400° for 12 to 15 minutes until brown.

Makes about 30.

SALT PICKLED VEGETABLE CRISPS

6 cups raw vegetables
4 cups ice water
½ cup vinegar

3 tablespoons brown sugar
3 tablespoons salt
¼ teaspoon Tabasco

Slice vegetables (carrots, celery, radishes, cucumbers) into sticks or circles. Combine other ingredients and soak vegetables in refrigerator for at least 1 hour. Drain and serve "as is" or with a dip.
    Makes 6 cups.

CHEESE CUTOUTS

2 cups flour
1 teaspoon salt
¼ teaspoon cayenne
½ teaspoon dry mustard
½ teaspoon sugar

⅔ cup butter or margarine
1 cup shredded Swiss or cheddar
    cheese
⅓ cup dry white wine
1 egg white, lightly beaten

Sift flour, measure, then sift into bowl with salt, cayenne, mustard, and sugar. Cut in butter until particles are size of small peas. Mix in cheese and wine with fork. Gather dough into a ball. On lightly floured board, roll out to ⅛-inch thickness. Cut out with cookie cutters. Brush with egg white. Bake on ungreased cookie sheet at 425° for 12 minutes, or until lightly browned.
    Makes about three dozen.

Frosted Coffee Bars

2 teaspoons instant coffee
½ cup hot water
½ cup shortening
1 cup brown sugar
1 egg
1½ cups flour
½ teaspoon baking powder
½ teaspoon baking soda
½ teaspoon ground cinnamon
⅛ teaspoon salt
½ cup chopped walnuts
½ cup raisins
1 cup powdered sugar
3 tablespoons cream
½ teaspoon vanilla

Dissolve coffee in hot water; cool. Cream shortening and brown sugar; add egg and beat well. Beat in coffee. Sift flour, measure, and sift again with remaining dry ingredients. Stir in nuts and raisins and add to coffee mixture. Spread dough in greased 9x12-inch pan. Bake at 350° for 15 minutes. Mix powdered sugar, cream, and vanilla. Frost bars while still warm. Cut when cool.

Makes about 36 pieces.

Almond Butter Cookies

2 cups flour
1 teaspoon baking powder
⅛ teaspoon salt
1 cup butter
1 cup sugar
2 egg yolks
½ teaspoon lemon extract
¾ teaspoon vanilla extract
¾ teaspoon almond extract
¼ cup whole, blanched almonds,
   roasted

Sift flour, measure, and sift again with baking powder and salt. Set aside. Cream butter and sugar together until fluffy. Add egg yolks, one at a time, beating well after each addition. Blend in extracts. Gradually add flour mixture, blending well. Pinch off pieces of dough and form into 1-inch balls. Set on ungreased baking sheet, about 2 inches apart, and press an almond in center of each. Bake at 300° for 15 to 20 minutes, until edges just begin to brown. Cool 5 minutes, then remove to racks.

Makes about 4 dozen cookies.

WE ONLY HAD TWO years in this fascinating, complicated, exhausting country. We were there through skirmishes along the Suez Canal, raids into and out of Lebanon, the hijacking of a Belgian airliner, the massacre of Puerto Rican pilgrims at Lod airport by members of the Japanese Red Army, and the assassination of Israeli athletes at the Munich Olympics. We crossed over to neighboring Arab countries, feeling an acute need to learn more about the perceptions of people on the other side of the contested borders, and returned with the understanding that both Arabs and Israelis desperately wanted the same thing—to raise their families in peace and have access to what each claimed as their religious, historical, and political birthright. It would take many years before the leaders of these people could come together and discuss their differences, opening their borders to mutual visits and cooperative ventures and dreaming of the possibility of peace.

12

Washington Encore

URING CLIFF'S SECOND TOUR of duty at the U.S. Information Agency in Washington, from 1973 to 1977, he was assigned first as Deputy Director of the Middle Eastern section. Later he was moved to the East Asia/Pacific region. Traumatic events were to happen in each area. In October of 1973, all eyes were on Israel during the Yom Kippur War. Our Tel Aviv and Jerusalem friends spent anxious hours in air raid shelters or were called to battle on the front lines, while we Americans grumbled over long waits at the gas station to keep fuel in our cars. In April of 1975, the last American diplomats left Saigon via helicopters taking off from the embassy roof. During those frantic final days of the Vietnam War, Cliff's colleagues on the scene were desperately tying to evacuate the Vietnamese who had worked as their friends and fellow employees of the U.S. Government. Cliff followed the tragedy in the crisis center at the Department of State.

Meanwhile, I had been asked to help create and teach a five-year world history cycle for students in grades five through nine at the Washington International School. While soldiers from some of their home countries fought on distant battlefields, our students from nearly seventy nations sat side by side in the gilded rooms of a rented mansion now serving as a schoolhouse. It had formerly been home to heiress Marjorie Merriweather Post and ex-ambassador Joseph P. Davies. The school, which taught classes in French and Spanish as well as English, catered to the children of the huge Washington diplomatic community and international financial institutions like the World Bank. It also attracted local residents who wanted a bilingual and cosmopolitan education for their children. A significant number of scholarships were available for talented children from the District of Columbia's poor African-American and Hispanic communities. Learning and communicating in new languages in the company of children from privileged backgrounds, these students blossomed, and they brought the real world of tough inner city neighborhoods into lively campus discussions.

One of the best things about teaching at WIS was getting to know faculty and staff from Turkey, Latin America, France, Haiti, Wales, Syria, China, Morocco, Nigeria—thirty-two countries represented. What great parties we had! At least once a season we would all gather at someone's home for a potluck dinner. The last day before Christmas holidays, the senior students provided their own festive potluck luncheon for teachers in the dining hall of the schoolhouse mansion. Treats such as chocolate-frosted Bûche de Noël and flaky Turkish pastry came from the bakery; many of the savory dishes were prepared by the students themselves.

WASHINGTON INTERNATIONAL SCHOOL POTLUCK

WIS Vichyssoise
Salad Niçoise
Argentine beef pie
Moroccan orange walnut salad
Iranian eggplant
Bûche de Noël (French Yule log)
Turkish pastries
Chilean Sangria

WIS Vichyssoise

1 pound potatoes, peeled and
cut up
1 pound onions and/or leeks,
chopped
Water to cover
1¼ teaspoons (hot) dry English
mustard

1¼ cups chicken broth
Salt and pepper
Approximately 2 cups milk,
cream, or half and half
Chives and/or tomatoes, chopped

Cover potatoes and onion with enough water to cover; cook gently until they are soft (10-15 minutes). Combine mustard with 1 tablespoon water to create a paste. In blender, mix vegetables, mustard, and chicken broth; add salt and pepper to taste. Add milk and/or cream to desired constituency. Chill. Garnish with chives and/or tomatoes.

Serves 8 to 10.

Salad Niçoise

2 teaspoons salt
¼ teaspoon pepper
3 tablespoons red wine vinegar
¾ cup olive oil
8 small russet potatoes
1 to 2 baskets cherry tomatoes
2 medium onions
1 large green pepper
1 (7-ounce) can tuna

½ pound Greek olives
1 can anchovies
1 tablespoon powdered mustard
1 teaspoon salt
2 teaspoons basil
1 tablespoon red wine vinegar
4 tablespoons olive oil
2 cloves crushed garlic

Combine first four ingredients to make marinade. Cook and slice potatoes. Sprinkle with marinade and mix until coated. Do not refrigerate. Cut cherry tomatoes in half and toss with 1 tablespoon marinade. Slice onions thin and cut green pepper into strips; toss together with 4 tablespoons marinade. Let each vegetable stand overnight. Drain and arrange on platter with drained tuna and decorate with olives and anchovies. Combine remaining ingredients to make dressing, served on the side.

Serves 8 to 10.

ARGENTINE BEEF PIE

4 potatoes, cooked and peeled	1 small onion
1 egg, lightly beaten	1 small tomato
Milk to moisten	1 canned pimento
Salt and pepper	1 pound ground beef
1 tablespoon oil	½ cup pimento stuffed olives, sliced

For the crust, mash the potatoes and stir in egg, milk, and salt and pepper to taste, beating until smooth and fluffy. Set aside. Chop onion, tomato, and pimento and brown in oil in heavy skillet. Add and brown the ground beef. Add olives and salt and pepper to taste. Transfer to casserole and top with potato crust. Bake at 350° for 45 minutes.

Serves 4 to 6.

MOROCCAN ORANGE WALNUT SALAD

6 large oranges
1 tablespoon honey
½ teaspoon cinnamon
1 pound mixed fresh greens
½ cup red onion, thinly sliced

½ cup radishes, thinly sliced
1 cup walnuts, toasted
3 tablespoons olive oil
Salt and pepper

Peel oranges with a sharp knife and cut into sections. Squeeze excess juice from peels into bowl with oranges. Drizzle honey over the oranges and sprinkle with cinnamon. Let stand at room temperature at least 1 hour. Combine washed and dried greens in serving bowl with onions, radishes, and nuts. Toss well with olive oil and salt and pepper to taste. Add oranges and their liquid just before serving. Mix well.

Serves 6 to 8.

IRANIAN EGGPLANT

3 tablespoons olive oil
1 large clove garlic, crushed
1 cup chopped onions
½ pound chopped mushrooms
2 to 3 cups diced eggplant
½ teaspoon dill weed
½ teaspoon ground cumin
¾ to 1 teaspoon salt
Black and cayenne peppers

Juice from 1 lemon
½ cup dried currants
½ cup uncooked bulgur
1 teaspoon honey
2 tablespoons butter
2 tablespoons flour
1¾ cups hot milk
1 hard-boiled egg, chopped fine

In a Dutch oven, sauté onions and garlic in oil. Stir in mushrooms, eggplant, seasonings, and lemon juice. Cook, stirring constantly, over medium heat 5 to 8 minutes. Add currants, bulgur, and honey. Stir well and cover. Simmer over low heat 10 to 15 minutes, stirring occasionally. When eggplant is tender, remove from heat and spread into a greased 9x13-inch pan. Melt butter in small saucepan over low heat. Add flour, stirring until smooth. While stirring, add small amounts of hot milk. Continue cooking and stirring until smooth and slightly thickened. Remove from heat and add eggs. Pour sauce over eggplant mixture, spreading it over entire surface. Dust top with paprika and bake, uncovered, at 350° for 35 to 40 minutes.

Serves 4 to 6.

CHILEAN SANGRIA

1 cup thinly sliced strawberries	1 whole lemon, thinly sliced
5 or 6 whole strawberries	1 bottle white wine
½ cup sugar	2 cups chilled sparkling water

In bowl, combine sliced strawberries, sugar, and lemon, reserving some slices for garnish. Stir to bruise fruit slightly. Pour in wine, cover, and chill at least 1 hour or overnight. Strain and discard fruit. In serving bowl or pitcher blend flavored wine with sparkling water. Drop in whole strawberries and reserved lemon slices. Add ice to individual glasses, if desired.

Serves 6.

SPENDING SO MUCH TIME overseas, we missed interacting with our extended family. During our Washington tours we cherished time spent with relatives in various parts of the country. By the mid-seventies, my father had moved from the cold northern winters of Ohio to the gentler climate of Sarasota, Florida. We visited there when we could. My stepmother and the neighbors produced tasty food and shared their recipes.

Recipes from the Florida Elders

Princeton Inn Welsh rarebit
Sally's ham (or Spam) quiche
Beef and avocado deluxe
Key lime pie à la Kendall

Princeton Inn Welsh Rarebit

1 tablespoon finely chopped
   onion
¼ pound butter or margarine
5 tablespoons flour
2 cups milk
½ cup cream
1 pound sharp cheese

¼ teaspoon paprika
¼ teaspoon dry mustard
½ cup beer
10 dashes Tabasco
Salt
Worcestershire sauce

Brown onion in butter. Add flour and stir until smooth. Gradually add milk and cream, stirring until thickened. Grate cheese and melt in top of a double boiler. Add sauce plus remaining ingredients. Serve over toast. (Recipe may be doubled and frozen.)

Serves 8.

Sally's Ham Quiche

1 unbaked 9-inch pie crust
½ cup mayonnaise
½ cup milk
2 eggs
1 tablespoon cornstarch

1½ cups (about ½ pound) cubed
   cooked ham or Spam
1½ cups diced Swiss cheese
⅓ cup sliced green onion
Dash pepper

Mix together mayonnaise, milk, eggs, and cornstarch until smooth. Stir in remaining ingredients and turn into pastry shell. Bake at 350° for 35 to 40 minutes.

Serves 4 to 6.

BEEF AND AVOCADO DELUXE

2 peeled, sliced avocados
2 pounds rare roast beef, sliced thin
1 red onion, sliced thin
⅓ cup vegetable oil
¼ cup olive oil

½ cup wine vinegar
2 teaspoons Dijon mustard
1 teaspoon salt
¼ teaspoon pepper
Chopped parsley

Arrange first three ingredients in casserole in layers: avocado, beef, onion; repeat. Mix other ingredients and pour over top. Marinate several hours.

Serves 6.

KEY LIME PIE À LA KENDALL

1 (14–ounce) can sweetened condensed milk
4 egg yolks
½ cup fresh lime juice
4 egg whites

1 prebaked 9-inch pie crust
6 to 8 tablespoons sugar
½ teaspoon cream of tartar
1 lime, sliced

Mix together milk, egg yolks, and lime juice. Beat 1 egg white until stiff, fold into the lime mixture, and turn into prebaked crust. Beat remaining 3 egg whites to a stiff peak, gradually adding sugar and cream of tartar. Spread meringue over filling, smoothing out to inner edge of crust. Bake in middle of 350° oven for 20 minutes or until egg whites are golden brown. Chill before serving. Garnish with lime slices.

Serves 6 to 8.

OUR CHILDREN WERE STARTING to leave the nest. Tom had graduated from high school while we were in Israel and was at Reed College in Oregon. Cindy returned to do her senior year of high school in Bethesda, then went on to Brown University. Doug would stay with us a bit longer, graduating from high school when we returned to Tokyo. The summer of 1974, everyone was on the move. Tom went to Guatemala to participate in a "dig" at the Mayan site of Utitlan. Cindy took a short course in archaeology at Oxford, then went out to do field work at burial mounds on England's east coast. Doug went to live with a French family on their farm north of Paris, then to a camp on the Normandy coast where he spent two weeks learning how to sail. His French improved somewhat, but the sailing lessons were the greatest success, launching an enduring love affair with sailboats and racing. On his return he succeeded in convincing his dad that we needed a boat so we could sail the inlets and explore the old towns along the Chesapeake Bay. I took on quartermaster and galley duty for the weekend explorations, and rejoiced that I was not afflicted by mal de mer.

FOOD FOR SAILING ON THE CHESAPEAKE BAY

Wine and beer for the parents, juice for the kids
Nuts and potato chips
Crackers and cheese
Spinach chestnut dip/spread
Lea's blender gazpacho
French potato salad
Cookies and fruit

SPINACH CHESTNUT DIP/SPREAD

1 package frozen spinach,
   thawed and squeezed dry
1 package Knorr vegetable soup

1 can water chestnuts, chopped
Yogurt to taste
Mayonnaise to taste

Mix all ingredients at least 1 hour before serving. Serve with vegetables and/or crackers.

Makes approximately 2 cups.

LEA'S BLENDER GAZPACHO

½ large onion, cut in hunks
1 clove garlic, sliced
3 tablespoons oil
2 tablespoons vinegar
1 teaspoon salt
¼ teaspoon pepper

1 egg
1 cucumber, diced
1 green pepper, cubed
2 peeled tomatoes
Tomato juice

Place in blender all ingredients through egg and blend to mush. Add cucumber, pepper, tomatoes, and enough tomato juice to fill the container; blend *only* to a count of five.

Serves 4 to 8.

FRENCH POTATO SALAD

8 small round red potatoes
1 Bermuda onion
Salt and pepper

Chopped parsley
2 tablespoons white wine vinegar
3 tablespoons olive or salad oil

Cook and thinly slice potatoes. Peel and thinly slice onion and separate into rings. In shallow dish, place alternate layers of potatoes and rings. Salt and pepper each layer and sprinkle parsley over it. Combine oil and vinegar to make dressing. Pour dressing over potato mixture and refrigerate overnight. Turn at least once.

Serves 5.

IN THE SPRING OF 1977 it was time for us to head overseas again, back to Tokyo where Cliff would have the challenges and satisfactions of running the entire USIS program. Our Maryland neighbors, who had moved into their newly built house on Broxburn Court at the same time we did in 1961 and had three children almost the same ages as ours, gathered Court dwellers for a farewell dinner. The dishes Pat Latendresse served that night have been among my mainstays for tasty and uncomplicated make-ahead dinner fare ever since.

FAREWELL FROM THE NEIGHBORHOOD

Pat's curried broccoli chicken Divan
Pat's rice salad

PAT'S CURRIED BROCCOLI CHICKEN DIVAN

2 packages frozen broccoli,
  cooked
4 whole chicken breasts, boned,
  cooked, and cut into 8 pieces
1 can cream of chicken soup
⅔ cup mayonnaise

⅓ cup milk
1 cup grated American cheese
1 tablespoon lemon juice
½ teaspoon (or more) curry
  powder
Bread crumbs for topping

Place broccoli in buttered 9x13-inch baking dish. Top with cooked chicken breasts. Combine soup, mayonnaise, milk, cheese, lemon juice, and curry powder. Spread over chicken. Spread bread crumbs on top. Bake at 350° 25 to 30 minutes.
    Serves 8.

PAT'S RICE SALAD

4 cups cooked rice
1¾ to 2 cups mayonnaise
2 cups chopped celery
1 medium onion, chopped
4 teaspoons prepared mustard

½ teaspoon salt
4 hard-boiled eggs, chopped
8 radishes, sliced
1 cucumber, sliced

Chill the rice. Add mayonnaise, celery, onion, mustard, and salt. Mix well and chill. Just before serving, stir in eggs, radishes, and cucumber.

Serves 8.

13

Tokyo Encore

B̲ECAUSE C̲LIFF WAS NOW a senior member of Ambassador
Mike Mansfield's Embassy team, we were allocated one of
the largest embassy residences. Along with the big house came a
blue-uniformed round-the-clock security guard at our gate, a professional cook, a full-time maid, and a part-time gardener—and
the expectation that we would open our home regularly to large
numbers of official guests. The house was perfect for this. A large
entryway led either into a sizeable study or the living room, which,
in turn, had wide doors leading to the dining room and outside to
a terrace and lawn. Traffic could flow easily during a large reception, and, when it was our turn to host the monthly play-reading
group that had been started three decades earlier by expatriates
starved for English-language theater, we could provide generous
space for actors and audience.

We brought Japanese guests into our home to meet members of
the Joffrey Ballet, Dillon Ripley of the Smithsonian Institution, the
advance team for President Carter's visit to Japan, Larry Halprin
and his architect colleagues who were revitalizing urban spaces
across the U.S., and well-known authors such as Susan Sontag and
Maxine Hong Kingston.

Our largest parties were the two that were scheduled every year for Japan's Fulbright scholars. In the fall we welcomed American professors and graduate students who came for their year of study and/or teaching, and we invited Japanese who had studied in American universities over the years. In the spring it was a send-off for this year's Japanese grantees who would be going abroad for their international education. The Fulbright Commission, which Cliff chaired, produced a list of invitees. I was asked to greet and prepare drinks and buffet food for about two hundred people. I culled recipes from my collection and scoured cookbooks and magazines for new ideas. I hauled in a carload of groceries, and Aiko-san did most of the cooking. Fuji Service—caterers long established and universally hired by the foreign community—provided butlers. These men quickly learned the favorite drinks of many of the guests; we could return to Tokyo after several years, attend a reception, and be handed our "usual" without making a request.

RECEPTION FOR FULBRIGHT SCHOLARS

Baked spinach balls
Sweet and sour sausage balls
Salmon mousse
Cheesy onion toasts
Stuffed grape leaves
Tomato-mushroom rarebit with toast
Frosted ham with party rye bread

BAKED SPINACH BALLS

2 packages frozen spinach,
  cooked and drained
2 cups packaged stuffing mix
1 cup grated Parmesan cheese

6 eggs, beaten
¾ cup butter or margarine,
  softened
Salt and pepper

Combine all ingredients, mixing well. Roll into balls the size of walnuts. Freeze if not using immediately. Before serving, arrange on cookie sheet and bake 10 minutes at 350°.

  Makes 60 to 70.

SWEET AND SOUR SAUSAGE BALLS

4 pounds bulk pork sausage
4 eggs, lightly beaten
1½ cups soft bread crumbs
3 cups ketchup

¾ cup brown sugar
⅓ cup white wine vinegar
½ cup soy sauce

Mix together sausage, eggs, and bread crumbs. Shape into balls the size of walnuts. Sauté in a frying pan until brown on all sides. Drain; combine remaining ingredients and pour over sausage balls. Simmer 30 minutes, stirring occasionally. Serve hot. (If made ahead, refrigerate or freeze sausage balls in their sauce and reheat in 350° oven for about 20 minutes.)

  Makes about 150.

SALMON MOUSSE

1 envelope gelatin
¼ cup cold water
½ cup boiling water
½ cup mayonnaise
1 tablespoon lemon juice
1 tablespoon minced onion
¼ teaspoon Tabasco, or to taste

¼ teaspoon paprika
1 teaspoon salt
2 tablespoons chopped fresh dill
2 cups finely flaked cooked or
    canned salmon
1 cup heavy cream

In a large bowl, soften the gelatin in cold water. Add boiling water and stir until gelatin dissolves. Cool. Stir again. Blend in mayonnaise, lemon juice, onion, Tabasco, paprika, salt, and dill. Refrigerate about 20 minutes, until mixture begins to thicken. Fold in salmon. Whip cream and fold into mixture. Transfer to a 6- to 8-cup mold. Cover and chill at least four hours. Serve on crackers or black bread. May also be served as a first course, garnished with lettuce or watercress.

Serves 24 at a reception, or 6 to 8 as a first course.

CHEESY ONION TOASTS

4 green onions, minced
½ cup grated Parmesan cheese
6 tablespoons mayonnaise

24 inches narrow diameter French
    bread, thinly sliced

Blend onions, cheese, and mayonnaise. Add more mayonnaise of needed to achieve spreading consistency. Toast one side of bread and spread cheese mixture on the other. Broil about 6 inches below heating unit until lightly browned.

Serves 24.

Stuffed Grape Leaves

6 cups white onions, finely
   chopped
2 green onions, finely chopped
1 bunch parsley leaves, chopped
1½ cups raw rice
¼ cup olive oil

¼ cup fresh lemon juice
2 tablespoons finely chopped mint
⅔ cup pine nuts (optional)
Salt to taste
3 (6-ounce) jars grape leaves

Cook white onions in lightly salted water until soft. Reserve cooking liquid. Combine onions with all remaining ingredients except grape leaves and mix thoroughly. Wash off brine in which leaves were packed and remove tough stems. Place leaves flat, vein side up. Put 1 or 2 tablespoons of mixture in each leaf, fold stem end over filling, then fold in sides and roll up like a cigar. Carefully and neatly layer grape leaves in a pot, placing parsley stems between layers of rolled leaves. Cover with cooking liquid. Weigh down grape leaves with a heat-proof plate. Cover, bring to a boil, reduce heat, and simmer for 50 minutes. Drain thoroughly. Serve hot or cold. May be frozen.

    Makes about 120.

Tomato Mushroom Rarebit

1 (20-ounce) can chopped
   tomatoes
4 tablespoons chopped onion
1½ teaspoons salt
1½ teaspoons Worcestershire
   sauce
¼ teaspoon dry mustard
¼ cup sugar

Pinch of red pepper flakes (to
   taste)
2 small cans button mushrooms
¼ pound butter
6 tablespoons flour
1 pound sharp cheese, cut in small
   pieces

Empty can of tomatoes into saucepan. Add onion, seasonings, and liquid from mushrooms. Cook over heat for 5 minutes and mash tomatoes into small pieces (not puree). In a double boiler, melt butter, blend in flour, and add tomato mixture. Cook, stirring, until mixture begins to thicken. Add cheese and cook, stirring, until it is melted. Add drained mushrooms and cook until they are heated. Serve (from a chafing dish) over toast.

Serves 24 at a reception, or 6 to 8 as an entrée.

FROSTED HAM WITH PARTY RYE BREAD

5- to 6-pound canned ham	3 tablespoons prepared
8 ounces cream cheese	horseradish
1 cup sour cream or yogurt	Pimento-stuffed green olives
	2 loaves party rye bread

Ask butcher to slice a canned ham into ¼-inch slices across, and slice in half down the middle lengthwise, then reassemble and tie the ham in its original shape. (This can be done at home by the cook, but it is time consuming and hard to achieve even slices.) Combine cream cheese, sour cream or yogurt, and horseradish to make "frosting." Place ham on serving platter, remove ties, and cover with frosting which should hold pieces together. Decorate top with sliced olives and serve with party rye bread slices. Guests pry off their slices of frosted ham; the frosting serves as seasoning and moisturizer for the bread.

Serves 24.

PROTOCOL IS THE OIL that greases the wheels of diplomatic life. But sometimes it can be a real headache for the hostess. Who should sit in the seats of honor at the right of host and right of hostess? Who will be insulted if they are far away from the center of action? Who might be bored if placed next to whom? The toughest seating plan I tackled was a party we gave for Jean and Bill Lane. Bill, the publisher of *Sunset* magazine, had been ambassador to the American pavilion at the Okinawa Ocean Expo in 1972, and on a return visit to Japan he wanted to meet again with people he had met and/or worked with before. The Lanes sent us their guest list: the mother and father of the Crown Princess of Japan, a U.S. Army sergeant and his wife (she had worked as Bill's secretary), and thirty-two other guests ranging from top rank to foot soldiers in the eyes of diplomatic protocol.

As I faced the task of seating this group, I remembered a technique Mrs. Mikimoto—the wife of the president of Mikimoto Pearls—had used at a dinner party we attended at her home. She had a collection of seashells, in matching pairs. She designated one group of paired shells for women and one for men. Alternating man-woman-man-woman, she put one of each matching pair at each place setting around her dinner table. Before we were seated, guests each selected at random one of the sea shells (one tray was passed for women, one for men). Shells in hand, we entered the Mikimotos' dining room and found our matching shells to determine our place at the table.

I adopted a version of this technique for the party for the Lanes. I put Mrs. Shoda (the mother of the Crown Princess) on Cliff's right, and Mr. Shoda on my right. Bill was host at a third table, and Jean was hostess at a fourth. For everyone else, it was the luck of the seashell draw.

Seated Dinner for Thirty-six

Cold cucumber soup
Roppongi beef curry with rice
Dinner rolls
Tossed green salad
Cherries jubilee

Cold Cucumber Soup

1½ cups peeled, grated
cucumber, seeds removed
1 quart buttermilk
1 tablespoon chopped green
onions

1 teaspoon salt
½ teaspoon MSG (optional)
¼ cup finely chopped parsley
Dash pepper

Combine ingredients. Mix well. Cover and chill thoroughly (at least 4 hours). Mix again just before serving. Garnish with slices of cucumber and parsley leaves.

Serves 8 to 10.

Roppongi Beef Curry

1½ pounds beef
8 tablespoons oil
2 medium onions, chopped
1 clove garlic, minced
1-inch piece of ginger, grated
5 bay leaves
20 coriander seeds
⅓ cup ketchup
⅓ cup Worcestershire sauce
1 small carrot, grated
1 cooking apple, grated
2½ teaspoons ground turmeric
⅓ teaspoon pepper

⅓ teaspoon caraway seeds
¼ teaspoon ground cloves
⅔ teaspoon allspice
1⅓ teaspoons paprika
½ teaspoon ground cinnamon
1½ teaspoons cayenne
½ teaspoon ground nutmeg
5 cups beef broth
1 cup milk
2 small potatoes, grated
Salt and pepper
Hot cooked rice

Cut beef into bite-sized pieces, brown in 2 tablespoons oil, and set aside. Sauté onion in 6 tablespoons oil. Add garlic, ginger, bay leaves, and coriander and cook 10 minutes. Then add ketchup, Worcestershire, carrot, and apple and sauté 20 minutes until liquid is almost gone. There should be a brown paste. Add all other spices (if some of the spices are unavailable, substitute 1 to 3 tablespoons curry powder) and sauté 5 minutes. Add broth and milk and bring

to a boil. Add potato and cook 20 minutes over low heat. Add beef
to sauce; cover and simmer until meat is tender, about 40 minutes.
Serve with rice.

Serves 6 to 8.

CHERRIES JUBILEE

1 can pitted black cherries
2 ounces brandy or rum
Vanilla ice cream

Heat the cherries in their own juice with 1 ounce of the liquor.
Pour into a heated dish, add the second ounce, ignite, and serve
over ice cream.

Serves to 6 to 8.

AIKO-SAN'S OWN CULINARY REPERTOIRE included Chinese cooking and the beef curry used above. She had eaten the curry at a
Tokyo restaurant and recreated it in her own style. She was assisted
in maintaining the house by Aree, a woman from Thailand. Our
lovely Thai maid moved into the kitchen on Aiko-san's day off and
cooked her own specialties for us.

AREE'S THAI SPECIALTIES

Basil chicken
Thai stir fry
Beef and vegetable salad

BASIL CHICKEN

3 tablespoons minced garlic
1 tablespoon salad oil
4 boned, skinned chicken breasts
1 cup lightly packed fresh basil
    leaves

3 tablespoons water
3 tablespoons lemon juice
1 tablespoon soy sauce
1 tablespoon sugar
½ teaspoon pepper

Brown garlic in oil in frying pan, stirring constantly, 3 to 4 minutes. Remove from pan. Add chicken and cook to brown, turning pieces over, about 5 minutes. Slice basil thinly. Add ½ cup basil to pan with garlic, water, lemon juice, soy sauce, sugar, and pepper. Cover and simmer until chicken is white in thickest part, 6 to 7 minutes. Baste with juices frequently. Remove chicken to a platter and keep warm. Boil pan juices over high heat until reduced to ¼ cup. Stir in remaining basil and pour over chicken.

Serves 4.

THAI STIR FRY

1 pound chicken breasts
¼ cup soy sauce
1 clove garlic, minced
¼ to ½ teaspoon crushed red
    pepper flakes
¼ cup peanut butter

3 tablespoons oil
1 tablespoon brown sugar
1 small onion, sliced
½ sweet red pepper, in thin strips
½ green pepper, in thin strips
1 head green cabbage, shredded

Cut chicken into bite-size pieces. Combine 3 tablespoons soy sauce, garlic, and pepper flakes in shallow pan and marinate chicken 15 minutes. Combine peanut butter, 1 tablespoon oil, sugar, and remaining soy sauce. Stir fry chicken in remaining oil until pink color disappears, about 4 minutes. Add onion and peppers and stir fry until vegetables are tender-crisp. Stir in cabbage and peanut sauce. Cover, reduce heat, and simmer about 2 minutes, just until cabbage is tender.

Serves 4 to 6.

BEEF AND VEGETABLE SALAD

½ cup julienned cucumbers,
  skin left on
½ cup bean sprouts
20 fresh mint leaves
20 fresh basil leaves
⅓ cup watercress leaves
2½ cups salad greens
2½ cups finely shredded cabbage
1 pound New York steak
Salt and pepper

6 tablespoons oil
1 teaspoon minced lemongrass (or
  lemon peel)
1 teaspoon minced scallion
½ teaspoon sugar
1 tablespoon soy sauce
½ teaspoon fish sauce or
  Worcestershire sauce
1 tablespoon lemon juice

Assemble salad mix (first 7 ingredients) and arrange on four plates. Cut steak into strips, season with salt and pepper, and sauté in oil over medium high heat. Add remaining ingredients and brown for 10 seconds to create dressing. Remove steak from pan and pour dressing over salad on individual plates. Mix well. Top each plate with beef strips.

Serves 4.

I WAS TEACHING AGAIN at Nishimachi School. Every fall the school had a Food Fair, a joyous gathering of parents and friends who prepared their special cuisine to sell: Japanese noodles, American hamburgers, barbequed chicken, Swedish meatballs, Chinese dumplings, French quiche, home-baked breads, cakes, and pies. This, with an accompanying White Elephant sale, raised money for the school and did much more. It helped to cement this diverse group of parents and children into a loving team.

In the spring, the Nishimachi PTA decided to try another kind of fundraiser, an auction: jewelry made by the principal's internationally acclaimed sister, Miye Matsukata; donations of packaged food and drink, hotel rooms, and airplane tickets by local firms; woodblock prints by famous artists; a tour of his training facilities by a father who was champion sumo wrestler; and a Chinese dinner for twelve at our house, cooked and served by the principal and her assistant. The following Saturday, the two school administrators took over our kitchen and cooked all day (with Aiko-san's help). In the evening, they served their meal to the chairman of their board who had made the winning bid and invited ten of his friends.

CHINESE FAVORITES FROM AIKO-SAN'S KITCHEN

Hot and sour soup
Chicken and cashew nuts (or walnuts)
Lettuce rolls
Mabo dofu (spicy tofu and meat)
Spicy eggplant and ground pork
Shinren (dessert) tofu
Summer noodle platter

HOT AND SOUR SOUP

4 diced Chinese mushrooms	1 tablespoon soy sauce
½ cup warm water	¼ teaspoon white pepper
5 ounces firm tofu	1 tablespoon white vinegar
½ cup canned bamboo shoots	1 egg, slightly beaten
2 tablespoons cornstarch	2 teaspoons sesame oil
3 tablespoons cold water	½ teaspoon hot chili oil
4 cups chicken broth	1 green onion, finely chopped
1 teaspoon salt	fried tofu strips (optional)

Combine mushrooms and warm water; soak 20 minutes. Cut tofu into ⅛-inch slices horizontally, ¼ inches vertically. Cut bamboo shoots into ⅛- by 1-inch slices. In small bowl, combine cornstarch and water; mix well and set aside. Remove mushrooms from water and squeeze out excess moisture. Cut off stems and cut mushrooms into ⅛-inch slices. In heavy 3-quart pot, combine broth, salt, soy, mushrooms, and bamboo shoots. Bring to boil over high heat. Cover, lower heat, and simmer 3 minutes. Add tofu, pepper, and vinegar; bring to a boil again. Re-mix cornstarch, adding water if needed, and add to soup. Stir, cooking on medium heat, until soup begins to thicken. Slowly pour in beaten egg, stirring while adding. Remove soup from heat and add the sesame and chili oils. Mix well. Ladle into soup bowls and garnish with green onions and tofu strips.

Serves 6 to 8.

CHICKEN AND CASHEW NUTS

1 pound chicken breasts, cubed	1 tablespoon cornstarch
½ teaspoon salt	½ pound bamboo shoots
3 teaspoons sake	¼ teaspoon salt
Salad oil	½ cup sugar
1 tablespoon soy sauce	1 cup cashew nuts or walnuts

Mix salt, sake, 2 teaspoons oil, soy sauce, and cornstarch; coat chicken cubes and let sit for about 5 minutes. Heat pan, add 3 tablespoons oil, and sauté the dredged chicken until it is tender. Set aside. Sauté bamboo shoots, cut into cubes, in 1 tablespoon oil and add salt and sugar. Remove from pan. Sauté nuts in 1 tablespoon oil (do not brown). Combine nuts, chicken, and bamboo shoots and serve hot.

Serves 4.

LETTUCE ROLLS

1 pound lean beef (or chicken)
2 tablespoons salad oil
1 clove garlic, minced
1 stalk celery, chopped
2 green onions, chopped
4 to 5 mushrooms, chopped

1 tablespoon sake
2 teaspoons soy sauce
3 tablespoons sugar
1 tablespoon sesame oil
2 tablespoons cornstarch
1 tablespoon water
Lettuce leaves

Heat salad oil and sauté garlic until brown. Add beef, celery, onion, and mushrooms and sauté until all are cooked. Add sake, soy sauce, and sugar and cook a few minutes. Sprinkle with sesame oil. Mix cornstarch with water and stir into meat mixture, cooking until thickened. Serve with lettuce leaves, which are filled individually with spoonfuls of mixture, rolled up, and eaten out of hand.

Serves 4 to 5.

MABO DOFU

1 pound ground pork or beef
3½ tablespoons oil
1 teaspoon cornstarch
1 teaspoon vinegar
¼ teaspoon hot chili oil
1 cake firm tofu
1 clove garlic, minced
1-inch piece of ginger, minced

1 green onion, chopped
1 cup broth
2 tablespoons miso
1 teaspoon sugar
3 tablespoons sake
3 tablespoons soy sauce
1 tablespoon cornstarch
2 tablespoons water

Combine pork or beef with ½ tablespoon oil, 1 teaspoon cornstarch, vinegar, and chili oil. Let stand 20 minutes. Cut tofu into ½-inch cubes, put in boiling water for a few minutes, and drain. Heat 3 tablespoons oil and sauté garlic, ginger, and onion until brown. Add meat mixture and brown. Add broth and cook for several minutes. Add miso, sugar, sake, soy sauce, tofu, and 1 tablespoon cornstarch mixed with 2 tablespoons water. Stir until thickened.

Serves 5 to 8.

SPICY EGGPLANT AND GROUND PORK

4 long (Japanese) eggplants
Oil for frying
3 cloves garlic, minced
1 tablespoon ginger, minced
½ pound ground pork

1 tablespoon green onion, finely
    diced
1 tablespoon sherry
2 tablespoons soy sauce
1 teaspoon sugar
2 to 3 chili peppers, minced

Halve eggplant lengthwise, then cut into 3-inch pieces. Fry in oil and remove from pan. Brown garlic and ginger in oil. Add pork and cook. Add eggplant, onions, sherry, soy sauce, and sugar and heat thoroughly. Add chili peppers and simmer on low for 3 minutes. Add more garlic, ginger, onions, and chili pepper to taste.

Serves 4.

SHINREN (DESSERT) TOFU

1 block kanten (Japanese gelatin)
4 cups water
2 cups milk
2 tablespoons plus ½ cup sugar

Canned fruit cocktail or mandarin
    oranges
½ teaspoon almond extract

Soak kanten 30 minutes in 2 cups of water, turning it over until it is dissolved. Add milk and 2 tablespoons sugar and cook for several minutes. Place in a square pan and chill until firm. Make a syrup of the remaining ½ cup sugar and 2 cups water. Cook until syrup is reduced to 1 cup, then add almond extract. Cut sweet tofu (chilled kanten mix) into cubes. Combine cubes, syrup, and fruit in a large bowl and ladle out individual servings into small bowls.

Serves 6 to 8.

SUMMER NOODLE PLATTER

Aiko-san created a cold noodle platter that makes a dramatic and delicious one-dish summer meal.

1 pound thin Chinese noodles or spaghetti	2 cups bean sprouts
Sesame oil	2 eggs
2 slivered chicken breasts	1 teaspoon sake
Salt	1 to 2 cucumbers
4 slices ham, slivered	¼ cup pickled red ginger
	Sesame and shoyu sauces (below)

Cook the noodles or spaghetti; drain, sprinkle with sesame oil, and mix well. Set aside to cool. Prepare the accompaniments, keeping each separate: Cook the chicken in 1 cup water with a pinch of salt until tender, then cut into slivers. Cut ham into slivers. Cook bean sprouts briefly in boiling water, then drain. Beat eggs lightly, combine with sake and a pinch of salt, cook like thin crepes, then roll and cut into strips. Cut cucumbers into long needles. To serve: Spread cold noodles on large serving dish. Top, in pie-shaped wedges, with accompaniments, placing pickled ginger in center. Each guest digs below accompaniments for noodles, tops them with samples from each wedge, and pours on sesame and/or shoyu sauce.

Serves 10.

SESAME SAUCE

½ cup white sesame seed	2 teaspoons sugar
Few drops water	½ cup water
6 tablespoons rice vinegar	

Grind sesame seeds with water to make a paste. Mix well with remaining ingredients and store in refrigerator. Stir again before serving.

SHOYU SAUCE

6 tablespoons soy sauce	1 teaspoon sesame oil
6 tablespoons rice vinegar	1 teaspoon minced garlic
4 teaspoons sugar	1 teaspoon minced fresh ginger
½ cup water	1 teaspoon minced green onion

Mix all ingredients well and store in refrigerator. Stir again before serving.

NUCY MEECH AND HER husband spent many years in Tokyo in the service of Honeywell of Minneapolis. Nucy had the eye of an artist, the passion of a collector, and a knack for finding and doing the unusual. One of her collections was plastic food models—the kind that Japanese restaurants put in their windows to show customers what is being served. These are faithful renderings of sushi, sashimi, pork cutlets (tonkatsu), bowls of noodles or chicken and rice (oyako domburi). The customers view the numbered models, place an order, pay the cashier, take a seat, and wait for the food to be brought to the table.

Nucy located the family factory of a descendent of the man who began this craft, and planned a "field trip" for a select group of friends. The current proprietor told us how his grandfather had launched the business—a coming together of medical and culinary skills. Grandfather was a medical-school dropout in the 1860s who used his knowledge of anatomy to create a prosthesis for a carpenter friend who had accidentally sawed off the tip of his thumb. He did such a good job that other accident victims came to him. As did a friend who had just returned from the United States; he had been a chef for the officials who were sent abroad on the first diplomatic mission from Japan to the West. This mission was sent to shop for the best of foreign institutions and techniques that could create a modernized Japan. The Japanese took along their own cooks and

supplies of rice and other necessities, fearing that their Western hosts would not be able to cater to their tastes.

This particular chef, when he wasn't busy cooking for his clients, had studied what Americans were eating. When he came home he opened a Western-style restaurant in the basement of Tokyo's most popular department store, featuring hamburger steak with a fried egg on top, vegetable curry and rice with pickles, and spaghetti with meat sauce. Potential customers were puzzled by the menu and hesitant to try something they had never seen. The chef's solution was to visit his artistic friend, cook up his standard fare in the friend's kitchen, then have the menu items created in durable three-dimension to be displayed to the public. Business flourished for both the craftsman and the chef, and artificial food displays are now ubiquitous in Japanese fast-food restaurants.

The second assignment in Tokyo was to be our last diplomatic post overseas. For fifteen years we had lived in Japan. Between 1953 and 1981 we were immersed in a society emerging from the harsh realities of war, to one characterized by self-confidence, innovation, and economic prosperity. Two of our three children were born here, Japanese friends we met in the fifties have maintained personal contact into the first decades of the twenty-first century, and Cliff and I took away from Japan memories of a wide range of experiences as we moved from a tiny apartment carved out behind library bookshelves in the shadow of Matsuyama Castle, to a Japanese style home on the island of Kyushu, to a spacious diplomatic residence in Tokyo.

14

Washington Finale

WE RETURNED TO WASHINGTON in 1981. Cliff was back in the East Asia office again, this time as the Area Director. He spent a lot of time visiting his far-flung territory—stretching east and west from Hawaii to the Bay of Bengal, and north and south from Korea to New Zealand. We had barely unpacked our belongings and arranged the furniture when he left on his first trip, to China. He was the escort officer for the head of the U.S. Information Agency, President Reagan's good friend Charles Wick; Supreme Court Chief Justice Warren Burger; a group of patrons of the Boston Museum of Fine Art; and all their wives. It was a tough assignment, being nursemaid to a group with high egos and high expectations, in a situation where there was ample opportunity for culture shock and the host country was in charge of all arrangements, both personal and official. The U.S. government mission was to sign an agreement launching a new era of cultural exchanges between China and the United States, and to open an exhibition in Beijing introducing "Three Centuries of American Art" from Boston's collection. The opening ceremony almost didn't happen. The night before, the Chinese said they would censor out the twentieth-century art, which conservative authorities had found threatening to socialist standards of morality. Intensive late-night negotiations saved the show. ("Take all three centuries, or none," was the U.S. position.) The Chief Justice cut the ribbon, with Premier Deng Xiaoping in attendance as scheduled.

I was back at the Washington International School, first as a coordinator of special activities for three separate grade levels, then as principal for grades six through twelve. It was wonderful to return to this school, which had graduated its first senior class in 1977, three students with the International Baccalaureate (IB) Diplomas. Now there was a thriving high school population with classes of twenty to thirty students. We were among the first schools to offer the IB in the U.S. It had been a real challenge, for teachers and students alike, to prepare those early candidates to take external examinations that would qualify them for universities throughout the world, and often allow them a full year of credit at American colleges. We were all apprehensive that first year. But now, with a good track record of successful candidates, the school had reached certified adulthood and went about its mission with self-confidence, as well as pride and pleasure.

Working long hours, I was always looking for recipes and meals that could be put on the table quickly and easily when I got home late.

WORKING WIFE'S SPEEDY DINNERS

Frank and cabbage supper
Meatball garden skillet
Country chicken casserole
Chicken garden skillet

FRANK AND CABBAGE SUPPER

1 medium cabbage cut in wedges
1 pound frankfurters
1 can cheese soup
2 tablespoons prepared mustard
Few drops of Tabasco

Cook cabbage, covered, in small amount of boiling water 10 minutes. Add franks and cook until cabbage is tender, 3 to 4 minutes more. Meanwhile heat soup and stir in mustard and Tabasco. Serve sauce over franks and cabbage.

Serves 4.

MEATBALL GARDEN SKILLET

¼ cup chopped onion
2 tablespoons oil
1 pound ground beef
4 tablespoons flour
1 teaspoon salt
Pepper to taste
1 egg
¼ cup milk
1 can condensed beef broth
1⅓ cups water
6 medium potatoes, quartered
5 carrots, cut up
6 sliced green onions
1 cup frozen peas

This is best prepared in an electric skillet. Brown onion in oil. Combine with beef, 2 tablespoons flour, salt, pepper, egg, and milk and form into 1-inch meatballs. Brown the meatballs, then push to one side. Blend remaining 2 tablespoons flour into fat in the pan and add the beef broth and water. Cook until liquids thicken. Add potatoes, carrots, and green onions. Cover and cook on medium heat for 30 minutes, until vegetables are tender. Add peas and simmer 5 minutes longer.

Serves 6.

COUNTRY CHICKEN CASSEROLE

1 package frozen peas	2 tablespoons chopped pimiento,
2 cups cubed cooked chicken	diced
1 can cream of chicken soup	1 cup flour
1 cup sour cream or yogurt	2 teaspoons baking powder
1½ teaspoons salt	2 eggs, beaten
⅛ teaspoon pepper	¾ cup milk
2 tablespoons chopped parsley	1¼ cups shredded cheese

Combine peas and chicken in 2 quart baking dish. Heat soup, sour cream or yogurt, 1 teaspoon salt, and pepper to boiling. Add 1 tablespoon each parsley and pimiento. Add ½ cup of this sauce to chicken and place in 350° oven. Blend flour, baking powder, ½ teaspoon salt. Mix eggs, ½ cup milk, 1 cup cheese, and remaining parsley and pimiento. Stir into flour mix. Drop by spoonfuls over hot chicken. Sprinkle with remaining cheese. Bake 40 to 50 minutes. Add ¼ cup milk to remaining sauce and serve with casserole as gravy.

Serves 6.

CHICKEN GARDEN SKILLET

4 cut up pieces of chicken	¾ cup sherry
2 tablespoons flour, seasoned	1 package frozen artichoke hearts
with salt and pepper	2 tomatoes, cut up
2 tablespoons oil	1 onion, sliced
¾ cup chicken broth	½ green pepper, sliced

Preheat electric skillet to 360°. Dredge chicken in seasoned flour and brown in hot oil, turning once. Reduce temperature to 230° and add chicken broth and sherry. Cover and cook 45 minutes. Push chicken to one side and add vegetables and salt to taste. Cover and cook 15 minutes.

Serves 4

Holiday celebrations were necessarily more elaborate than the above, but a foolproof and time-saving formula for the Thanksgiving or Christmas turkey feast became my tried and true favorite, repeated year after year. The soup recipe was adapted from one in the *Washington Post,* and my sister's holiday salad became a family mainstay.

Holiday Turkey Dinner

Williamsburg peanut soup
Hawkins ribbon salad
Roasted turkey and vegetables
Sour cream pumpkin pie

Williamsburg Peanut Soup

½ cup roasted peanuts   ½ teaspoon chili powder
3 cups beef broth   ½ teaspoon salt
1 cup half and half

Blend peanuts in blender with 1 cup of broth until smooth. Pour into saucepan and add remaining ingredients. Bring to a boil, then reduce heat to simmer and cook slowly 15 minutes. Serve hot, with dab of whipped cream, or cold, garnished with thin slices of cucumber or radishes.

Serves 6.

Hawkins Ribbon Salad

1 box red Jell-O   ½ pint cream, whipped
1 can whole cranberries   1 cup walnuts, chopped
8 ounces cream cheese

Mix Jell-O according to package directions, and add cranberries. Place mixture on bottom of a bread loaf pan. Refrigerate. Cream the cheese until it softens, then stir in whipped cream and nuts. Place this mixture on top of the Jell-O layer, after it has jelled. To serve, invert pan and unmold.

Serves 8 to 10.

ROASTED TURKEY AND VEGETABLES

12- to 14-pound turkey	½ teaspoon thyme
2 packages Pepperidge Farm stuffing mix	½ teaspoon sage
	6 medium onions
Butter or margarine	8 medium sweet potatoes or yams
2 stalks celery, chopped	3 cans whole water chestnuts
1 large onion, chopped	6 green peppers

Prepare stuffing mix according to package directions. Cook celery and onion in butter until soft; add to stuffing, along with herbs. Stuff turkey just before roasting. Place turkey, breast side up, in a shallow roasting pan that is at least 11½ x17 inches. Roast at 325° on lower rack of oven, allowing about 15 minutes per pound (3 to 3½ hours for a 12- to 14-pound bird). About 1½ hours before turkey will be done, add onions, unpeeled, to roasting pan and put potatoes on rack above pan. About 1 hour before, add drained water chestnuts and peppers to pan, tucking them around the bird. When turkey is done, lift from pan and allow to stand about 30 minutes before carving. Keep vegetables warm. Skim and discard fat from pan juices, then pour into gravy container. Cut onions and potatoes in half, slit potato tops, and insert a pat of butter to serve.

Serves 10.

SOUR CREAM PUMPKIN PIE

1 (1 pound) can pumpkin	¼ teaspoon ground cloves
½ cup packed brown sugar	2 tablespoons molasses
½ cup granulated sugar	3 eggs, slightly beaten
1 teaspoon ground cinnamon	1½ cups sour cream
½ teaspoon ground ginger	1 unbaked pie crust
½ teaspoon salt	

Combine all ingredients but pie crust and mix well. Pour into pastry-lined pie plate and bake 15 minutes at 425°. Reduce temperature to 350° and bake about 40 minutes longer, until filling is firm. Cool before serving.

Serves 6.

THE IB WAS GROWING rapidly. It was moving beyond its original constituency of international schools in capital cities catering to an expatriate community that wanted their children to qualify for the most competitive universities back home, wherever home might be. Local schools—in Spain, England, Argentina, the Netherlands, Canada—were adopting this creative, well-balanced, and challenging program. In the United States, public schools were looking for ways to strengthen their curriculum and to make tomorrow's leaders more aware of the international community in which they would need to operate. Chicago, southern California, and Florida communities were setting up IB magnet programs in their inner-city high schools, and many other school districts were doing the same.

The president of a small liberal arts college in Hawaii had heard about the IB and thought it would be beneficial to create an "academy" division, with high-school juniors and seniors coming to his campus to do the International Baccalaureate. It had been suggested that he visit our school when he came to Washington on business—as one of the most experienced, we could show him how the program operated. It was my task to take him around and to describe the IB in general and the school's operation in particular. That day's work led to an invitation for me to come to Hawaii and introduce the IB at Hawaii Loa College on Oahu.

Cliff, at a point in his career where he qualified for full retirement benefits, was ready and willing. "You," he said to me, "have followed me around the world for thirty-four years. With an offer like this—living in Hawaii—I'm willing to switch roles and follow you for a change."

15

A Decade of Aloha

WE LIVED IN HONOLULU from 1983 to 1995—longer than we had ever lived in one place. The house we bought was on a ridge, overlooking Diamond Head and Waikiki. The gentle climate made for a relaxed lifestyle where the boundaries between the inside of our home and our tropical surroundings became blurred. From our own garden we picked guava, papaya, sweet limes, oranges, grapefruit, tangerines, bananas, and Surinam cherries (which were small and very tart). We couldn't begin to eat all the fruit ourselves, so I made countless jars of preserves and loaves of banana bread, which we took as gifts to family and friends whenever we traveled to the U.S. mainland. The Alexanders next door had a prolific mango tree and during the season they would regularly come to the door with a grocery bag full of their fruit.

Harvesting Our Tropical Garden

Guava jelly

Lime marmalade

Mango chutney

Avocado grapefruit soup

Hawaiian fruit platter

Lime-ginger, Javanese, and papaya-seed dressings

Banana nut bread

Banana coffee cake

Oranges in red wine

Guava Jelly

2 quarts under-ripe guavas	Lime juice
Sugar	(Pectin)

Wash and cut guavas in quarters. Place in heavy kettle and cover with water. Bring to boil then simmer for about ½ hour, scooping off film as it accumulates. Strain juice though very fine strainer or jelly bag, without pressing fruit. Add 1 cup of sugar for each cup of juice and bring again to a boil. Add 1 teaspoon lime juice for each cup of guava juice. Cook only 4 cups at a time. Cook at a simmer long enough to bring jelly to a point of sheeting off a spoon (temperature 220° to 225°). Time required will range from 8 to 30 minutes. Allow jelly to cook a bit longer, then pour into jars. Cover and let stand overnight. When completely cool, store in refrigerator. (If jelly failed to jell, I would go shopping for pectin in the grocery store, reheat the jelly with pectin according to package instructions, cool, and refrigerate the jelled jelly.)

Makes about 6 jars.

LIME MARMALADE

6 small limes
3 lemons
Sugar

Cut the outer rind from the limes and lemons. Remove seeds and slice into very small pieces. Measure the fruit and juice and add 3 times the amount of water. Soak for 12 hours. Simmer for 20 minutes. Let stand again for 12 hours. For every cup of fruit and juice add ¾ cup sugar. Cook these ingredients until they form a jelly (see recipe for guava jelly).

Makes about 3 jelly glasses.

MANGO CHUTNEY

6 cups sugar
2 cups cider vinegar
½ cup ginger root, peeled and chopped fine
½ teaspoon dried crushed red peppers
1 clove garlic, minced

1 teaspoon ground cloves
1 teaspoon ground cinnamon
1 tablespoon salt
1 pound raisins
12 cups mangoes, peeled, seeded, and cut into chunks

In large kettle, combine sugar and vinegar. Heat while stirring, until sugar is dissolved. Add remaining ingredients. Bring to a boil and simmer gently for 1½ hours. Stir occasionally to prevent sticking.

Makes about 6 pints.

AVOCADO GRAPEFRUIT SOUP

3 medium avocados
2 cups chicken broth

1 cup freshly squeezed grapefruit
   juice
Salt and pepper

Peel and pit avocados. Quarter them and place in blender or food processor with broth and juice. Blend to puree and season to taste. Serve cold.

Serves 4.

HAWAIIAN FRUIT PLATTER

1 medium-sized fresh pineapple
2 medium bananas
1 medium papaya
2 cups pink or white grapefruit
   sections

2 cups melon balls
Lime twists
Mint leaves

Prepare lime-ginger or Javanese dressing (below) and let stand an hour or longer. Twist crown from pineapple. Peel and quarter pineapple lengthwise, cut out core, and cut fruit into spears. Slice bananas. Peel, halve, and slice papaya. Arrange all fruits on chilled platter, decorate with lime and mint, and serve with one of the dressings.

Serves 8.

LIME-GINGER DRESSING

1 ounce ginger root
Juice of 4 lemons
Juice of 4 limes

¼ cup honey
1 tablespoon sugar
¼ cup olive oil

Peel and chop ginger root. In small saucepan, combine ginger, juices, honey, and sugar. Bring to boil, lower heat, and simmer 3 minutes, stirring. Cool and remove chopped ginger. Add ¼ cup olive oil, gradually blending with wire whisk. Let stand an hour or longer to mellow the flavors

Makes 1 cup.

JAVANESE DRESSING

½ cup oil
½ cup rice vinegar
2 tablespoons chopped fresh
   pineapple
2 tablespoons mango chutney
1 tablespoon pineapple juice

1 tablespoon lime juice
1 tablespoon honey
¼ teaspoon paprika
¼ teaspoon curry powder
¼ teaspoon grated lime peel.

Combine all ingredients except lime peel in blender. Cover and blend well. Add lime peel and stir to mix. Let stand an hour or longer to mellow the flavors

Makes 1 cup.

PAPAYA SEED DRESSING

1½ cups sugar
1½ cups red wine vinegar
1½ teaspoons dry mustard
1 tablespoon salt

½ onion, quartered
1½ cups vegetable oil
3 tablespoons papaya seeds

Combine first 5 ingredients in blender and blend until smooth. Add vegetable oil slowly, still blending, and papaya seeds. Pour into covered container. Serve on fruit salad or mixed greens.

Makes about 3 cups.

Banana Nut Bread

½ cup white sugar
½ cup brown sugar
½ cup butter or margarine
2 eggs
3 to 4 bananas, mashed
3 tablespoons buttermilk
2 tablespoons lime juice

2 cups flour
½ teaspoon baking powder
½ teaspoon salt
1 teaspoon baking soda
1 cup chopped pecans or walnuts
1 teaspoon vanilla

Combine sugars and mix with butter which has been beaten until creamy. Beat in eggs, one at a time. Add mashed bananas, buttermilk, and lime juice. Sift together dry ingredients and add, a bit at a time, to mixture. Stir in nuts and vanilla. Turn into greased loaf pan and bake at 350° for 30 to 40 minutes, until firm.

Banana Coffee Cake

½ cup butter
2 eggs
1 cup mashed ripe bananas
  (about 3)
1½ teaspoons lime or lemon
  juice

1⅓ cups flour
1¼ cups sugar
1 teaspoon baking soda
½ teaspoon salt

Beat butter until creamy, then beat in eggs. Blend in bananas and juice. Sift flour, measure, and sift again with remaining ingredients. Using a rubber scraper or wooden spoon, quickly fold dry ingredients into banana mixture. Do not over mix; batter will be lumpy. Turn into lightly buttered 9-inch-square pan. Bake 40 minutes, until done. Let stand 5 minutes, then loosen edges with knife. Turn cake onto cooling rack.

Serves 8.

Oranges in Red Wine

¾ cup sugar
1 cup water
1 cup red wine
2 cloves

3-inch stick of cinnamon
1 inch vanilla bean
4 lemon slices
6 large seedless oranges

Combine sugar and water in saucepan and cook, stirring, until sugar dissolves. Add wine, cloves, cinnamon, vanilla, and lemon. Bring to boil and cook 5 minutes, then strain. Meanwhile peel oranges and remove all white. Slice thinly. Pour hot syrup over orange slices and refrigerate at least 4 hours.

Serves 8.

Each week in the winter months I picked dozens and dozens of tangerines. These went with me to school to share with fellow teachers and with my students during our afternoon class in the Theory of Knowledge (a core requirement for the International Baccalaureate Diploma).

Two of our earliest IB students came from China. They had been in the second year of a program to train teachers of English at Beijing Teachers College and were told that if they achieved the IB Diploma after two years, they would receive their BTC diploma and a job teaching upon their return. Wang Yue Ping and Chen Meng were provided with round trip plane tickets by the Chinese and allowed to exchange currency worth $32 to bring with them. For two years! Any spending money during their stay would have to be earned. So, in addition to tackling a strange culture (neither had been abroad before), taking a heavy academic load in a foreign language (English literature, Chinese literature, world history, biology, mathematics, marine science, theory of knowledge) and doing community service plus a 4,000-word research project, they had jobs at the school to earn spending money.

Chen Meng lived with us and became our "Chinese daughter." Discovering America through her eyes was an adventure for us. When she was assigned reading and analysis of *The Communist Manifesto* by her history teacher, she asked Cliff (the ex-cold warrior) to clarify some of the points. Though she had been one of the young elite in China and marched in parades as a Red Guard, she objected to Marx's disregard for the family.

It was great to have another pair of hands in the kitchen. Chen Meng was a quick learner at home as well as at school, and was ready to take on any task. Except handing raw chicken. Cooked chicken was fine, but years of watching her mother bring home newly butchered ones with heads and feet still attached had turned her stomach, and even our neatly packaged supermarket poultry revived too many unpleasant visions. She loved to experiment with American food. The Chinese dish she liked best to prepare for us was dumplings to serve as a full dinner, ten to fifteen per person. She bought us a dumpling press as a gift so we could continue to make them after she left.

CHEN MENG'S CHINESE POTSTICKERS

¾ cup Chinese cabbage,
   blanched
⅓ pound ground beef or poultry
½ cup chopped green onions
2 teaspoons cornstarch
1 tablespoon sesame oil
½ teaspoon salt

1 tablespoon sherry
1 tablespoon soy sauce
¼ teaspoon sugar
1 package Chinese dumpling
   wrappers
2 tablespoons salad oil
½ cup water

Finely chop cabbage; squeeze and drain. In a bowl, combine cabbage, meat, green onions, cornstarch, sesame oil, salt, sherry, soy sauce, ginger and sugar. Place 1 tablespoon of filling in center of each wrapper. Fold wrapper in half and squeeze edges together. In a skillet, heat oil. Arrange dumplings in a single layer and cook over medium heat until bottoms are brown. Add water, cover, and cook over low heat for 10 minutes or until water has evaporated. Repeat until all dumplings are cooked.

Makes about 30 dumplings.

AT CHRISTMAS, GERRY ALEXANDER brought us gifts from her kitchen, marmalade and seasoned walnuts. My gift to friends and neighbors was a bowl of chutney chicken pate or cheese-pesto appetizer.

CHRISTMAS GIFTS FROM THE KITCHEN

Gerry's calamundin (kumquat) marmalade
Rosemary walnuts
Chutney chicken pate
Layered cheese-pesto appetizer

GERRY'S CALAMUNDIN MARMALADE

1 pound calamundin
  (kumquats)
½ lemon, seeded, chopped

4 cups cold water
2¼ cups sugar

Soak fruit overnight in water. Cook, adding sugar as it is heating. Boil until mixture sheets from a spoon (about 1 hour).
    Makes 3 jelly jars.

ROSEMARY WALNUTS

2½ tablespoons unsalted butter
2 teaspoons dried rosemary,
  crumbled

1 teaspoon salt
½ teaspoon cayenne
2 cups shelled walnuts

Melt butter with seasonings. Pour mixture over walnuts, tossing to coat them. Spread them on a cookie sheet and bake 10 minutes at 350°.
    Makes 2 cups.

CHUTNEY CHICKEN PATE

2 cups cubed cooked chicken
¼ cup minced onion
1 large sweet pickle, minced
½ cup minced parsley
1 teaspoon oregano
1 teaspoon thyme

3 tablespoons chopped almonds
½ teaspoon salt
Pinch black pepper
½ cup mango chutney
¾ cup mayonnaise
Crusty bread

Mince chicken in food processor. Stir in remaining ingredients and pack into a bowl. Chill overnight. Serve with crusty French bread.
    Makes about 3 cups.

LAYERED CHEESE-PESTO APPETIZER

1 pound cream cheese, softened
1 pound butter or margarine, softened
2½ cups lightly packed fresh basil leaves
1 cup grated Parmesan or Romano cheese

⅓ cup olive oil
¼ cup pine nuts (or finely chopped walnuts)
Fresh basil sprigs
Thinly sliced baguettes
Crisp raw vegetables (optional)

With electric mixer, cream the cheese and butter until smoothly blended. To make pesto filling, blend basil, Parmesan or Romano, and olive oil in food processor or blender, then stir in nuts and season to taste with salt and pepper. Line a 5- to 6-cup bowl with cheesecloth that extends over edges of bowl. (Recipe may be split between two smaller bowls.) Spread ¹/₆ of cheese mixture in bottom of lined bowl. Cover with ¹/₅ of pesto, extending each layer to bowl's edge. Repeat layers of cheese and pesto, finishing with cheese. Fold ends of cloth over bowl and press down lightly to compact the layers. Chill 1 to 2 hours, then invert onto serving plate and remove cheesecloth. Do not let cloth remain longer; it will cause pesto color to bleed into cheese. If making ahead, cover appetizer with plastic wrap and chill as long as 5 days. Garnish with sprigs of basil and spread on bread and vegetables.

Serves 15 to 20.

IT WAS GREAT TO be located halfway between the U.S. mainland and Asia. Friends from both regions relished an opportunity to visit Hawaii, and many came either on business or for pleasure, or to combine the two. We invited our visitors and local friends to convivial evenings, serving buffet style and eating outside on our lanai as the sun set over the ocean and the lights of Waikiki below began to sparkle. Since we lived an eternal summer, much of the food was served cold (which meant it could be prepared ahead and I could relax with our guests).

Buffet Dinner for Visiting Guests

Avocado bisque
Sausage in pastry with honey mustard
Turkey tonnato (with tuna sauce)
Layered mozzarella and tomato salad
Shredded carrots with lemon dressing
Anchovy stuffed eggs
Kiwi rum tart

Avocado Bisque

2 tablespoons butter or
  margarine
¼ cup minced onion
2 tablespoons flour
3 cups chicken broth
1 tablespoon fresh lemon juice
1 tablespoon tarragon vinegar
1 clove garlic, minced

1 tablespoon horseradish
¼ teaspoon curry powder
¼ teaspoon tarragon
1 teaspoon salt
Freshly ground black pepper
1 large, ripe avocado
1 cup milk
1 cup light cream

Melt butter in heavy 4-quart saucepan. Add onion and sauté until tender but not brown. Blend in flour. Stir in chicken broth and heat, stirring, until mixture thickens. Add lemon juice, vinegar, and seasonings; cover and simmer 10 minutes. Peel avocado and cut into chunks. Puree with 1 cup of broth in blender. Stir puree into soup. Add milk and cream, bring to a boil, then simmer 5 minutes. Cover and chill.

Serves 8.

Sausage in Pastry with Honey Mustard

1⅓ cups flour
½ teaspoon salt
½ cup cold butter, cut into bits
2 eggs
1 tablespoon sour cream or
  yogurt

1 (1-pound) Polish sausage
1 teaspoon water
⅓ cup Dijon-style mustard
3 tablespoons honey
¼ teaspoon fresh thyme leaves
Fresh thyme sprigs for garnish

For dough: Sift together flour and salt; blend in butter until mixture resembles coarse meal. Beat together 1 egg and sour cream; add to flour and stir until mixture forms soft dough. Form into a ball, dust with flour, and flatten slightly. Chill, wrapped in wax paper, for 1 hour or overnight. Cut sausage in half, removing ends; prick with fork and boil in 1 inch of water in skillet for 8 minutes. Drain and cool, then peel off outer casing. Combine remaining egg and 1 teaspoon water to make egg wash. Roll half dough into ⅛-inch rectangle and center 1 sausage half in it. There should be 3-inch borders on each side and 1½ inches at each end—enough to enclose the sausage. Bring one side over sausage and brush edge with egg wash. Bring other side up to overlap by 1 inch and press edges together. Seal ends with egg wash and transfer the roll, seam side down, onto baking sheet. Brush entire package with egg wash. Repeat for second sausage half. Chill sausages 15 minutes, then bake at 375° for 25 to 30 minutes, until pastry is golden and flaky. Transfer sausage pasties to platter, slice with serrated knife into ¾-inch pieces, and garnish with thyme sprigs. Combine honey, mustard, and thyme leaves and serve with the sausage.

Serves 8.

TURKEY TONNATO

4- to 6-pound frozen boneless
   turkey roast, thawed
1½ cups dry white wine
1 bay leaf
1 clove garlic, minced
Water to cover
1 (3-ounce) can tuna, in oil

Olive oil to make 1 cup
5 anchovy fillets
3 tablespoons lemon juice
2 eggs
2½ tablespoons capers
Lemon slices

Place turkey in 6-quart kettle; add wine, bay leaf, and garlic and cover with water. Bring to a boil, then lower heat, cover, and simmer 1½ hours until meat is very tender when pierced (170° on meat thermometer placed in thickest part). Let meat cool in stock, cover, and chill. To make sauce: Drain oil from tuna into a measuring cup and add olive oil to make 1 cup. Combine tuna, anchovies, lemon juice, eggs, and 1½ teaspoons capers in blender and whirl until smooth. Gradually add oil, while blending. Cover and chill at least 4 hours. When meat is cold, remove from stock and slice thinly. Pour about ⅓ of sauce into bottom of large shallow serving dish and arranged sliced meat over top. Cover with remaining sauce and chill 2 to 24 hours. Before serving, garnish with lemon slices and remaining capers.

Serves 10 as an entrée, 16 as an appetizer.

LAYERED MOZZARELLA AND TOMATO SALAD

4 large ripe tomatoes, sliced
2 pounds mozzarella cheese, in
   ¼-inch slices
¼ cup chopped basil

¼ cup chopped parsley
½ cup Niçoise olives, pitted and
   quartered
Vinaigrette dressing (below)

On a large serving platter, alternate overlapping slices of tomato and cheese. Sprinkle basil, parsley and olives over all. Drizzle with vinaigrette dressing and serve at room temperature.

Serves 6 to 8.

VINAIGRETTE DRESSING

1 tablespoon Dijon mustard
4 tablespoons red wine vinegar
1 teaspoon sugar
½ teaspoon salt

½ teaspoon black pepper
Minced parsley or chives
½ cup olive oil

Measure mustard into bowl and whisk in vinegar, sugar, and seasonings. Continue to whisk while slowly dribbling in olive oil until mixture thickens. Cover until ready to use. (Best made just before serving.)

Makes 1 cup.

SHREDDED CARROTS WITH LEMON DRESSING

3 cups shredded carrots
3 tablespoons lemon juice
2 tablespoons olive or salad oil

Pepper to taste
Chopped parsley

Mix carrots, lemon juice, oil, and pepper; cover and chill up to 24 hours. Garnish with chopped parsley.

Serves 10.

ANCHOVY STUFFED EGGS

6 hard-boiled eggs
¾ cup minced anchovy fillets
1 clove garlic, minced

2½ tablespoons olive oil
Additional anchovy filets and
    capers

Shell and halve eggs lengthwise. Remove and mash yolks. Add anchovy, garlic, and oil, mixing well. Fill whites with yolk mixture. Garnish each with a small piece of anchovy and a few capers.

Makes 12 halves.

Kiwi Rum Tart

1 cup sugar
½ cup cornstarch
¼ teaspoon salt
3 cups milk
4 egg yolks
1 teaspoon vanilla

½ cup rum
7 kiwis
¼ cup light corn syrup
1 teaspoon lemon juice
Tart shell (below)

To make rum custard filling: In small bowl, stir together sugar, cornstarch, and salt. Scald milk in a saucepan over medium heat. Slowly add sugar mixture, constantly stirring. Boil, stirring, for 2 minutes. Remove from heat. Beat egg yolks until thick and lemon colored. Stir half of cooked mixture into yolks, then stir all back into pan. Return to low heat and cook, stirring, until mixture is thick enough to mound from a spoon, about 5 to 7 minutes. Turn mixture into a bowl and add vanilla and rum. Cover with waxed paper directly on custard and chill about 45 minutes, until slightly set. Spoon into prepared shell and chill at least 1 hour. To create topping: Peel and slice kiwis crosswise into ¼-inch slices. Arrange slightly overlapping in a spiral, working from the crust towards the center. Warm corn syrup over low heat and stir in juice. Brush over the top of the tart. Chill, uncovered, 1 to 3 hours.

Serves 10.

FRUIT TART SHELL

1⅓ cups flour
¼ cup sugar
1 tablespoon grated orange peel

½ cup firm butter or margarine
1 egg yolk

Sift together flour and sugar. Stir in orange peel and cut in butter until mixture resembles coarse meal. With fork, blend in egg yolk, then work dough with hands into smooth ball. Press evenly over bottom and sides of 10-inch tart pan with a removable bottom. Bake at 300° for 30 minutes. Cool on a rack, and fill with custard and fruit.

SOON AFTER WE CAME to Hawaii, Cliff was diagnosed as having high levels of cholesterol and some blockage of his arteries. I had mildly elevated blood pressure. Cliff started an aggressive campaign with a fat-free diet to combat the effects of too many burgers and shakes and creamy casseroles in earlier years. He collected health food books, heart-disease reversal volumes, compendiums of prohibited foods and recommended ones. I began searching for new, user-friendly recipes that would be good for our health without taking all the fun out of family dining and entertaining company. Pasta and tofu dishes, salads and stir-fries moved to the top of the family menu agenda.

Heart-friendlier Food

Sarah Ross's miso dressing
Julie Reisner's Eugene tofu
Tofu sukiyaki
Spaghetti with broccoli and tomato
Pasta primavera
Chinese chicken salad à la Petti
Nancy Mason's spinach-chicken pinwheels
Barbara Moore's chicken and vegetable soup

Sarah Ross's Miso Dressing

1 tablespoon white miso (or soy sauce)
2 tablespoons lemon juice
2 tablespoons olive oil
1 tablespoon dill or mixed fresh herbs
1 tablespoon tahini

Blend all ingredients and serve on salad greens or as a dressing for rice.

Julie Reisner's Eugene Tofu

1 (12-ounce) block tofu
½ cup sake
¼ cup soy sauce
1 tablespoon minced fresh ginger
1 tablespoon sugar
1 small bunch chopped green onions

Drain the tofu and cut into ½-inch cubes. Put in a serving bowl. Mix all the remaining ingredients and pour over tofu. Refrigerate to marinate for at least 1 hour. This is a cool dish for summer, making a meal when served with hot rice and vegetable sticks or a salad.
    Serves 4.

Tofu Sukiyaki

¼ cup soy sauce	1 to 2 tablespoons sherry
1 cup water	1 pound tofu
3 minced scallions	1 stalk celery
1 large clove garlic, minced	1 large carrot
1½ teaspoons freshly grated ginger	1 large green bell pepper
1 tablespoon cider vinegar	⅓ pound green beans
1 tablespoon honey	½ pound mung bean sprouts
	Hot cooked rice

Combine soy sauce, water, scallions, garlic, ginger, vinegar, honey, and sherry in large saucepan. Cut tofu into 1-inch cubes. Slice celery, carrots, bell pepper, and green beans. Add all the vegetables and tofu to the liquid, bring to a boil, cover, and lower heat. Simmer until all vegetables are tender (10 to 15 minutes). Serve in bowls, over rice, including broth with each serving.

Serves 4.

Spaghetti with Broccoli and Tomato

1 pound broccoli, cut in small flowerets, stems peeled and diced	2 large tomatoes, peeled, seeded, coarsely chopped
½ pound spaghetti	½ cup chopped fresh parsley leaves, preferably flat-leaved
2 tablespoons olive oil	12 Niçoise or 6 kalamata olives, pitted and quartered
2 cloves garlic, minced	Salt and pepper to taste
½ teaspoon dried hot red pepper flakes	Grated Parmesan

Boil broccoli 3 to 5 minutes, until just tender, and transfer to colander with slotted spoon. Refresh under cold water. Add pasta to kettle and cook until al dente. In large heavy skillet heat oil with garlic and pepper flakes, stirring, until oil is hot but not smoking.

Add tomatoes and cook, stirring occasionally, 3 minutes. Add broccoli to boiling pasta, boil 12 seconds, and drain the mixture. In serving bowl toss pasta and broccoli with tomato mixture, parsley, olives, and salt and pepper to taste. Serve with Parmesan.

Serves 6.

PASTA PRIMAVERA

2 tablespoons olive oil	2 cups cauliflower pieces
1 cup minced onion	¼ pound mushrooms, sliced
3 to 4 cloves garlic, minced	2 cups raw or frozen peas
½ teaspoon salt	1 red pepper, diced
Freshly ground black pepper	3 tablespoons tamari or soy sauce
1 teaspoon dried basil	1 pound spaghetti
2 cups sliced asparagus (or	1 cup finely chopped parsley
zucchini, or broccoli)	2 cups grated low-fat cheese

Cook onion and garlic in oil in heavy skillet with salt, pepper, and basil until onions are soft. Add asparagus, cauliflower, and mushrooms and cook until asparagus and cauliflower are barely tender. Add peas and red pepper and cook until they are heated through. Remove from heat and stir in tamari or soy sauce. Toss with hot cooked pasts, mixing in parsley and cheese.

Serves 4 to 5.

CHINESE CHICKEN SALAD À LA PETTI

1 pound boneless chicken breast
2 cups water
3 green onions, sliced on
  diagonal
¼-inch slice ginger, crushed
1 tablespoon dry sherry or sake
1 teaspoon salt
1 teaspoon pepper
1 small head of lettuce

1 small cucumber, seeded and
  sliced
2 tablespoons toasted sesame seed
½ can crisp chow mein noodles
1 teaspoon dry mustard
1 tablespoon sugar
½ cup vegetable oil
2 teaspoon sesame oil
6 tablespoons rice wine vinegar

Place chicken in pot with water, one of the green onions halved, ginger, sherry, ½ teaspoon each salt and pepper. Bring to boil, cover, and simmer 20 minutes. Remove from heat and cool. Strain and save broth. Shred chicken and refrigerate. Shred lettuce into salad bowl and add cold chicken, cucumber, sesame seeds, and remaining green onions. Top with noodles. Just before serving, mix together remaining ingredients (including remaining salt and pepper, to taste) to make dressing. Shake well; pour over salad and toss gently.

Serves 6.

NANCY MASON'S SPINACH-CHICKEN PINWHEELS

1 package frozen chopped
  spinach, thawed
1 teaspoon vegetable oil
1 small onion, minced
1 teaspoon fresh lemon juice

2 ounces blue cheese, crumbled
Salt and pepper
4 boneless chicken breast halves
Paprika
Hot cooked rice

Press liquid from spinach. In hot oil stir fry onion 30 seconds. Add spinach and stir fry 1 minute. Spoon into medium bowl and add lemon juice, cheese, salt, and pepper. Pound chicken pieces flat (¼ inch). Spread with spinach mixture. Roll up, jellyroll style, and secure with toothpicks. Place in single layer in shallow steaming dish. Place dish on rack in wok or steamer over simmering water; cover and steam 20 minutes or until meat is firm and white through center. Remove and cool slightly. Sprinkle with paprika. Cut each roll into 3 to 4 slices and serve cut side up on a bed of rice accompanied by a salad.

Serves 4 (or, as appetizers, makes 12 to16 pieces).

BARBARA MOORE'S CHICKEN AND VEGETABLE SOUP

6 to 7 cups chicken broth (left from cooking the chicken)
½ cup rice
3 carrots, sliced
3 stalks celery, sliced
2 zucchini, sliced
6 tablespoons butter
6 tablespoons flour
1 pint light cream or milk
4 cups cooked chicken, in bite-sized pieces
½ cup thinly sliced green onion
Salt and pepper
¼ cup minced parsley

In a 5-quart soup kettle, heat broth to boiling. Add rice, cover, and simmer for 10 minutes. Add vegetables and simmer, covered, 10 minutes more. In another pan melt butter, blend in flour, and cook until bubbly. Gradually blend in milk, then a cup of broth from kettle. Heat and stir until this boils and thickens, then stir into mixture in soup kettle. Add chicken and green onions, salt and pepper to taste. Heat quickly, just until heated through. Sprinkle with parsley.

Makes 6 hearty servings and freezes nicely.

16

Riding the Jet Stream

WE DID A LOT of overseas traveling during our Hawaii years. To see our family on the mainland. To take advantage of accumulated mileage awards and visit various parts of Europe, which had not been our territory during Foreign Service days. To attend IB annual conferences for the North American Region (to which Hawaii's program officially belonged) and Asia Region (which, because of our Pacific location, we were invited to join unofficially). For meetings of the heads of all IB schools around the globe. We met with colleagues in the Canadian and Colorado Rockies, in Chicago and Los Angeles and Washington, D.C.; in Singapore and Seoul, Bangkok and Kuala Lumpur, Jakarta and Beijing; in Paris and Geneva, Barcelona, Quito, and Buenos Aires. During my sabbatical year in 1993-94, we visited IB schools and institutions providing distance learning in Europe, the U.S. and Mexico, Australia and New Zealand. My project was to investigate ways our worldwide community could make creative use of the new tool of computer technology for faculty networking and student collaboration. As we traveled, we enjoyed foreign cuisines on their home territory.

INTERNATIONAL FLAVORS

Parisian kir royale
Kilarney tomato-mint salad
Greek peasant salad
Eggs Spanish style
Nasi goring (Indonesian rice)
Sate ajam (Indonesian chicken on skewers)
Gado gado (Indonesian vegetables with peanut sauce)
Kerry Tolleth's chicken tandoori
Betty Lou Hummel's tandoori-roasted turkey breast
Swiss Alps dessert plate

PARISIAN KIR ROYALE

2 teaspoons crème de cassis (blackcurrant liqueur)
2 ounces sparkling wine

Place cassis and 1 ounce chilled wine into chilled champagne flute. Stir gently. Top with remaining wine.
Serves 1.

KILARNEY TOMATO-MINT SALAD

1 pound tomatoes
Salt and pepper
1 tablespoon cream
Pinch sugar

¼ teaspoon grated lemon rind
1 tablespoon lemon juice
Freshly chopped mint

Slice tomatoes and arrange on serving plate. Salt and pepper to taste. To make dressing, combine cream, sugar, rind, and juice. Pour dressing over tomatoes and sprinkle with mint.
Serves 4.

GREEK PEASANT SALAD

1 clove garlic, halved
3½ cups torn romaine lettuce
3 cups torn Boston lettuce
2 medium tomatoes, in wedges
1 medium cucumber, sliced
1 medium green pepper, cut in
    rings
1 small onion, cut in rings

1 cup crumbled feta cheese
½ cup black Greek olives
⅓ cup snipped parsley
½ cup olive oil
¼ cup red wine vinegar
½ teaspoon salt
¼ teaspoon freshly ground pepper
¼ teaspoon crushed oregano

Rub wooden salad bowl with cut clove garlic; discard. Combine greens in bowl and add vegetables. Top with cheese, olives, and parsley. Cover and chill. To make dressing, combine remaining ingredients, cover, and shake well.

Serves 8 to 12.

EGGS SPANISH STYLE

⅓ cup chopped onion
⅓ cup chopped green pepper
1 clove garlic, minced
2 tablespoons butter or olive oil
1 (8-ounce) can tomato sauce
1 teaspoon vinegar
2 tablespoons chopped fresh
    parsley

¼ teaspoon oregano
¼ teaspoon basil
½ teaspoon salt
Dash pepper
12 hard-boiled eggs
2 packages frozen artichoke
    hearts, thawed
¼ cup grated Parmesan cheese

Sauté onion, green pepper, and garlic in oil. Stir in tomato sauce, vinegar, and seasonings. Cut eggs in half lengthwise and arrange with artichoke hearts in 9x13-inch baking pan. Spoon sauce over top and sprinkle with cheese. Bake uncovered at 425° for 15 minutes.

Serves 6.

NASI GORENG

¼ cup butter or margarine
2 onions, chopped
½ to 1 tablespoon curry powder
2 tablespoons peanut butter
1½ cups cooked chicken, diced
1 cup diced cooked ham
5 cups cooked rice
1 clove garlic, minced

1 teaspoon salt
1 teaspoon cumin seed
Dash each of mace and pepper
Garnish: 1 peeled cucumber,
    sliced thin; 2 hard-boiled eggs,
    chopped; 1 banana, sliced; ½
    cup chutney; ½ cup chopped
    peanuts

Brown onions in butter and add curry. Add peanut butter, chicken, and ham and mix thoroughly. Add rice and brown for 10 minutes. Add seasonings and turn into casserole. Bake at 350° for 15 minutes. Serve garnished with cucumber, egg, banana, chutney, and peanuts.

Serves 4 to 6.

SATE AJAM

2 pounds chicken, boned
¾ teaspoon vinegar
¾ cup water
½ teaspoon powdered cumin
½ teaspoon minced garlic
¼ teaspoon salt
5 tablespoons peanut butter

½ cup bouillon
1 teaspoon sugar
½ teaspoon minced garlic
1 teaspoon soy sauce
1 teaspoon paprika
1 bay leaf

Cut chicken into 1½-inch pieces and thread onto 6-inch skewers. Mix vinegar, water, cumin, garlic, and salt; dip chicken into this mixture, then broil 15 to 20 minutes. (Open fire is best.) To make peanut sauce for dipping, cook remaining ingredients together until smooth and thick.

Serves 4.

GADO GADO

3 large potatoes, boiled
½ pound bean sprouts
1 pound green beans
3 carrots
½ small cabbage

1 cucumber
Small bunch watercress
3 hard-boiled eggs
Peanut sauce (below)

Peel and slice cooked potatoes. Wash bean sprouts, pour boiling water over them, then rinse in cold water and drain. Cut string beans in diagonal slices and cook in lightly salted boiling water until crisp. Scrub carrots, cut into thin strips, and cook until tender. Slice cabbage, discarding center, then blanch in boiling water for a minute or two until tender but not limp. Chill until crisp. To serve: Place watercress on platter and arrange vegetables on top. Surround with slices of cucumber and wedges of egg. Serve cold with peanut sauce.

Serves 6 to 8.

PEANUT SAUCE

½ cup peanut butter
2 tablespoons rice vinegar
2 tablespoons sesame oil
2 tablespoons sugar

1 tablespoon soy sauce
1 teaspoon minced garlic
Dash of ground chili pepper to
    taste

In a small bowl, combine peanut butter, vinegar, and oil with water as needed for thinning. Add remaining ingredients and stir until smooth.

Makes ½ cup.

Kerry Tolleth's Chicken Tandoori

1½ pounds skinned chicken
   pieces
2 cups low-fat yogurt
¼ cup lemon juice
1 medium onion, chopped
3 cloves garlic, crushed
1 thin slice ginger, crushed

½ teaspoon ground cloves
½ teaspoon ground cardamom
1¼ teaspoon black pepper
1 teaspoon ground coriander
1 teaspoon ground cumin
1 teaspoon ground cinnamon
1 teaspoon paprika

Slash chicken in several places to allow marinade to penetrate. To make marinade: Combine all remaining ingredients in blender and process until smooth. Pour over chicken and marinate in refrigerator 1 to 2 hours or overnight. Preheat grill or broiler. Grill until tender and golden, about 25 minutes.

Serves 6 to 8.

Betty Lou Hummel's Tandoori-Roasted Turkey Breast

1 boneless turkey breast, about 5 pounds
Marinade from Kerry's chicken tandoori, above

Combine marinade ingredients in blender and process until smooth. Make deep gashes in turkey breast and rub in marinade. Use remaining marinade to coat turkey. Place in a plastic roasting bag and refrigerate overnight. Turn the bag occasionally to distribute seasonings. To roast: Make small cuts in top of bag to vent air and put bagged turkey in baking dish in 325° oven. Roast for 2 hours. Cool, slice thin, and serve as main dish or as sandwich filling for a reception/buffet.

Serves 4 to 6 for dinner, 10 to 12 for buffet sandwiches.

Swiss Alps Dessert Plate

2 slices kiwi   Pureed strawberries
2 slices melon   Chopped walnuts
Scoop of cottage cheese

Place thin slices of kiwi and melon on plate and top with cottage cheese, strawberry puree, and chopped walnuts.

Serves 1.

When not traveling, we were still heavily involved in international activities. Cliff worked with several foreign-affairs organizations during our time in Hawaii and was instrumental in arranging conferences and setting up programs with speakers from abroad as well as with American experts on world issues and policies. We both enjoyed these sessions and were pleased that, though geographically isolated from the rest of the world in our island community, we still were able to interact regularly with people who devote themselves to identifying and solving global problems.

After two years at Hawaii Loa College, it became clear that the IB program would be more successful if it were located on a high-school campus. In 1986, the senior class and I moved as a package to Mid-Pacific Institute, a private school with 1,100 students in grades seven to twelve, which was about to celebrate the 125th anniversary of its founding by American missionaries. The earliest students had been Hawaiian girls being trained to be good Christian wives, joined by the sons of Chinese and Korean ministers assigned to remote island congregations, and later the children of blue- and white-collar workers, Japanese plantation laborers, and members of the U.S. military. All these parents and students valued the practical, increasingly academic, and multiethnic environment of "Mid-Pac."

The International Baccalaureate was a perfect fit for this school, which was now repositioning itself to prepare committed, creative, and skilled citizens for a new kind of future. This program would be an option for the most highly motivated students and gave Mid-Pac entrée into a worldwide community of students and faculty.

The heart of the IB program is of course the international student population, which it serves with an international curriculum. In June of 1993, our students planned an international conference on the environment, following up on the "Earth Summit" in Rio the previous year. During our closing session the student from Czechoslovakia (his country had not yet split into two nations) addressed the group with passion: "Learn a lesson from my country. We used to have the most beautiful forests and rivers in Europe, but now the rivers are dirty, the forests destroyed, and the air is so bad that my young cousins are sick all the time. You are in peril if you ignore the warning signs!"

On the final evening of our conference we held a luau (Hawaiian feast) followed by performances of traditional and modern Hawaiian dance. Several of the boys from Jordan imitated what they had observed. When they returned to their school in Amman, they danced hula for their fellow students during an assembly.

Luau Menu for an IB Student Conference

Oven kalua pork
Lomi lomi salmon
Poi
Chicken long rice
Haupia (coconut milk dessert)
Fresh pineapple and cake

OVEN KALUA PORK

8 pounds pork butt
4 tablespoons rock salt
5 to 6 tablespoons liquid smoke

6 to 8 ti leaves (or banana leaves
or spinach)

Kalua pig, the pride of the luau, is properly a whole pig cooked in a hole that is dug in the ground for the purpose, wrapped in the leaves of the ti plant, cooked over hot lava rocks on a hardwood fire, and covered with wet burlap bags and dirt. For this simplified version, rub the rock salt and liquid smoke into the pork, wrap it in leaves, then enclose in heavy-duty foil. Bake in a covered pan at 500° for 30 minutes. Reduce temperature to 400° and cook another 3½ hours. Shred cooked meat into pieces and serve with its juice. Bake sweet potatoes while pig is roasting.
Serves 20.

LOMI LOMI SALMON

1 pound salted salmon
4 pounds tomatoes, finely
  chopped
2 medium Maui (sweet) onions,
  minced

1 cup crushed ice
1 bunch green onions, finely
  chopped

Soak salmon in water for 2 to 3 hours, changing the water several times. If using unsalted salmon, rub it with rock salt and let it stand overnight. Rinse it thoroughly and soak in water 1 hour, changing 2 to 3 times. Drain and remove skin and bones. Shred into small pieces. Place in bowl with tomatoes and onions, then refrigerate. Cover with thin layer of crushed ice 1 hour before serving. Add green onions just before serving.
Serves 20.

POI

7 pounds poi
1 to 2 cups water

The Hawaiian staple starch is made from the taro plant and can be bought in bags in Hawaiian markets. Place prepared poi in mixing bowl and gradually add water, mixing with hands until smooth and paste-like. Cover and keep in cool place. Serve at room temperature.
Serves 20.

CHICKEN LONG RICE

5 pounds chicken thighs
1 to 2 inches fresh ginger, crushed
2 tablespoons rock salt

2 cloves garlic
20 ounces long rice (noodles made from mung-bean flour)
1 bunch green onions, chopped

Cover chicken with water, adding ginger, half the salt, and garlic. Simmer 45 minutes, until tender. Cool, bone, and cut chicken into bite-size pieces, reserving broth. Remove ginger and add long rice to broth. Let stand 30 minutes. Remove long rice and cut into 4-inch lengths. Return long rice to broth and add onions, remaining salt, and chicken. Bring to boil and simmer 15 to 20 minutes. Serve with broth as sauce.
Serves 20.

Haupia

| 12 ounces frozen coconut milk | ½ cup plus 2 tablespoons sugar |
| 1½ cups water | ½ cup plus 2 tablespoons cornstarch |

Combine all ingredients in a saucepan. Stir over medium heat until custard thickens. Lower heat and continue cooking and stirring for 10 minutes. Pour into 8x8-inch dish and chill until set. To serve, cut into squares.

Serves 20.

After a week of listening to lectures and panel discussions, participating in small group sessions, and coming up with resolutions, many of the participants went on to the island of Kauai for a week working with a community of Hawaiians—helping to repair damage from the ravages of Hurricane Iniki which tore across that island the previous autumn. They lived in a YMCA camp on the beach, did their own kitchen cleanup chores for meals, and were joined by Hawaiian families who planned menus, did the cooking, and stayed on to "talk story" and sing songs when dinner was over.

Every year the IB seniors at Mid-Pacific Institute faced their ultimate challenge during the month of May, when they sat down for a four-hour exam in world literature, gave recitals in theater arts, discussed visual-arts portfolios with a visiting professional, took oral examinations as well as written ones in two languages, and wrote many more hours of external exams in history, math, and science. When it was all over, the group gathered at our house for a pot-luck dinner celebration. The students brought fried rice, sushi, cheese and meat, salads, and dips. The most spectacular presentation was an Australian girl's decadent dessert named for the Russian ballerina Ana Pavlova.

Nerida Onley's Pavlova

8 egg whites, room temperature
¼ teaspoon salt
¼ teaspoon cream of tartar
2 cups refined sugar

2 teaspoons lemon juice
2 teaspoons vanilla
1 cup cream, whipped
Fresh fruit (kiwi, strawberries, and/or bananas)

Beat egg whites with salt and cream of tartar until fluffy, gradually adding sugar. Beat until stiff, then add lemon juice and vanilla and beat together approximately 20 minutes. Pile high in a circle on an ovenproof plate (to make a crisper meringue, spread flatter). Depress the center slightly to make a bowl. Bake in center of 300° degree oven 1½ to 2 hours until firm to touch. Leave in oven several hours or overnight. Fill with whipped cream, top with fruit, and slice in wedges

Serves 8 (to serve 4, recipe may be halved).

OUR CHILDREN AND GRANDCHILDREN living in California and the Pacific Northwest were delighted to have an excuse to visit Hawaii. They rejoiced when we moved there. But, in actuality, it wasn't that easy for them to get their families (and finances) organized for coordinated vacation time, and to make the five-hour plane trip. We went to see them more than they came to us, and our visits were too short for us to participate in the lives of our four grand-children. Much as we enjoyed Hawaii, we decided that we needed to be closer to family. In the spring of 1995, we made final visits to some of our favorite Hawaiian islands, including the home of friends on the slopes of Haleakala volcano, said farewell to neighbors and colleagues, packed up our household goods, and headed for California.

The recipes from special friends in Hawaii are souvenirs of their Aloha spirit and reminders of shared times of contemplation and celebration. The annual opening night gala of the opera season, hosted by Greg and Rhoda Hackler. The kind and generous good neighborship of the Alexanders next door and the Herbigs up the hill. The wonderful weekend with the Crowes at Kula on Maui. The special friendship with our Swedish realtor, Helena Cence.

RECIPES FROM ISLAND FRIENDS

Rhoda Hackler's artichoke spread
Rhoda's teriyaki meatballs
Rhoda's parmesan yogurt chicken
Gerry Alexander's banana smoothie
Helena Cence's Swedish pork
Helena's Swedish cabbage
Ann Crowe's escalopes of chicken Parmigiana
Ann's sage potatoes
Hannelore Herbig's lentil soup
Kula curried peanuts and raisins

RHODA HACKLER'S ARTICHOKE SPREAD

1 (14-ounce) can or 2 small jars   ¾ cup grated Parmesan cheese
   artichoke hearts   Dash of Tabasco
1 cup mayonnaise

Drain and finely chop artichoke hearts. Mix all ingredients and place in ovenproof serving dish. Bake until hot and bubbly at 350°. Serve with crackers.

Makes 3 cups

Rhoda's Teriyaki Meatballs

1 cup soy sauce
½ cup water
2 tablespoons crushed ginger

2 cloves minced garlic
3 pounds lean hamburger

Combine first 4 ingredients to make a sauce, them mix thoroughly with the hamburger. Marinate for several hours. Form into small balls. Place in large roasting pan and bake, uncovered, for 30 minutes at 275°. Serve warm on a platter with toothpicks.

Makes about 100 meatballs.

Rhoda's Parmesan Yogurt Chicken

10 skinned, boneless chicken breasts.
Juice of 1 lemon
Salt and pepper
1 cup yogurt
½ cup mayonnaise
2 tablespoons Dijon mustard

2 tablespoons Worcestershire sauce
1 teaspoon ground thyme or other dried herbs
½ cup thinly sliced green onions
½ teaspoon cayenne
1 cup Parmesan cheese

Arrange chicken breasts in a single layer in a baking dish. Drizzle with lemon juice and lightly sprinkle with salt and pepper. Blend yogurt, mayonnaise, mustard, Worcestershire, herbs, and green onions into a sauce and spread over chicken. Sprinkle with cayenne. Bake uncovered for 30 minutes at 350°. When done, drain off pan juices and sprinkle with the Parmesan cheese. Put under broiler for a few minutes to brown the cheese.

Serves 10.

GERRY ALEXANDER'S BANANA SMOOTHIE

1 banana   ⅛ teaspoon vanilla
1 cup skim milk   ⅛ teaspoon ground nutmeg
2 cubes ice

Blend all ingredients at high speed and drink right away.
   Serves 1.

HELENA CENCE'S SWEDISH PORK

2 pounds pork filet, cut into   2 to 3 tablespoons ketchup or
   pieces   chili sauce
1 teaspoon rose peppercorns   ½ cup cognac
Butter for browning   ½ cup cream
2 to 3 bananas, in 1-inch slices   Hot cooked rice or noodles

Crush peppercorns and coat meat with them, then brown meat in
butter. Remove from pan. Brown bananas in same butter. Add chili
sauce for color, cognac, and cream. Return meat to pan and stew,
covered, for 1 hour. Check liquid and add water if needed. Serve
with rice or noodles.
   Serves 6.

HELENA'S SWEDISH CABBAGE

1 head red cabbage   2 tablespoons lemon juice
1 large onion   2 to 3 tablespoons brown sugar or
3 green apples   molasses
Salt and pepper to taste

Cut up cabbage and onions; core, peel, and chop apples. Gently
brown in butter and add remaining ingredients. Cook 2 hours over
slow heat and adjust seasonings as necessary.
   Serves 6.

Anne Crowe's Escalopes of Chicken Parmigiana

4 chicken breasts
1 egg
Flour, salt, and pepper
Olive oil
1 eggplant
1 cup tomato sauce
1 tablespoon chopped onion

1 clove minced garlic
Pepper, parsley, and oregano to
  taste
Dash of red wine.
Parmesan cheese
½ cup white wine

Skin, bone, and flatten chicken. Dip each piece in beaten egg, then mixture of flour, salt, and pepper. Sauté in olive oil and transfer to flat casserole dish. Flour and sauté eggplant slices, drain on paper towels, and place on top of chicken. Combine tomato sauce, onion, garlic, pepper, parsley, oregano, and red wine. Top each portion of chicken and eggplant with 2 tablespoons tomato mixture and grated cheese. Deglaze sauce pan with white wine and pour over all. (This may be done ahead, refrigerated overnight.) Bake 45 minutes to 1 hour at 350°.

Serves 4.

Ann's Sage Potatoes

4 medium potatoes, scrubbed and sliced thin
Olive oil
Fresh sage leaves (or basil)

Brush potatoes with olive oil. Sandwich a sage leaf between each 2 slices. Arrange on baking sheet lined with foil. Bake at 350°, turning once, about 20 minutes.

Serves 6 to 8.

Hannelore Herbig's Lentil Soup

2 cups lentils   1 onion, chopped
Ham bone   2 potatoes, diced
2 carrots, sliced   Chopped parsley
2 stalks celery, sliced

Rinse and cook lentils at low heat with ham bone, about 15 to 20 minutes. Add vegetables and cook until done, about 20 minutes more. Season with 1 beef cube if no ham bone. Garnish with parsley.

Serves 6

Kula Curried Peanuts and Raisins

2 cups roasted peanuts   1 teaspoon curry powder
1 cup yellow raisins   ½ teaspoon cumin

Place nuts and raisins in frying pan (with small amount of oil if peanuts are dry roasted). Sprinkle with curry and cumin and stir over medium high heat until nuts and raisins are coated and have been toasted, about 5 minutes.

Makes 3 cups.

Aloha! This wonderful phrase is filled with meaning: hello, goodbye, welcome, farewell, and may the spirit of good health and well being blow upon you.

17

Retirees in Tiburon

OUR NEW HOME in Tiburon was perched on a hillside, fifteen minutes north of the Golden Gate Bridge, overlooking Mount Tamalpais and Richardson Bay. This was a new lifestyle for me— no school bells to govern my hours, no fixed daily schedules, more time to explore. I tried out new recipes and resurrected old ones that were too much trouble for a working wife to manage. We shopped in vegetable markets stocked with dazzling varieties of California produce. We drove and walked through the towns and cities of Marin County, each with its own personality, discovering wonderful local restaurants. With days free, we entertained at lunch as well as dinner and enjoyed leisurely preparation of meals for family, close friends, and fellow retirees—many of them living within an hour's drive.

For our own meals, we continued to read labels carefully, to monitor fat and sodium and cholesterol, and to look for appetizing ways to present meals with less meat. Dinner, especially in winter, was often just a hearty soup, bread, and salad.

WINTER SOUP SUPPERS

Cabbage borscht
Red lentil and carrot soup
Hearty hamburger soup
Curried broccoli and cheddar soup
Hawaiian Portuguese bean soup
Ricotta dumpling and spinach soup
Black bean soup with sherry and lime
"Last of the turkey" minestrone
Popovers
Grandma's onion biscuit squares
Cornbread

CABBAGE BORSCHT

3 to 4 pounds short ribs
3 quarts water
4 teaspoons salt
4 whole black peppercorns
1 bay leaf
1 to 2 bunches unpeeled beets
1 medium potato

1 large onion
2 large carrots
2 stalks celery
1 (1-pound) can tomatoes
1 small head cabbage
2 tablespoons lemon juice
1 tablespoon sugar

Put meat, water, salt, peppercorns, and bay leaf in large kettle, bring to boil, and simmer 1 hour. Cut beets in large dice, add to soup, and cook 1 more hour (I often use canned beets, reducing cooking time). Remove meat from broth with slotted spoon; set aside. Cut potato and onion in large dice, carrots in ¾-inch slices, and celery in ½-inch slices; add to soup along with tomatoes and simmer 1 hour longer (can do this ahead). 20 minutes before serving, heat to boiling. Cut cabbage into 1-inch wedges and remove core; add to soup and simmer about 10 minutes. Stir in lemon juice and sugar just before serving.

Serves 12.

RED LENTIL AND CARROT SOUP

2 tablespoons butter or olive oil
1 onion, chopped
1 to 3 cloves garlic, minced
2 stalks of celery, halved
    lengthwise and thinly sliced
5 medium carrots, grated
5 cups chicken or vegetable broth

1 teaspoon grated lemon rind
1 bay leaf
1 cup dried red lentils
Juice of 1 lemon
Sweet basil
Salt and pepper

Sauté onion, garlic, celery, and carrots in butter or oil until onions are limp. Add broth, lemon rind, bay leaf, and lentils and cook about 40 to 60 minutes, adding water if necessary. Add lemon juice, basil, and salt and pepper to taste; simmer another 20 minutes.

Serves 4 to 6.

HEARTY HAMBURGER SOUP

3 tablespoons butter or olive oil
1 medium onion, coarsely
  chopped
1½ pounds ground beef
1 (28-ounce) can tomatoes
3 (10-ounce) cans consommé
  plus 3 cans water

4 medium carrots, sliced
1 bay leaf
4 celery tops
6 sprigs parsley
½ teaspoon thyme
10 peppercorns
1 teaspoon salt

Heat butter or oil in soup kettle and cook onion until soft. Add ground beef and stir until it browns. Add remaining ingredients. Cover and cook over low heat about 45 minutes. Serve plain or with toast rounds covered with grated Parmesan cheese, or with rice.

    Serves 6 to 8.

CURRIED BROCCOLI AND CHEDDAR SOUP

1½ pounds broccoli
¼ cup butter or olive oil
1 tablespoon curry powder
1 medium onion, chopped
6 cups chicken broth

2 large potatoes, peeled and cubed
4 slender carrots, thinly sliced
1 cup milk
3 cups shredded sharp cheddar
  cheese

Trim flowerets from broccoli and cut into small pieces. Peel stems and slice thinly. In large kettle, heat butter or oil over medium heat. Add curry powder and onions and cook, stirring, 5 minutes. Add broth, potatoes, broccoli stems, and carrots. Cover and simmer until potatoes are tender, about 30 minutes. Whirl the soup in blender and return to kettle. Heat to boiling and add broccoli flowerets and milk. Simmer, uncovered, until flowerets are tender. Stir in cheese, a handful at a time, until melted.

    Serves 8 to 10.

Hawaiian Portuguese Bean Soup

1 pound Portuguese sausage (or
  ½ pound each sausage and
  lean ham)
1 large carrot, diced
2 potatoes, diced
1 small onion, chopped
1 quart water

1 (8-ounce) can tomato sauce
2 cups cooked macaroni
2 (15-ounce) cans kidney beans,
  drained
1 large head cabbage, chopped
1 tablespoon chopped parsley

In large pot, combine all ingredients except macaroni, beans, and cabbage. Bring to a boil; lower heat and simmer, covered, for 20 minutes. Add remaining ingredients and simmer additional 20 minutes.

Makes 4½ quarts.

Ricotta Dumpling and Spinach Soup

⅔ cup bread crumbs
¼ cup milk
⅔ cup ricotta cheese
4 egg yolks
2 egg whites
1 teaspoon salt
½ teaspoon pepper
¾ cup flour
1 tablespoon baking powder

8 cups broth
2½ tablespoons sherry wine
  vinegar
2½ tablespoons minced shallots
⅓ cup walnut or olive oil
1 (6-ounce) package baby spinach,
  rinsed and dried
1 tablespoon chopped parsley

For dumplings: Place crumbs in bowl, add milk, and let stand 3 minutes. Stir in cheese, eggs, salt, and pepper. Add flour and baking powder and blend well. Bring broth to boil in large saucepan. Add dumpling mixture by level tablespoonsful (16 total) in 2 batches. Simmer about 8 minutes and remove dumplings to a bowl. For spinach: Mix vinegar and shallots; whisk in oil and salt and pepper to taste. Add spinach and parsley and toss to coat with dressing. To serve: Put 2 dumplings into each of 8 bowls; spoon spinach alongside; ladle broth over dumplings and spinach.

Serves 8.

BLACK BEAN SOUP WITH SHERRY AND LIME

½ cups prepared black beans,
   including cooking liquid
   (below)
1 to 2 cups water

4½ tablespoons sherry, to taste
1 tablespoon fresh lime juice, to
   taste
Salt to taste

Puree beans in batches in blender and transfer to 2½- to 3-quart heavy saucepan. Stir in 1 cup water, sherry, lime juice, and salt, then thin soup to desired consistency with additional water, if necessary. Simmer over moderate heat, stirring occasionally, for 5 minutes. Serve with cornbread (below).

    Serves 4.

PREPARED BLACK BEANS

1 pound dried black beans,
   about 2½ cups
1 medium onion, finely chopped
3 tablespoons olive oil
8 cups water

1½ teaspoons salt
1 cup sherry
1 to 2 tablespoons soy sauce
1 to 2 tablespoons balsamic
   vinegar

Bring beans, onion, oil, water, and ½ teaspoon salt to boil in heavy 6- to 8-quart pot, then reduce heat and simmer, covered, until beans are tender, 1½ to 2 hours. Thin to desired consistency with additional water. Stir in sherry and remaining teaspoon salt, then soy sauce and vinegar to taste, and simmer, covered, stirring occasionally, for 5 minutes.

"Last of the Turkey" Minestrone

1 to 3 quarts turkey stock
1 medium potato, cubed
1 medium carrot, sliced
1 cup celery, chopped
1 cup cabbage, chopped
1 cup green beans, in 1-inch
  pieces
1 (15-ounce) can tomatoes

2 teaspoons dried basil
1 cup zucchini or crookneck
  squash
1 cup pasta in small pieces
1 (15-ounce) can white or red
  kidney beans, rinsed and
  drained
Grated Parmesan cheese

Add to broth: potato, carrot, celery, cabbage, beans, tomatoes, and basil. Bring to a boil and cook 15 minutes. Add squash, pasta, and beans. Boil until pasta is tender. Season with salt and pepper and ladle into bowls. Pass the cheese.

Serves 6 to 10.

Popovers

1 cup sifted flour
½ teaspoon salt
2 beaten eggs

1 cup milk
1 tablespoon melted butter

Sift together flour and salt. Combine eggs and milk and add to flour. Beat to a smooth batter. Add melted butter. Beat 3 minutes with a rotary beater. Pour into well-greased popover pan or custard cups, filling ½ full. Bake at 425° for 20 minutes. Reduce heat to 350° and bake additional 25 to 30 minutes until brown and firm.

Makes 6.

GRANDMA'S ONION BISCUIT SQUARES

2 cups flour
4 teaspoons baking powder
½ teaspoon salt
¼ cup shortening
½ to ⅔ cup milk

2 tablespoons butter
2½ cups onion slices
1 egg
1 cup sour cream or yogurt

Mix flour, baking powder, salt, shortening, and milk to a soft dough. Put into greased 9-inch square pan and flatten to ¼-inch thickness. Melt butter, add onion and a pinch of salt, and cook until delicate brown. Cool and spread over the dough. Beat egg and sour cream, blend well, and pour over onions. Bake at 450° for 20 minutes. Cut into squares when cool.

Makes 16 squares.

CORNBREAD

¾ cup sifted flour
2½ teaspoons baking powder
1 to 2 tablespoons sugar
¾ teaspoon salt

1 cup yellow corn meal
1 egg, beaten
2 to 3 tablespoons melted butter
1 cup milk

Sift together flour, baking powder, sugar and salt, and add corn meal. Beat together egg, butter, and milk and add to flour mixture. Place batter in heated 9x9-inch greased pan and bake at 425° about 15 minutes.

Serves 8.

IN GOOD CALIFORNIA STYLE, we bought a barbeque and during the summer we grilled many an evening meal, experimenting with various meats and grilled vegetables. A recipe for a Greek-style, family-sized hamburger that had languished in my recipe collection since early Washington days was perfect for dinner on the deck.

SUMMER DINING ON THE DECK

Julie Reisner's watercress dip
Cold carrot orange soup
Greek platter burger
Kerry Tolleth's crusty mustard chicken
Garlic-lime pork tenderloin
Jalapeño onion marmalade
Salmon grilled or baked in foil
Herbed potatoes grilled or baked in foil
Cabbage, carrot, and ginger slaw
Heather Collins' pesto potato salad

JULIE REISNER'S WATERCRESS DIP

8 ounces cream cheese, room
  temperature
3 to 4 green onions, chopped
1 small clove garlic, crushed
1 bunch watercress, washed and
  dried

3 tablespoons lemon juice
1 tablespoon prepared horseradish
½ teaspoon salt
¼ teaspoon white pepper

Break up the cream cheese; put in blender with other ingredients.
Blend until smooth.

Makes about 2 cups.

COLD CARROT ORANGE SOUP

1 to 2 carrots, grated
1 celery stalk, diced
1 quart vegetable or chicken
   broth
2 garlic cloves, minced
¼ cup thinly sliced mint leaves

2 cups diced tomatoes
Juice of 4 oranges
Grated zest of ½ to 1 orange
Lemon juice
Salt
Dash Tabasco

Combine carrots, celery, broth, garlic, and half of mint in saucepan. Heat to a boil, then reduce heat and simmer until vegetables are tender. Cool, then add tomatoes, orange juice, and zest. Chill in refrigerator. Before serving, season with remaining mint, lemon juice, salt, and Tabasco to taste. Float an ice cube in each soup bowl.

Serves 4.

GREEK PLATTER BURGER

3 tablespoons lemon juice
½ onion, diced
3 cloves garlic, minced
2 teaspoons dried oregano
¼ teaspoon ground coriander
1½ teaspoons salt
¼ cup chopped fresh mint
1 pound ground lean beef
1 pound ground lean lamb
1 round loaf sourdough French
   bread

½ cup softened butter or
   margarine
2 cloves minced garlic
3 ounces cream cheese
¼ pound crumbled feta cheese
1 large onion, sliced
2 medium tomatoes, sliced
1 (7-ounce) jar marinated
   artichoke hearts

Combine first seven ingredients with meat. Mix thoroughly and shape into a large meat patty (2 inches larger in diameter than the bread loaf). Grill over coals until desired state of doneness, about 15 minutes on each side for rare to medium rare. Meanwhile, cut bread loaf in half horizontally. Combine softened butter and 2 cloves minced garlic and spread equal portions on each bread half. When burger is done, grill bread, cut side down, until browned. Cut upper half into wedges and keep warm. Beat cream cheese until smooth and stir in crumbled feta. To assemble, slide burger onto bottom half of bread. Top with sliced onions, tomatoes, feta mixture, and artichokes. Cut into serving-size wedges and accompany with garlic bread wedges.

Serves 8 to 10.

KERRY TOLLETH'S CRUSTY MUSTARD CHICKEN

8 boned chicken breasts	2 tablespoons fresh thyme leaves
½ cup unsalted butter	1 teaspoon freshly ground black
2 tablespoons vegetable oil	pepper
6 tablespoons Dijon mustard	1 teaspoon crushed red pepper
3 tablespoons minced shallots	4 cups fresh white bread crumbs

Broil chicken over hot coals 3 minutes on each side; set aside. Melt butter in oil. In mixing bowl, combine mustard, shallots, thyme, and peppers. Stir in half the oil mixture and blend thoroughly. Brush chicken breasts with mustard mixture and coat them thoroughly in bread crumbs. Dab with remaining butter and oil. Grill chicken over coals 10 to 12 minutes, turning two to three times and basting with mustard mixture. Chicken is done when juices run clear when pricked with a knife. (Alternatively, grill under broiler in oven 10 to 12 minutes, turning as above.)

Serves 8.

GRILLED GARLIC-LIME PORK TENDERLOIN

3 cloves garlic, chopped
2 tablespoons soy sauce
2 tablespoons grated fresh ginger
2 teaspoons Dijon mustard
⅓ cup fresh lime juice

½ cup olive oil
Salt, pepper, and cayenne to taste
4 pork tenderloins (¾ pound),
   trimmed
Jalapeño onion marmalade
   (below)

Combine first 6 ingredients in blender or food processor to make marinade, adding salt, pepper, and cayenne to taste. Combine pork with marinade in large plastic bag. Seal, pressing out excess air, and place in shallow baking dish. Marinate pork in refrigerator 1 to 2 days, turning occasionally. Remove pork from marinade and drain. Grill on an oiled rack 5 to 6 inches over glowing coals, turning every 5 minutes, for 15 to 20 minutes. Let meat stand 5 minutes before slicing. Serve with jalapeño onion marmalade.

Serves 6.

JALAPEÑO ONION MARMALADE

4 cups onions, chopped fine
3 tablespoons olive oil
Salt and pepper
2 fresh jalapeño chilies, seeded,
   minced

2 tablespoons honey or sugar
3 to 4 tablespoons red wine
   vinegar
¼ cup water

Cook onions in oil until limp. Add salt and pepper to taste and jalapeños. Cook, stirring 1 minute. Add honey and cook, stirring, I minute. Add vinegar and simmer, stirring until most liquid has evaporated. Add water and simmer, stirring, until mixture thickens and onions are tender, about 10 minutes. Adjust seasonings. May be made ahead and refrigerated up to 2 days.

Makes 3 cups.

SALMON GRILLED OR BAKED IN FOIL

2 teaspoons sesame oil
2 cups spinach leaves, rinsed
  and dried

2 (8-ounce) salmon steaks
Salt and pepper

Spread 1 teaspoon of oil in center of each of two 12x16-inch sheets
of foil. Place half of spinach leaves to left of center and top with
salmon. Season with salt and pepper. Top with remaining spinach
and oil. Fold foil over fish and spinach and pinch edges together to
form sealed packages. Grill packages over hot coals, turning once,
for about 10 minutes, or bake in oven at 400° for 20 minutes. Serve
with herbed potatoes (below).
    Serves 2.

HERBED POTATOES GRILLED OR BAKED IN FOIL

1 tablespoon butter, softened
½ pound tiny red or yellow
  potatoes, about 8, rinsed and
  halved

Salt and pepper
1 teaspoon chopped fresh or ½
  teaspoon dried herbs

Spread butter in center of 12x16-inch sheet of foil. Place potatoes
to left of center and season with salt, pepper, and herbs. Fold foil
over potatoes and pinch edges to seal. Roast over hot coals or bake
in oven at 400° for 30 minutes.
    Serves 2.

Cabbage, Carrot, and Ginger Slaw

6 cups finely shredded Chinese cabbage

1 cup shredded carrots

1 large red pepper, stemmed, seeded, slivered

½ cup slivered pickled ginger

½ cup seasoned rice vinegar

Mix all ingredients, cover, and chill up to 6 hours.
Serves 6.

Heather Collins' Pesto Potato Salad

4 medium red potatoes

¼ to ½ cup prepared pesto sauce

2 tablespoons rice vinegar

¼ cup yogurt

Boil, cool, and slice or dice potatoes. Dress with pesto sauce, adding vinegar and yogurt to taste and for a creamy consistency.
Serves 4.

Just before our first Christmas in Tiburon, a harsh wind and rain storm knocked out power over a large portion of Northern California and shut down all the schools. Doug and Kerry's home a few miles away was powerless for several days. Cliff and I were fortunate enough to have light and heat restored after the second day, so Kerry brought her two children to us to get warm and for hot food and baths. Taylor, Wyn, and I spent the day making Christmas cookies—using the cookie cutters and recipes that had been a baby shower gift to me on the eve of their dad's birth in Washington D.C. in 1961.

18

Tasting California—And Beyond

ONCE RETIRED, WE ATE out more often than before, tempted by the many types of cuisine available and the artistry of local chefs. In our own neighborhood restaurants, we traveled to Mexico, Italy, China, France, Japan, and Sweden for this new chapter in our culinary journey.

Leaving the neighborhood, we had easy access to the wine country north of us—where we sampled creations of chefs who specialized in happy marriages of food and wine—and to the former gold-mining towns in the foothills and the ski slopes and hiking trails of the Sierras to the east of us. On our way to cross-country skiing between redwoods in the Calaveras Big Trees State Park and the groomed cross-country ski trails at Bear Valley, we stayed overnight in the town of Murphys, where the owner/chef of our inn fortified us for the day with a hearty breakfast. As we took off on a camping trip through Utah and New Mexico, a friend from Tokyo days presented us with a sustaining jar of peanut brittle. On a summer weekend, we dined elegantly with new friends from Marin County who were building themselves a mountain house near the entrance to Lassen Volcanic National Park. Though a trip to her nearest supermarket took an hour and a half, Carolyn Stohler had a three-star dinner ready for road-weary guests.

On the Road in California

Napa Valley butternut squash soup
Wine country beef stew
Wild rice salad
Jan Drammer's southwestern egg bake
Jeanne Gosho's peanut brittle
Carolyn Stohler's prune-stuffed pork tenderloins
Carolyn's watermelon salad
Carolyn's potato-squash stir fry
Dana Victorson's avgolemono soup
Dana's spanakorizo (spinach with rice)
Kathy Poole's melon-sauced spaghetti
Susan Englebright's easy lemon soufflé

Napa Valley Butternut Squash Soup

½ cup minced onion
1½ teaspoons minced fresh
  ginger
3 tablespoons unsalted butter
4 cups peeled, seeded, thinly
  sliced butternut squash
2 cups chicken broth

2 cups water
3 cloves garlic, minced
2 tablespoons fresh lime juice
Salt and pepper
Vegetable oil
3 tablespoons julienne strips fresh
  ginger

In a large saucepan, cook onion and minced ginger in butter over low heat until onion is limp. Add squash, broth, water, and garlic. Bring mixture to a boil and simmer covered until squash is tender, 15 to 20 minutes. Put mixture in batches through blender or food processor. Return to pan. Add lime juice, salt, and pepper and reheat soup. In small skillet, fry julienned ginger in hot oil over high heat. Garnish soup with lime slice and fried ginger.
  Serves 4.

Wine Country Beef Stew

4 pounds lean beef, cut in 1-inch
  cubes
4 tablespoons olive oil
4 garlic cloves, sliced
2½ cups pinot noir wine
1 cup beef stock

½ pound mushrooms, sliced
1 bay leaf
1 teaspoon thyme
Salt and pepper
Hot cooked rice or noodles

Brown meat in oil in large skillet. Remove meat to a covered casserole and sauté garlic 1 minute in skillet. Add 1 cup pinot noir, scraping bottom of skillet. Pour mixture and remaining wine over meat. Marinate, covered, overnight. Next day, add stock, mushrooms, and seasonings and cook, covered, at 325° for 2 to 2½ hours. Optional: thicken with a roux of flour and butter. Serve with rice or noodles.

    Serves 4.

Wild Rice Salad

5 cups salted water
½ pound (about 1½ cups) wild
  rice, rinsed
2 celery stalks, cut in ¼-inch dice
2 small tomatoes, diced
½ carrot, diced
½ red onion, chopped fine
½ cup red bell pepper, diced

½ green bell pepper, diced
½ yellow pepper, diced
½ cup sliced almonds, toasted
½ cup raisins
6 tablespoons balsamic vinegar
7 tablespoons vegetable oil
1 teaspoon garlic, minced
Salt and pepper to taste

Bring water to boil in large saucepan; add rice and cook uncovered, stirring occasionally, until tender, about 40 minutes. Drain and transfer to bowl then chill, covered, about 2 hours. In large salad bowl, combine vegetables, almonds, and raisins with wild rice. In another bowl, combine vinegar, oil, garlic, salt, and pepper. Pour over salad. May be made two days ahead and chilled, covered.

    Serves 6.

JAN DRAMMER'S SOUTHWESTERN EGG BAKE

2 tablespoons butter	1 teaspoon baking powder
1 green pepper, chopped	Seasonings to taste: oregano, salt,
3 to 4 green onions, sliced	lemon pepper, black pepper,
½ red onion, chopped	cayenne
2 Roma tomatoes, chopped	1 cup grated cheese
1 can whole-kernel corn, drained	Cornbread (page 264) or
16 to 20 eggs	packaged cornbread mix
1 cup nonfat yogurt	¼ cup pine nuts

Fry pepper and onions in butter; add tomatoes and corn. Beat eggs and add yogurt, baking powder, and seasonings. Add vegetables and pour into greased baking dish. Top with ¾ cup grated cheese and bake at 350° for 1 hour. Make cornbread according to recipe or package directions, adding pine nuts and ¼ cup cheese to batter. Cut baked eggs into squares and serve with cornbread.

Serves 12.

JEANNE GOSHO'S PEANUT BRITTLE

1 cup sugar	1 teaspoon vanilla
1 cup white corn syrup	1 teaspoon baking soda
1 cup roasted peanuts	12x15-inch sheet of silver foil, on
½ teaspoon salt	a cookie sheet
1 tablespoon butter	

Have all ingredients measured and ready before starting. Using a wooden spoon with medium-length handle (which is left in bowl during cooking process), mix together sugar and corn syrup in 2-quart microwaveable bowl with handle. Microwave on high 4 to 4½ minutes. Add peanuts and salt; microwave 2 minutes more. Peanuts will be lightly browned and syrup very hot. Add butter, vanilla, and baking soda and stir until light and foamy. Quickly pour mixture onto aluminum foil (do not attempt to spread thin); brittle will harden quickly. Cool 1 hour, then break into small pieces and store in plastic bags or airtight containers.

Makes 1 pound.

Carolyn Stohler's Prune-Stuffed Pork Tenderloins

16 pitted prunes
½ cup warm water
2 (12-ounce) pork tenderloins, trimmed and halved crosswise
2 cups canned beef broth
2 cups canned chicken broth
4 tablespoons butter or margarine

4 large shallots, chopped
1 cup chopped green onions
⅔ cup chopped carrots
¾ cup vodka
¼ cup yogurt
Tabasco, salt, and pepper to taste

Combine prunes and water; let stand 30 minutes, then drain, reserving liquid. Cut lengthwise pocket in center of each tenderloin piece. Stuff with 4 prunes each; cover and refrigerate. Combine broths in saucepan; boil and reduce to 1 cup (about 35 minutes). Sauté shallots, onions, and carrots in 2 tablespoons butter in heavy skillet. Add vodka, prune liquid, and broth. Boil about 10 minutes until 1 cup remains. Strain sauce, discarding solids; cover and refrigerate. (All of the above can be done a day ahead.) Sauté pork in remaining butter or margarine, browning on all sides. Transfer to ovenproof pan and roast at 425° for 15 minutes. Add yogurt to sauce and cook until thickened. Season with Tabasco, salt, and pepper. Slice pork crosswise; arrange on plates and spoon sauce over.

Serves 4.

CAROLYN'S WATERMELON SALAD

4 cups seeded watermelon, in
1-inch cubes
½ cup thinly sliced red onion

4 teaspoons unseasoned rice
vinegar
2 teaspoons chopped fresh mint
½ teaspoon pepper

Combine all ingredients. Refrigerate if making ahead.
Serves 4.

CAROLYN'S POTATO-SQUASH STIR FRY

4 medium potatoes
4 zucchini or summer squash

1 red pepper
Dried herbs, salt, and pepper

Parboil potatoes, cut in ½-inch dice. Dice zucchini and red pepper.
Stir-fry vegetables with minimal margarine and season with herbs,
salt, and pepper.
Serves 4.

DANA VICTORSON'S AVGOLEMONO SOUP

6 cups chicken broth
1 cup orzo macaroni
Salt and pepper

2 eggs
Juice of 2 lemons

Bring broth to a boil. Stir in orzo, salt and pepper. Bring to a
second boil, cover, and simmer for 10 minutes, or until orzo is
tender. Remove from heat. Separate eggs. Beat egg whites until
peaks form; add yolks. Beat until blended. Add lemon juice and
stir only until barely mixed. Gently stir two ladlesful of soup into
egg mixture. Pour this back into the soup pot. Stir gently and ladle
into bowls.
Serves 4.

DANA'S SPANAKORIZO

2 medium onions, chopped   1 tablespoon chopped fresh
¼ cup olive oil   parsley and dill
1 pound spinach   ¼ cup rice
½ cup water   Salt and pepper

Sauté onions in heated oil until golden. Add spinach and water and bring to boil. Sprinkle the parsley and dill and add the rice. Stir, season to taste, and allow to simmer for about 15 minutes until rice is tender.
Serves 4.

KATHY POOLE'S MELON-SAUCED SPAGHETTI

3 cups cantaloupe cubes   1 tablespoon lemon juice
4 tablespoons butter   4 tablespoons tomato paste
1 tablespoon oil   1 pound egg pasta
1 cup heavy cream (¾ cup if   Salt and pepper
   using flour pasta)

Cook melon 2 minutes in butter and oil. Add cream, lemon juice, and tomato paste. Stir and cook until volume is reduced by half; this should not be too creamy. Add salt and pepper. Cook pasta until al dente, drain, and toss with sauce.
Serves 4 to 6.

Susan Englebright's Easy Lemon Soufflé

½ cup sugar
2 tablespoons flour
½ teaspoon salt
2 egg yolks, lightly beaten
1 cup milk

2 tablespoons lemon juice
2 teaspoons lemon zest, grated
2 egg whites
Whipping cream

Mix sugar, flour, and salt and sift together into a large bowl. Add beaten egg yolks and milk. Add lemon juice and zest. Beat egg whites until stiff, then fold into batter. Pour into a greased 1-quart soufflé dish. Place in a pan of hot water. Bake in a 350° oven for 45 minutes. Chill. Serve with whipped cream.

Serves 4.

Now that we were back in the continental United States and in charge of our own schedules, we were nearer to Europe and had the time for leisurely exploration. Driving through small towns and villages, we enjoyed the local cuisine.

On the Road in France and Spain

French cheese wreaths
Mixed vegetable salad
Lamb daube Provençal
Potatoes Provençal
Mediterranean fillet of sole
Chicken Marbella
Spanish flan

FRENCH CHEESE WREATHS

1 scant cup flour
1 teaspoon salt
1¼ cup milk
¼ cup butter, cut up

3 large eggs
¼ pound Gruyère cheese, coarsely
    grated

Prepare baking sheet: Line with parchment paper and draw 2 8-inch circles in pencil, using cake pan or pie tin as guide. Sift together flour and salt. Heat milk and butter until just boiling. Add flour mixture all at once and stir over medium heat until mixture forms smooth paste that leaves the sides of the saucepan. Remove from heat. Add eggs, one at a time, beating until smooth. Beat in grated cheese. Place overlapping spoonsful of dough just inside prepared circles, to create two cheese wreaths. Bake in preheated 400° oven until puffed and golden, about 35 minutes. Turn off heat and leave wreaths in oven with door partially open another 10 minutes. Serve with red wine.

Serves 10 as a snack.

MIXED VEGETABLE SALAD

1 carrot, cut into sticks
1 cooked beet, sliced
½ boiled potato, sliced
½ red onion, sliced thin
1 hard boiled egg, quartered
1 canned anchovy fillet

Parboiled broccoli and/or
    cauliflower
Green and black olives
Lettuce
Oil and vinegar for dressing

For each serving, arrange a selection of the first nine ingredients on individual plates and drizzle with dressing.

LAMB DAUBE PROVENÇAL

5 to 6 pounds lamb, in bite-sized pieces
½ cup brandy
1 to 1½ bottles red wine
1 head garlic, peeled and coarsely chopped
1 onion, coarsely chopped
Peel from ½ orange
½ teaspoon herbes de Provence
½ teaspoon pepper

3 tablespoons olive oil
1 to 2 tablespoons flour
½ red bell pepper, diced
3 carrots, diced
1 leek, white and green part diced
½ turnip, diced
2½ to 3 cups tomatoes, diced
Pinch cinnamon
4 ounces bacon, in small pieces

Combine first 8 ingredients. Let marinate 4 hours at room temperature or overnight in refrigerator. Remove lamb from marinade, then brown in oil in heavy skillet. Toss with flour and layer it in heavy casserole with tight-fitting lid. Add onion and garlic from marinade. Strain marinade and pour over meat. Add remaining ingredients. Bring to a boil. Cover and either simmer over low heat on top of stove or bake at 325° two to three hours until meat is very tender. Pour cooking liquid into saucepan. Spoon off fat, then boil to reduce. Serve meat and vegetables on platter with sauce spooned over.

Serves 8.

POTATOES PROVENÇAL

4 tablespoons olive oil
1 medium onion, chopped fine
1 clove garlic, minced
1 tablespoon herbes de Provence
¼ teaspoon sugar
6 plum tomatoes, chopped
Salt and pepper to taste

⅓ cup Niçoise olives
2 large baking potatoes, scrubbed
3 ounces mild goat cheese, crumbled
2 tablespoons finely chopped fresh parsley

Grease bottom and sides of 11x8-inch shallow baking dish. In skillet, cook onion in 2 tablespoons oil until softened. Add garlic and cook, stirring, 1 minute. Add herbs, sugar, tomatoes, salt, and pepper. Cook mixture covered for 20 minutes, stirring occasionally. Add olives. Cut potatoes in ⅛-inch slices and arrange ⅓ in bottom of baking dish. Spread with half of tomato mixture and top with half of goat cheese. Continue a second layer of potatoes, tomatoes, cheese, and top with potatoes. Drizzle remaining olive oil over all and bake, covered with foil, in middle of oven at 350° for 40 minutes. Remove foil and continue baking an additional 20 to 30 minutes until potatoes are tender. Sprinkle with parsley.

Serves 8.

MEDITERRANEAN FILLET OF SOLE

4 (8-ounce) fillets of sole or flounder	1 cup dry white wine
2 cups fresh mushrooms	8 plum tomatoes, diced
2 tablespoons butter	Additional salt and pepper, to taste
1 small onion, minced	1 scallion, minced
Salt and pepper to taste	1 cup flat-leaf parsley

Cut each fillet into 4 pieces lengthwise. Rinse and dry mushrooms and chop coarsely. Cook onion until soft in 1 tablespoon butter, about 5 minutes. Sprinkle with salt and pepper. Add mushrooms, reduce heat, and cook, stirring constantly, until mushrooms are soft, about 8 minutes. Add wine and cook 2 minutes more. Add tomatoes and scallions, stir, cover, and simmer 10 minutes, adding additional liquid (water, wine, or tomato juice) if needed. Stir in parsley and remove from heat. Grease ovenproof pan with remaining butter. Arrange 16 small fillets on bottom, lightly salt and pepper, and pour sauce over. Cover with foil and bake at 350° for 15 minutes.

Serves 4.

Chicken Marbella

8 boneless, skinless chicken
  breast halves
8 cloves of garlic, minced
2 tablespoons dried oregano
Salt and pepper to taste
¼ cup red wine vinegar
¼ cup olive oil
 ½ cup pitted prunes

¼ cup pitted green olives
¼ cup capers with a bit of juice
3 bay leaves
½ cup brown sugar
½ cup white wine
¼ cup Italian parsley or cilantro,
  finely chopped

In a large bowl combine chicken breasts, garlic, oregano, salt and pepper, vinegar, olive oil, prunes, olives, capers and juice, and bay leaves. Cover and let marinate, refrigerated, overnight. Arrange chicken in a single layer in one or two shallow baking pans and spoon marinade over it evenly. Sprinkle chicken pieces with brown sugar and pour wine around them. Bake for 50 minutes to 1 hour at 350°, basting frequently with pan juices. With a slotted spoon, transfer chicken, prunes, olives, and capers to a serving platter. Moisten with a few spoonfuls of pan juices and sprinkle generously with parsley or cilantro. Pass remaining pan juices in a gravy dish.
    Serves 8.

Spanish Flan

½ cup sugar for caramel
2 tablespoons hot water
2 cups milk
⅓ cup sugar for custard
⅛ teaspoon salt

3 eggs, beaten
1 teaspoon vanilla
⅛ teaspoon ground nutmeg
Whipped cream
Toasted slivered almonds

Caramelize sugar: Heat ½ cup sugar over very low heat, stirring constantly with long-handled spoon, until sugar is melted and straw-colored, about 10 minutes. Remove from heat and very slowly and carefully add 2 tablespoons very hot water. To make syrup heavier, return to low heat and stir until it is the color of maple syrup. Place syrup in 6 individual custard cups or larger mold and tip up and push with wooden spoon to coat base of dish. Blend together milk, ⅓ cup sugar, and salt. Add eggs and beat well. Add vanilla and nutmeg. Pour carefully into cups or mold, place in a pan of hot water, and cook in 325° oven for an hour or more, until knife blade inserted near edge comes out clean. Unmold onto plate so that caramel is on top. Garnish with whipped cream and almonds.

Serves 6.

OUR GARDEN IN TIBURON gave me a chance to redeem my disastrous horticultural initiation with the stunted vegetables on our carport deck in Davao. All kinds of plants flourished the Bay Area climate. We lovingly collected those that liked northern winters—roses, camellias and azaleas, spring blooming bulbs—and planted them on our hillside. With almost no danger of frost, we created a miniature citrus orchard on our sunny deck, mostly lemons. When freezing temperatures were forecast in January of 2007, I harvested all the ripe lemons. My first challenge was to research recipes for preserving lemons, North-African style. With the preserves on hand, I then sought out recipes that would use them, experimenting with variations on Moroccan, Turkish, and Lebanese recipes and sharing the results with family and friends.

HARVESTING LEMONS

Preserved lemons
Tagine of chicken with preserved lemon and olives
Tomatoes stuffed with pimentos, tuna, capers, and olives
Tagine of beef with apples and raisins
Meatball tagine with herbs and lemon

PRESERVED LEMONS

6 to 7 juicy lemons
¼ cup salt
6 coriander seeds, crushed
1 cinnamon stick, broken
(optional)

4 black peppercorns, crushed
1 bay leaf, crushed
Extra lemons for juice
1-pint jar

Put 1 tablespoon salt in bottom of jar. Starting at the top of the lemons, cut crosses to within ½ inch of the bottom, so the four quarters remain joined. Sprinkle salt on exposed flesh and pack lemons tightly into the jar, adding spices and more salt between layers. Add lemon juice on top to cover lemons. Leave airspace at top and seal jar. Shake jar to distribute salt. Keep at room temperature 24 hours, then refrigerate. To use lemons, rinse off salt, then remove pulp.

TAGINE OF CHICKEN WITH PRESERVED LEMON AND OLIVES

tablespoons extra-virgin olive oil
2 onions, finely chopped
2 to 3 cloves garlic, crushed
½ teaspoon crushed saffron
threads
¼ to ½ teaspoon ground ginger
4 to 6 chicken breasts
Salt and pepper

3¼ cups water
Juice of ½ lemon
2 tablespoons cilantro
2 tablespoons flat-leaf parsley
Peel of 1 large preserved lemon
12 to 16 green or violet olives
4 to 6 artichoke bottoms, frozen
or canned (optional)

In wide heavy-bottomed pan that can hold all chicken pieces in one layer, heat oil and sauté onions over low heat till they soften, then stir in garlic, saffron, and ginger. Add chicken pieces, season with salt and pepper, and add water. Simmer, covered, turning pieces a few time and adding water if needed, about 20 min. Stir in lemon

juice, cilantro, parsley, lemon peel cut into thin strips, and olives. (For artichoke option, slide artichoke bottoms beneath chicken at this stage.) Simmer uncovered for 5 to 10 min until sauce is thick. Present chicken on serving dish with olives and lemon peel on top.
   Serves 4.

Tomatoes Stuffed with Pimientos, Tuna, Capers, and Olives

1 (4-ounce) jar pimentos
Salt
2 tablespoons extra-virgin
   olive oil
1 (7-ounce) can tuna, flaked
2 tablespoons capers

4 tablespoons chopped black
   olives
Peel of ½ preserved lemon,
   chopped
2 tablespoons flat-leaf parsley
6 large tomatoes

Combine all ingredients except tomatoes. Cut small circle around stalk of each tomato and cut out a cap. Remove center and seeds with pointed teaspoon. Fill cavities with tuna mixture and some of the removed tomato. Arrange in shallow baking dish and bake in preheated oven at 350° for 20 to 30 minutes or till tomatoes are a little soft. Keep watch that they do not fall apart. Serve hot or cold.
   Serves 6.

TAGINE OF BEEF WITH APPLES AND RAISINS

2 pounds chuck or blade steak, in 1-inch cubes
3 teaspoons oil
4 tablespoons butter
1 medium onion, sliced
¼ teaspoon saffron
½ teaspoon ground ginger
1½ teaspoons ground cinnamon
½ cup water
1½ teaspoons salt
Black pepper
4 tablespoons chopped cilantro
1 cup raisins
¼ cup honey
3 tart apples, cut into wedges
4 teaspoons roasted sesame seeds

Heat half the oil and half the butter in saucepan and brown beef over high heat. Remove beef. Add remaining oil as needed. Reduce heat to medium; add onion and cook for 5 minutes to soften. Add saffron, ginger, and 1 teaspoon cinnamon and cook 1 minute. Stir in water, salt, and a generous grinding of black pepper. Add beef and cilantro; cover and simmer for 1 hour. Add raisins and 4 teaspoons honey. Cover and simmer an additional 30 minutes or until meat is tender. Heat remaining butter in frying pan and cook apples for 10 minutes, turning often. Drizzle with remaining honey, dust with remaining cinnamon, and cook 5 minutes or until glazed and softened. Transfer meat and sauce to serving dish, arrange apples on top, and sprinkle with sesame seeds.

Serves 6.

MEATBALL TAGINE WITH HERBS AND LEMON

1 onion, coarsely chopped
6 tablespoons parsley, coarsely
  chopped
2 slices white bread, crusts
  removed
1 egg
1 pound 2 ounces ground lamb
  or beef
¾ teaspoon ground cumin
1 teaspoon paprika

½ teaspoon freshly ground pepper
1 teaspoon salt
4 teaspoons olive oil
½ teaspoon turmeric
¼ teaspoon cayenne pepper
1½ cups chicken broth
3 tablespoons cilantro, chopped
3 tablespoons lemon juice
½ rind of preserved lemon, cut
  into slivers

For meatballs: Process ½ onion and 3 tablespoons parsley in food processor. Add bread, torn into pieces, along with egg and process briefly. Add meat, ½ teaspoon cumin, ½ teaspoon paprika, and 1 teaspoon salt and process to a thick paste. Form into walnut-size balls and refrigerate until needed. (I often use frozen meatballs from the grocery store as a shortcut.) For herb and lemon sauce: Sauté remaining ½ onion in olive oil over low heat. Add ½ teaspoon paprika, ¼ teaspoon cumin, turmeric, and cayenne and cook 1 minute, stirring. Add chicken broth and cilantro and bring to boil. Add meatballs to pan and stir into sauce. Simmer 45 minutes. Add remaining 3 tablespoons parsley, lemon juice, and preserved rind. Transfer into serving bowl (tagine if available).

Serves 4.

WE WOULD RETURN TO the Sierra foothills hills many times after that first visit in 1997. Cliff's nephew Charles and his wife Joan bought a house in Murphys in 2000 and welcomed us as part of the extended family. With a modern kitchen large enough for a team, Joan presided over many a gastronomic experiment. We baked Christmas cookies together, "cooked" raw tuna for hors d'oeuvres by letting it sit on a Himalayan salt slab, and devised new ways to cook vegetables to accompany the meats Charles cooked on his grill. We combined fruits, pastry, and whipped cream for dessert, and experimented with seasonings purchased from The Spice Tin just off Murphys' main street.

The proprietors, Patty and Jan Schulz, travel the world on spice-buying trips, visiting exotic locales such as the spice market (Misir Carsisi) in Istanbul's Grand Bazaar.

RECIPES FROM THE SPICE TIN IN MURPHYS

Menemen (Turkish eggs) with sumac yogurt
Middle Eastern fatoush salad
Chicken tikka masala
Spicy hot brownies

MENEMEN WITH SUMAC YOGURT

4 tablespoons olive oil
1 teaspoon whole fennel seeds
½ teaspoon cumin seeds
¼ teaspoon mustard seeds
½ teaspoon chili flakes
   (optional)
1 tablespoon grated fresh ginger
1 red onion, diced
2 cloves garlic, chopped
1 red bell pepper, diced

8 tomatoes or 1 (15-ounce) can
   tomatoes
1 tablespoon water
¾ cup Greek yogurt
2 teaspoons sumac
½ teaspoon garlic, crushed
Lemon juice
6 eggs
Flat-leaf parsley, chopped

Heat the oil in large pan. Add the first 4 spices and toast for about 4 minutes. Add ginger, onion, and chopped garlic. Saute until soft. Add red pepper, tomato, and water. Cook for 10 minutes. While the veggies are cooking, make the sumac yogurt by whisking together yogurt, 1 tablespoon olive oil, sumac, ¼ teaspoon crushed garlic, and a bit of lemon juice. Set aside. Make 6 hollows in the menemen mixture, crack the eggs into them, cover, and simmer gently until the eggs are cooked to your preference (about 6 to 10 minutes). Remove from heat, drizzle with remaining oil, and sprinkle with parsley. Serve with sumac yogurt.

Serves 6.

MIDDLE EASTERN FATOUSH SALAD

¼ cup lemon juice
½ cup olive oil
1 teaspoon salt
1 clove garlic, minced
2 tablespoons sumac
½ teaspoon rice vinegar
4 cups pita bread, cut in 1-inch pieces
½ head romaine lettuce

1 red bell pepper, seeded and diced
1 small cucumber, peeled and diced
1 handful fresh chopped mint leaves
1 handful fresh chopped parsley
A few thinly sliced red onion rounds

To make dressing: Combine lemon juice, ¼ cup olive oil, salt, garlic clove, sumac (this makes salad authentic), and vinegar in a cup or jar with lid and stir or shake. Set aside. To make fried or baked pita chips: Fry pita pieces in remaining olive oil on low to medium heat until golden in color; drain on paper towel. For a healthier option, bake in oven at 350° for approximately 5 minutes, until crispy. For an easy substitution, use packaged pita chips. In large bowl, combine lettuce, tomatoes, bell pepper, cucumber, mint, parsley, onion, and pita chips. Toss with dressing, and serve.

Serves 4.

CHICKEN TIKKA MASALA

1 cup yogurt
1 tablespoon lemon juice
4 teaspoons ground cumin
1 teaspoon ground cinnamon
2 teaspoons cayenne pepper
2 teaspoons ground black pepper
1 tablespoon minced fresh
  ginger
4 teaspoons salt, or to taste
3 boneless skinless chicken
  breasts, cut into bite-size pieces

4 long skewers
1 tablespoon butter
1 clove garlic, minced
1 jalapeño pepper, finely chopped
2 teaspoons ground cumin
2 teaspoons paprika
3 teaspoons salt, or to taste
1 (8-ounce) can tomato sauce
1 cup heavy cream
¼ cup chopped fresh cilantro

In a large bowl, combine yogurt, lemon juice, 2 teaspoons cumin, cinnamon, cayenne, black pepper, ginger, and salt. Stir in chicken, cover, and refrigerate for 1 hour. Preheat a grill for high heat. Lightly oil the grill grate. Thread chicken onto skewers, and discard marinade. Grill until juices run clear, about 5 minutes on each side. To make sauce: Melt butter in a large heavy skillet over medium heat. Saute garlic and jalapeño for 1 minute. Season with 2 teaspoons cumin, paprika, and salt. Stir in tomato sauce and cream. Simmer on low heat until sauce thickens, about 20 minutes. Add grilled chicken and simmer for 10 minutes. Transfer to a serving platter and garnish with fresh cilantro.

Serves 4.

SPICY HOT BROWNIES

1 stick butter	½ teaspoon baking powder
8 ounces dark chocolate	½ teaspoon salt
1 cup flour	1¼ cup sugar
¼ cup cocoa powder	3 eggs
1 teaspoon cayenne pepper	1 teaspoon vanilla
1 tablespoon cinnamon	Salt on top

Preheat oven to 350°. Line 9x9-inch pan with parchment. Melt dark chocolate and butter together, then allow to cool slightly. Mix flour, cocoa powder, cayenne, cinnamon, baking powder, and salt together in small bowl. Stir sugar, eggs, and vanilla into butter and chocolate. Add dry ingredients and stir until mixed. Pour into pan. Bake for 15 to 20 minutes, until toothpick has crumbs. Cool in pan, then remove and cut. If desired, salt tops before serving.

Makes 16 large brownies.

IN THE THE TWENTY-FIRST century, the Forster children and grand-children have embarked on their own business-propelled global journeys. To southern California, Central and South America, Washington D.C., New York, Pennsylvania, the Middle East and East Asia, Europe, Africa, and southern Florida. Both generations and both genders of Forster offspring and spouses like to cook and like to entertain, experimenting with exotic new cuisines or consulting their own recipe collections—sometimes using a recipe from their own photocopied editions of the earliest draft of this cookbook. When families gather to celebrate holidays at homes in Brooklyn and Fort Myers, household favorites are dished out to nurture three generations, or a special cake is baked and decorated to celebrate a birthday.

FAMILY FEASTING IN FLORIDA AND NEW YORK

Kristin Daer's blueberry corn pancakes
Kristin's heirloom tomato, herb, and burrata pasta
Kate Mackenzie's mushroom risotto
Tom and Makala Forsters's chocolate bourbon cake

KRISTIN DAER'S BLUEBERRY CORN PANCAKES

¾ to 1 cup polenta or corn meal
¾ cup whole-wheat flour
¾ cup white flour
1 teaspoon baking soda
½ teaspoon salt
1 egg, lightly beaten

2 tablespoon maple syrup or honey
3 tablespoons canola oil
3 tablespoons butter
2 cups buttermilk
2½ cups blueberries
Grade-A maple syrup

Mix dry ingredients together in a bowl until combined; set aside. Thoroughly mix together egg, 2 tablespoons syrup or honey, 2 tablespoons oil, and buttermilk. Quickly add to the dry ingredients and mix well. Set aside for 10 minutes. Wash fresh blueberries and drain well. If using frozen blueberries, thaw and drain juice *very* well. Add about 1 tablespoon each of canola oil and butter to a hot 10-inch cast-iron skillet. Pour approximately ¾ of a cup of batter into the pan (make 1 large pancake at a time). Let the pancake cook until bubbles form on the top of the uncooked side. Drop a generous amount of blueberries onto the top of the pancake. Carefully flip the pancake over. Cook a few more minutes until done. Serve with warm maple syrup.

Makes approximately 6 large pancakes (1 pancake is typically one serving).

Kristin's Heirloom Tomato, Herb, and Burrata Pasta

⅓ cup extra-virgin olive oil
2 to 3 cloves crushed garlic
2 tablespoons fresh chopped
   Italian parsley, plus additional
2 tablespoons fresh chopped
   basil, plus additional
2 tablespoons fresh squeezed
   lemon juice

Zest from 1 lemon
¼ cup plus 2 tablespoons fresh
   grated Parmesan cheese
Salt and pepper to taste
1 box good quality linguine pasta
4 heirloom tomatoes
1 pound burrata cheese

In a small bowl combine olive oil, garlic, parsley, basil, lemon juice and zest, 2 tablespoons Parmesan, salt, and pepper and set aside. Bring a large pot of salted water to boil. Add pasta to boiling water and cook according to directions on box. Before draining, reserve approximately 1 cup of the pasta water and set aside. Combine olive-oil mixture and pasta in a large pasta bowl. Chop the tomatoes and burrata cheese and add to pasta. Toss well. Add the remainder of the Parmesan and toss. Add reserved pasta water in ¼-cup increments as needed. Garnish with remaining basil and Italian parsley.

Serves 6.

Kate Mackenzie's Mushroom Risotto

½ cup dried porcini mushrooms
4 to 6 tablespoons butter or
  extra-virgin olive oil
1 medium onion, chopped
1½ cups Aborio or other short-
  or medium-grain rice
Salt and freshly ground black
  pepper
½ cup dry white wine or water

4 to 5 cups chicken, beef, or
  vegetable broth
1 cup sliced shitake or portobello
  mushroom caps
Freshly grated Parmesan cheese
  (optional)
Optional vegetables (see note
  below)

Rinse dried mushrooms, then soak in hot water to cover. Melt 2 tablespoons butter or heat oil in deep nonstick skillet over medium heat. Add onion and cook, stirring, until soft, 3 to 5 minutes. Add rice and cook, stirring occasionally, until coated and glossy, 2 to 3 minutes. Add salt, pepper, and wine. Stir until liquid is gone. Drain and chop porcini, then stir into rice with about half of their soaking liquid. Begin adding broth, ½ cup at a time, stirring until absorbed after each addit1on. Mixture should not be soupy or become dry; it should be tender but with a bit of crunch. Stir frequently over medium to medium-high heat. Melt or heat remaining butter or oil in small skillet, add fresh mushrooms, and cook, stirring occasionally, until brown and becoming crisp, about 10 minutes. Add cooked fresh mushrooms and ½ cup Parmesan to rice mixture. Serve at once, passing additional parmesan at the table.

Serves 4 to 6.

Note: Other fresh vegetables (artichoke hearts, green beans, snow peas, etc.) may be cooked and added along with cooked fresh mushrooms. Or dried porcini may be replaced with 1 celery stalk, 1 chopped carrot, and ½ teaspoon dried or 1 sprig fresh herbs. If used, these should be cooked and added along with the onions.

Tom and Makala Forster's Chocolate Bourbon Cake

2 cups sifted flour
2 teaspoons baking powder
½ teaspoon salt
½ cup unsalted butter
2 cups sugar
4 squares (4 ounces) unsweetened baking chocolate, melted

2 large egg yolks, well beaten
1 teaspoon vanilla
2 tablespoons bourbon
1½ cups milk
2 large egg whites, stiffly beaten
1 cup chopped pecans (optional)

Preheat oven to 350°. Sift flour with baking powder and salt; set aside. Cream butter in a large bowl until light and fluffy. Gradually add sugar and continue beating until mixture is smooth. Stir in melted chocolate. Add egg yolks and beat well. Stir in vanilla and bourbon. Gradually blend in flour mixture, alternating with milk, beginning and ending with flour. Fold in beaten egg whites, and pecans if desired. Pour batter into a well-oiled 13x9x2-inch pan or a 10-inch tube pan. Bake 25 to 30 minutes for the oblong pan, 55 to 60 for the tube pan until a cake tester comes out clean. Do not overbake. Remove from oven and cool in pan on a wire rack for about 10 minutes. Remove from pan and frost with Chocolate Bourbon Frosting.

Serves 6 to 8.

CHOCOLATE BOURBON FROSTING

4¾ cups (1 pound) sifted
  powdered sugar
1½ cups unsalted butter at room
  temperature
2 squares (2 ounces) unsweetened chocolate, melted

1 large egg, well beaten
1 teaspoon vanilla
1 teaspoon lemon juice
2 to 3 tablespoons bourbon
1 cup chopped pecans (optional)

Combine the first 7 ingredients and mix until smooth. Ice the cake and, if using, sprinkle pecans on top.

THE FINAL RECIPE OF this book—the chocolate bourbon cake—deserves to have its story told. In April, 2012, I was in New York for my grandson Nathan's twenty-seventh birthday. After Tom baked his son the cake, and Makala lovingly frosted and decorated it for her brother, they looked for a safe hiding place until dinnertime, in case Nathan and his girlfriend arrived while the rest of us were out enjoying cherry blossoms in the Brooklyn Botanical Garden. The cake was stashed in the one spot in the snug apartment kitchen where it wouldn't be found—the oven. That evening, when all had gathered in the living room for pre-dinner drinks and to view photos from my recent trip to India, clouds of smoke billowed from the kitchen. The cake! Tom had turned the oven on to preheat for the appetizer pizza he was about to cook. Violet flowers and green leaves and pink words of birthday love melted into chocolate. But our "twice baked" cake tasted delicious, and I had iPhone photos of the original masterpiece to show Nathan what had been.

Afterword: Enjoying a Global Feast

THIS CULINARY TRAVEL TALE—a finite compendium of meals served and savored in the company of treasured friends, adventurous family members, and distinguished visitors—ends here. But the memories endure, as do the recipes, and it is my wish that they will serve as a travel guide for others who enjoy adventures in food, and wish to share such adventures with congenial traveling companions.

Food is an international language, understood and appreciated by us all. I cherish recollections of sharing meals from my kitchen with Americans and Japanese who had recently fought a devastating war; with Burmese, Pakistani and Indian women who wrote out their family recipes for a young American woman; with Arabs and Israelis having lunch together on a Jerusalem rooftop overlooking a Christian holy procession. Breaking bread together is a wonderful way to bridge the chasms created by distance and history and culture, and to participate in a global feast.

Bon Voyage and Bon Appétit!

Acknowledgements

WITH THANKS AND ACKNOWLEDGEMENTS to my inspiration and support system:

THE PROFESSIONALS

A bare manuscript was transformed into an attractive book by a team of insightful and skilled professionals. Lydia Bird was an incomparable editor and project manager, polishing rough edges and making wise recommendations. Cindy Salans Rosenheim created the charming illustrations for the cover and interior. Gregory Fields designed the compelling cover, and Jill Ronsley did the interior design.

FAMILY TASTERS

Cindy, Doug, Tom, and especially Cliff, who endured fourteen straight days of hash in 1949 and was a cheerful consumer of my culinary trials and errors from then onward.

RECIPE CONTRIBUTORS

Kate Blanke (my mother), Rose Keeney (my stepmother), the Japanese ladies in Fukuoka, Daryl Kleinpell, Ginger Herndon, the members of my Rangoon cooking class, Betty Martin, Ele Nickel, Franny Nichols, Irene Moran, Cindy Hawkins Petti, Maggie McVeigh, Hatsue Horikawa and her mother, Maria Behrens, Chick Kimes, Kay Kendall, Lea Sneider, Pat Latendresse, Aiko

Mitsuya, Nucy Meech, Gerry Alexander, Sarah Ross, Julie Reisner, Kerry Tolleth, Nancy Mason, Barbara Moore, Annie O'Leary, Sue Yung Li, Betty Lou Hummel, Nerida Onley, Rhoda Hackler, Helena Cence, Anne Crowe, Hannelore Herbig, Jan Drammer, Jeanne Gosho, Heather Stanisbury Collins, Dana Victorson, Carolyn Stohler, Vera Fields, Susan Englebright, Kristin Daer, Kate Mackenzie, Patty Schulz.

INSPIRATION FROM PUBLICATIONS
Sunset and *Gourmet* magazines (subscriptions which have sustained me through the years of wandering from one city to another); recipes and food sections in *The Washington Post, Honolulu Advertiser,* and *San Francisco Chronicle;* my shelf of cookbooks, which started with *The Joy of Cooking* and *The Fannie Farmer Cookbook* and expanded to include Asian, vegetarian, institutional, and other comprehensive and specialized volumes.

GRACIOUS GUESTS AND DEAR FRIENDS
Many wonderful friends and acquaintances crossed our thresholds in the Philippines, Japan, Burma, Washington, Israel, Honolulu, and Tiburon. Their coming to participate in a dining and drinking and conversing ritual stimulated my search for appropriate and interesting fare. Without such an audience, there would have been far less feasting.

GENEROUS GUIDES ALONG THE ROAD TO PUBLICATION
Joan and Charles Howard urged me to pick up and complete a long-languishing book, and John and Lucie Hall made this possible by retrieving lost computer files. Michaela Grudin, Sue Yung Li, and Bill Lane provided wise and welcome counsel.

MUCH THAT IS RIGHT about this book is thanks to all these special friends and colleagues. That which is not right is mine alone.

Index of Recipes

Nancy Keeney met Clifton Forster while they were both students at Stanford University. They were married in 1949 and immediately launched on his thirty-four-year career in the U.S. Foreign Service. As she faced the challenges of learning to cook and acting as diplomatic hostess during their journey from one Asian city to another, Nancy Keeney Forster took on two additional careers: mother of three and teacher of high-school history. In recent years, she has gathered and published stories of her husband's unusual childhood and their family's diplomatic journey (*Encounters: A Lifetime Spent Crossing Cultural Frontiers,* 2009) and the experiences of students, alumni, and teachers in the International Baccalaureate Program (*Journeys in Learning Across Frontiers: Stories, Strategies and Inspiration from the IB Community,* 2012). In 1995, the Forsters moved to Tiburon, California, where they continued to travel, to entertain family and friends, and to experiment with new dishes. Cliff died in 2006. Their three children and five grandchildren are also crossing cultural and culinary frontiers at home and abroad.

Visit the author's website at www.windshadowpress.com.

Made in the USA
Charleston, SC
12 February 2013